THE SWIMMER
An Integrated Computational Model of a Perceptual-Motor System

SCIENTIFIC PSYCHOLOGY SERIES

Stephen W. Link & James T. Townsend, Editors

MONOGRAPHS

William R. Uttal et al. • The Swimmer: An Integrated Computational Model of a Perceptual-Motor System

Stephen W. Link • The Wave Theory of Difference and Similarity

EDITED VOLUMES

F. Gregory Ashby • Multidimensional Models of Perception and Cognition

Hans-Georg Geissler, Stephen W. Link, and James T. Townsend • Cognition, Information Processing, and Psychophysics: Basic Issues

THE SWIMMER
An Integrated Computational Model
of a Perceptual-Motor System

William R. Uttal
Arizona State University

Gary Bradshaw
University of Colorado

Sriram Dayanand
Robb Lovell
Thomas Shepherd
Arizona State University

Ramakrishna Kakarala
Kurt Skifsted
University of Michigan

Greg Tupper
Kailua, Hawaii

LEA LAWRENCE ERLBAUM ASSOCIATES, PUBLISHERS
1992 Hillsdale, New Jersey   Hove and London

Lawrence Erlbaum Associates, Inc., Publishers
365 Broadway
Hillsdale, New Jersey 07642

Library of Congress Cataloging-in-Publication Data

The swimmer : an integrated computational model of a perceptual-motor
    system / William R. Uttal . . . [et al.].
        p.   cm.
    Includes bibliographical references and indexes.
    ISBN 0-8058-1070-6 (hard)
    1. Perceptual-motor processes—Computer simulation.   I. Uttal,
William R.
    BF295.S93   1992
    152.1'01'13—dc20   91-35670
                                                                          CIP

Printed in the United States of America
10   9   8   7   6   5   4   3   2   1

FOR MIT-CHAN, THE REAL THING.

BOOKS BY WILLIAM R. UTTAL

Real Time Computer: Techniques and Applications in the Psychological Sciences

Generative Computer Assisted Instruction (with Miriam Rogers, Ramelle Hieronymus, and Timothy Pasich)

Sensory Coding: Selected Readings (Editor)

The Psychobiology of Sensory Coding

Cellular Neurophysiology and Integration: An Interpretive Introduction

An Autocorrelation Theory of Form Detection

The Psychobiology of Mind

A Taxonomy of Visual Processes

Visual Form Detection in 3-Dimensional Space

Foundations of Psychobiology (with Daniel N. Robinson)

The Detection of Nonplanar Surfaces in Visual Space

The Perception of Dotted Forms

On Seeing Forms

The Swimmer: An Integrated Computational Model of a Perceptual-Motor System (with Gary Bradshaw, Sriram Dayanand, Robb Lovell, Thomas Shepherd, Ramakrishna Kakarala, Kurt Skifsted, and Greg Tupper)

Table of Contents

Preface

This book is the first report from a moderately large simulation project. It is based upon a number of premises and is beset by a number of difficulties. The two main premises are:

1. There is much to be gained by approaching a theoretical modeling task from a broader perspective than is usual in this field. Rather than attempt to fine-tune a single-purpose algorithm, we sought to integrate many different procedures and processes into a comprehensive model of a entire organism.
2. From a purely psychobiological point of view, a model that integrates many different weak and idiosyncratic processes into a powerful and capable system is a more realistic expression of the way the real organic perceptual motor system works.

Thus, from computational-theoretical and psychobiological points of view, it was felt that it was timely to undertake what to many might seem to be an overly ambitious and broad attempt at computational modeling. Nevertheless, we hope to convince our readers that the task was well chosen and that we were able to make a reasonable amount of progress.

The difficulties arise to the degree that the project has been successful in proceeding in the directions specified by the two guiding premises. For example, we are faced with the problem of reporting the results of a large computational project in a way that neither trivializes what we have done nor numbs our reader's senses with excruciating details of computer programs and algorithmic details. To a degree it must be historical; to a degree it must be expository; to a degree it must be technical; to a degree it must even be autobiographical (if the project can be considered as an entity); and, finally, it must be readable.

How do we satisfy all of these criteria without destroying any of the others. The choice of a middle ground between these many hazards is a difficult one, and we can only hope that we achieved some semblance of readability. We decided that we will eschew the details of program listings and, instead, describe the model from the same point of view that it was programmed—the point of view that emphasizes the processes that we had to simulate. We discuss the technical approach, therefore, but not the specific programs. We have put in only so much mathematics as is necessary to make a serious reader aware of what we have done. However, we make no attempt to mathematize each and every process. As we shall see, some of our simulations are intrinsically heuristic or nonmathematical, and it would be pointless to try to force this nomenclature on them.

A further difficulty concerns performance testing of our model, either in its entirety or in terms of some of the parts. Professional computer scientists may wish to have more in the way of precise estimates of algorithm execution times or competence under varying conditions. We feel, however, that this is not necessary or possible with our programs. We acknowledge their non-real-time character and stress that it is the quality of the concept rather than the quantity of time taken for execution that concerns us most at this phase of the project. Our attention was always directed at the overall structure, rather than the efficiency, of the model. A major goal was not to minimize execution time but to make the model follow, in broad principle, the organization of a putative organism that it might be simulating.

Another difficulty, or challenge if you wish, in writing this book was to avoid the tendency to wander too far off into the project's technical aspects. The day-by-day development of algorithms and procedures to accomplish some task always tended to divert our attention from the primary goal—to develop a comprehensive, integrated theory of organic perceptual-motor performance. The proverbial computer "rat hole" down which many a psychologist has fallen is always yawning at our feet. So, at the outset, we remind our readers that this is a progress report of a computer modeling project from an experimental psychology perspective.

It should also be acknowledged that our approach constrained in a major way the tools we used. From the outset, this has been a simulation project. In that spirit, some of the algorithms that we programmed may not be mathematically rigorous or, for that matter, even formally mathematical. We have used our computers in a way that emphasizes local pixel interaction in a way that is often not straightforwardly formulizable. The computer was merely a medium for carrying out the interactions among the picture elements. In some cases this approach actually allowed us to go on much further than we could have if we had demanded mathematical formularization or, worse, mathematical rigor.

Finally, this book must be accepted as a progress report. We have certainly not yet achieved our ultimate goal of simulating a complete perceptual-motor system. Some important aspects remain unfulfilled. Most notably, the objects in the present version of the model are two-dimensional entities in most cases. Even more significant to some is that our segmentation routines are almost completely static; movement, a powerful cue for segmentation, is not yet a part of our system. There is much work yet to be done, and we hope to have a second monograph on our progress available in a couple of years.

Most of the work reported in this book was carried out at the Perception Laboratory of the Department of Psychology at Arizona State University. However, some of the progress we report is based on work done in an earlier incarnation of the project at the Naval Ocean Systems Center—Hawaii Laboratory in Kailua, Hawaii. In Hawaii, others contributed programs and materials. Specifically, we acknowledge the programing contributions of Nancy Davis and Lois Genzmer, both of whom were employees of SEACO Inc. of Kailua during that phase of the project's history.

Although this book is a collective effort, we note that the programming work on stereoscopic modeling that is reported here was jointly carried out by Ramakrishna Kakarala and Sriram Dayanand, the material on texture segmentation is mainly due to Robb Lovell, the work on reconstruction is that of Kakarala and Dayanand, the work on form recognition is that of Tom Shepherd, and Sriram Dayanand designed the Macro Processing System. The appendix is a contribution of Gary Bradshaw. Others contributed to smaller sections in ingenious and fundamental ways. The task of tying this all together into a usable synthesis fell on Bill Uttal.

We are especially grateful to the Office of Naval Research (ONR) for their continued support of this project when the principal investigator (Uttal) moved from Kailua, Hawaii, to Tempe, Arizona. The project was funded by Contract #N00014-88-K-0603 between ONR and Arizona State University. We particularly acknowledge the wise guidance and continued enthusiastic encouragement that has come from Dr. Harold Hawkins, the ONR scientific officer for the project. We also acknowledge the willingness of Lawrence Erlbaum, a caring and contributing publisher of the old school, to extend his company's resources to books of limited circulation like the present one. Three such resources— Arthur Lizza, Judith Amsel, and Cathy Dolan are specifically acknowledged. We also appreciate the constructive contributions of Stephen W. Link and James T. Townsend, the editors of what we expect will become a distinguished series of volumes in scientific psychology, in giving us the opportunity to be among their first contributors. Steve, in particular, acted as the technical editor for this book, adding much to its clarity and value.

Numerous others deserve some credit for this project. Some have passed through our lab for only a few hours but unknowingly made a suggestion or contributed an idea that later had a major influence on the development of the program. Some are members of the faculty of an invisible international university whose teachings, through their written or spoken communications, influenced us in indirect ways. It is not possible to identify everyone who had some kind of impact on our work, but it is clear that much of our progress is based on the contributions of those who preceded us and to whom we owe important intellectual debts.

Finally, as first author and the one person who has been with the project from its inception, Uttal claims the right of dedication for this volume. Once again, he acknowledges the companionship, love, and support of a lifetime from his dear wife, May.

1 Introduction

A recent explosion of activity in the development of computational models of human perceptual, decision making, and response processes has been made possible by modern developments in cognitive theory and computer technology. A wide variety of programmed algorithms has been developed that simulate and describe what are usually only the parts and pieces of perceptually guided behavior. In the visual domain, for example, algorithms have been developed that perform such visual functions as edge enhancement (e.g., Argyle, 1971), object segmentation based on brightness, color, or texture (e.g., Landy & Bergen, 1991), and the generation of object depth from disparity, shading, or contour lines (e.g., Horn & Brooks, 1989). Other models have been developed that describe and analyze performance during motor tasks such as walking or manipulation or that imitate such performance in the form of a mechanical device.

A characteristic of this present joint theoretical science and practical engineering endeavor is that most current energy has been aimed at the fine-tuning of the algorithms representing separate segments, aspects, or components of the total perceptual-motor process. Current goals have mainly been to invent or improve the individual algorithms that carry out isolated components of the total process rather than to integrate them into a coherent aggregate that performs some behavioral task in its entirety.

Similarly, much of the effort to study perception and performance in humans or animals has been directed at examining the components of human cognition. Researchers in this field tend to study fragments of mentation rather than the whole process. However, in the last decade it became clear that most cognitive processes, no less than complete perceptual-motor tasks in general, are actually accomplished by the integration of numerous attributes or mechanisms rather

1

than driven by a single dimension of the stimulus or psychobiological mechanism. We showed this to be the case for a sampled surface reconstruction perceptual task (Uttal, Davis, Welke, & Kakarala, 1988). Anderson (1981) makes this concept a central point of his important work, and Massaro and Friedman (1990) have added greatly to our understanding of attribute and dimensional integration by their careful comparison of a number of alternative theories of information integration.

The promise of this present work, in this same spirit, is that there is much to be learned, both by the student of artificial intelligence and by the student of natural intelligence, by considering an entire perceptual-motor process at once. The premise upon which the present work is founded, therefore, is that perceptually guided behavior is not simply line detection, nor stereopsis, nor control of movement in space. Rather, it is a complex of functionally integrated processes, of which these are only a few examples, that mutually affect and interact with each other. Visual inputs evoke *perceptual* or *interpretive* responses that are necessary to define the parameters of the environment and the objects it contains. The interactions between the stimuli, the natural or synthetic organism, and the environment set goals, the achievement of which requires specific meaningful and relevant responses. The process is a highly adaptive and dynamic feedback system in which the very act of *behaving* in an appropriate manner to close on those goals can alter the sensory inputs as new relationships occur during that behavior.

The integrated computational model that we present here emphasizes traditional psychological variables such as a figure from ground extraction, reconstruction of forms, closure, discrimination, recognition, and some primitive decision making. It is not unique, it must be acknowledged in another closely related context—the engineering of artificially intelligent systems. Several other efforts in that context were directed at the design of autonomous, automobile robots. Among the most notable of these projects comparable to our own, have been those summarized in a recent article by Busby and Vadus (1990). However different our long-term goals may be, all of these efforts obviously share common methods and techniques.

The best way to communicate our plan is pictorially. Figure 1.1 presents the global outline of our project as initially planned. At present, all of the blocks have been programmed and installed in an operating version of the model with the exception of the *motion* and *contours and optical flow* modules. This flowchart indicates the rudiments of both the horizontal and vertical integration, but the full implications of this very abbreviated flowchart can only be appreciated when it is realized that any of the connecting lines may also itself be instantiated in the form of a set of serial and parallel processes.

The flowchart is also a theory of human perceptual processes in that it analogizes some of the perceptual mechanisms that are necessary for human vision. It outlines, however briefly, the relationships we believe to exist among the various components that underlie perceptual-motor behavior.

In the rest of this book, we report the development of this computational model of an entire perceiving and responding organism. Although we place primary emphasis on the integration of a suite of algorithms and processes, we also report considerable progress in improving the structure of a number of individual programming modules. Each of the functional steps in our simulation is considered to be tentative and replaceable as the technology for executing that particular subprocess evolves. The simulated perceiving and behaving entity we describe in this report is thus an integrated, but easily modified, concatenation of a wide variety of actions, interactions, and transformations. The computational model representing that entity simulates or analogizes the actions that "must" be carried out (in Marr's, 1982, terms) by an organic nervous system that would function in an equivalent manner when confronted with the same environment. However, it is important to note that it may do so by means that are quite different than those used by an organism. Indeed, we have made no effort in this work to specifically imitate psychological or physiological *mechanisms*. Rather, it is the sequence and integration of processes and transforms that we are simulating. Thus, our mathematical tools are typically chosen from the ordinary forms of classical analysis (e.g., integral equations and Fourier transforms) or from a set of simple computational interactions rather than from some currently popular connectionist concept of parallel neural nets.[1]

The actions that have to be simulated range from the initial transduction of photic energy to the appropriate interpretation of a stimulus scene to the construction of a map of the world of the simulated entity to a specific effector response. Thus, our simulation—to the degree that it is successful—represents a *descriptive* transformational theory of this kind of behavior in an entire organism as opposed to a restricted model of a single internal stage of information processing. We repeat: It is not intended to be a valid *reductive explanation* of the actual inner workings of the brain or mind of any real organism, but a *description* of the transformations and processes that have to be accounted for if we are to understand the complexities involved in perceptual-motor behavior.

Another general premise of our project is that both psychological theory and computer technology have developed to a point where it is now possible to consider collecting many existing algorithms, procedures, ideas, and theories into an integrated model of a complex perceptual-motor skill. While we feel that we are pushing the frontiers in this kind of theorizing, we do not feel that we are beyond the current limits of science and technology. We are convinced that what

---

[1]Parallel computational models may come later. Our plan is to keep our system sufficiently modular so that algorithms that may be totally different in architecture but alike in the transformations they produce can easily be substituted at any time in the future.

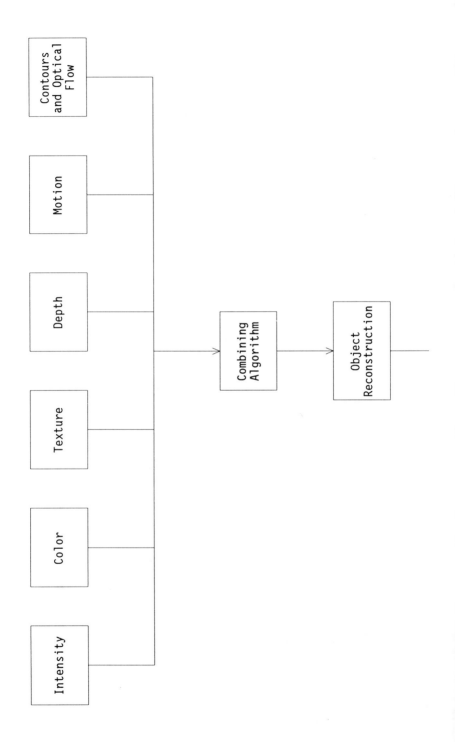

4

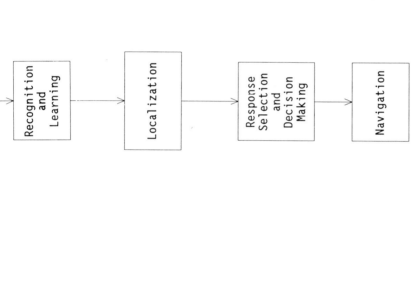

FIG. 1.1. A flowchart showing the horizontal and vertical integration of the various components of our model of perceptual-motor processes. With the exception of the *motion* and *contours and optical flow* modules, which have not yet been programmed, all of the other components of the system are described in this book.

5

we have chosen to do has been, from the outset, a realizable goal simply because it is synchronous with modern developments in both computer technology and cognitive science.

To pursue such a project without violating those state-of-the-art boundaries, we have had to limit the universe in which we work. It would be inappropriate and grandiose to suggest that a universal model of perceptual-motor performance could be developed with current knowledge and technology. Therefore, we have chosen, as a prototypical *microworld* system to be studied, an underwater SWIMMER capable of acquiring images of food objects, recognizing and discriminating among salient (edible) and irrelevant (inedible) objects, establishing a three-dimensional *world model* of its environment and the objects in it (including itself), and then demonstrating its *understanding* by *swimming* through a turbulent *ocean* to those objects. Involved in such a simulation must be consideration of visual, localization, interpretative, decision making, and motor functions as well as some challenging new problems of how one integrates all of these functions.

An important technological goal of our work is to incorporate these functions into a single integrated programming structure that operates completely automatically, but is easily modified as new techniques for improving the various transformation stages become available. To this end, we also had to develop an executive operating system environment that permits flexible and convenient construction of alternative theories or models as our understanding evolves.

We discovered that new empirical, practical, and theoretical problems arise when simulating such an integrated ensemble of psychological and/or computational processes. The difficulty of experimenting with such a complex perceptual-motor function is vastly greater than the clean-cut experimental task of examining, for example, isolated psychophysical relationships. Indeed, much of psychophysics' progress is based on what was called the Method of Detail by John Stuart Mill or the Methode of René Descartes. That is, on techniques that sought, in the ideal, to hold all variables and components of a complex process constant except the one that was intentionally manipulated.

Successful studies of quasi-realistic and less constrained (i.e., in terms of the numbers of variables allowed to covary) complex systems, however, often require more naturalistic and explorative approaches in which many variables of the system's perceptual input may be difficult to control and its behavioral output difficult to measure. Simulations of the kind explored here provide an alternative and convenient means of studying some of the more complex interactions than might be possible in the conventional laboratory or field situations.

Practically, and here we refer to the practical details of the simulation (i.e., the programming) process itself, researchers concerned with the study of elaborate programing efforts of the kind we describe are confronted with a new set of problems that are not faced when working with carefully isolated components of the total system. For example, how can the output of one process be automatically transformed into the input to the next in such an integrated simulation? This is the problem referred to as *automation* (a slightly different use of the word than in other contexts), faced by engineers developing working robotic or tele-operator systems. Automation is an especially challenging and unstudied issue because most component-oriented projects can, by definition, ignore the many difficulties involved in communication between the separate program segments.

The same problem of defining the sequencing of information flow also exists for cognitive modelers and theoretical neuroscientists. These more biologically oriented scientists confront virtually identical challenges; for example, how do we explain the neural coding and integration mechanisms by means of which the signals from the receptors are conveyed to and interpreted by subsequent levels of neural processing? It is quite clear that the two groups of researchers—engineers, on the one hand, and psychologists and neurophysiologists, on the other—are often attacking exactly the same problems, although from the differing perspectives of their respective sciences.

Theoretically, a computer model of a complex perceptual-motor action is also a much more intricate mixture of many different challenges than a putative description or explanation of only one step of the overall behavior. Not only does such a model require that determinations be made of the nature of the individual processes that compose the composite behavior, but also how they interact. As we have learned more and more about the codes and activity patterns at the periphery of the nervous system, our attention has necessarily turned to the ways in which the various centers and nuclei operate in the central nervous system. Biological and cognitive hypotheses leap forth from this change in the conceptualization of the relationship between cognitive process and neural structure.

This change in emphasis immediately raises a major philosophical or conceptual issue. We assume implicitly that the complex perceptual-response behavior we simulate is, in biological fact, a composite or concatenation of segmentable and separately assayable components; that is, that our program modules represent mental processes that may be literally characterized as being *microgenetic* as opposed to a single inseparable process with different aspects from which it may be examined. Surprisingly, some recent, although preliminary, evidence (Posner, Petersen, Fox, & Raichle, 1988) using positron emission tomography (PET) adds a kind of physiological reality to the microgenetic concept by showing separate physiological response for separate cognitive components. Other earlier, less direct arguments for this kind of psychological process can be found in the work of Bachmann (1980, 1992), and of course most experimental psychologists behave as if they accept this point of view when they go about their laboratory research studying putatively isolatable cognitive components. Thus, the idea of microgenetic components (i.e., constituent psychological processes) is a fundamental component of contemporary views of mind. They are also a necessary conceptual, if not physiologically and anatomically instantiated, strategy for psychological research; at the present time our methodology and mathematics simply do not have the power to deal with a totally holistic model of cognition.

A related epistemological point concerns the significance (as opposed to the mechanical details) of computational or mathematical models of cognitive processes. Uttal (1990) has discussed the issue of the *meaning* of computational models. He argued that there is no way to verify or validate the actual internal neural mechanisms suggested by a model because of constraints that were elucidated by workers in the fields of automata theory (Moore, 1956), chaos theory (Gleick, 1987), and combinatorics (Stockmeyer & Chandra, 1979; Tsotsos, 1990), among many other arguments drawn from psychology, mathematics, physics, and computer science. If this view is sustained, then any simulation or computational model could be, at best, only an *analog* (i.e., a process description that follows the same course as some internal mechanism) describing, to a more or less successful degree, the series of events unfolding within a process. But, it could never be substantiated or verified as a *homolog* (i.e., a true and valid reductionistic explanation of the actual internal neural or cognitive mechanisms). It is, thus, not only conceivable but likely that any hypothetical subprocess embodied in a programmed algorithm (as well as the overall system of a model such as the present one) will always be indeterminate with regard to the validity with which it can represent the actual internal structure and logic of the perceiving brain. This is not a startling new revelation, but an idea that has long standing in the history of science. Unfortunately, it is often forgotten in the enthusiasm for a new computational or mathematical theory, particularly in cognitive science or neuroscience.

Another conceptual issue must be frankly faced here. This concerns the ambitiousness of our project. So far our experience on this project confirms that it is clearly infeasible, given the current technological state of the computational modeling art and psychological theory, to produce a broadly competent perceptual-motor model[2] able to operate in many different microworlds. There is no question that a simulation of a truly intelligent entity that even begins to approach completeness is still beyond our capability. Nevertheless, what we accomplished does support our contention that it is plausible to pursue the development of a model capable of a circumscribed, but integrated, kind of perceptual-motor behavior that goes well beyond the scope of the individual processes themselves. To do so, we built upon the base of currently available specialized algorithms and pyramided the results obtained with several decades of research on hypothetical cognitive components into both a more broadly based theoretical model and a more broadly representative and realistic simulation than has heretofore been presented.

In this book, we report some of the progress made toward such an integrated theory and a simulation of such a well-defined, but strongly constrained,

---

[2]By broadly competent, we are suggesting a vision system with the ability to function in many visual environments and to carry out many visually guided tasks.

perceptual-motor process. We describe the main steps that we took in modeling the simulated organism we call the SWIMMER.

In pursuing this goal we adhere to a philosophy of theory and simulation originally proposed in the seminal work of the late David Marr (1982). Marr suggested that we could understand and imitate biological functions (specifically vision), at least in part, by approaching the problem from a perspective that emphasizes the *information transformations that must occur* as an image passes from one representational state to another and finally culminates in behavior. In other words, Marr suggested that we should concentrate on understanding the information transformations in a *functional* sense rather than being overly concerned with the specific cognitive and neural instantiations and mechanisms that might actually account for these transformations within the nervous system. He was, we are convinced, asserting that we should center our efforts not on a neuroreductive analysis of the mechanisms of real vision systems but on the mathematical description of the operations, processes, and functions they execute.[3]

This approach is in sharp contrast to those who attempt to analyze vision by working at the neurophysiological (cell or network) level or by inferring specific internal cognitive mechanisms from psychophysical responses. Our earlier work (Uttal, 1990) argues that, *in principle,* neither of these two goals can be achieved; the former because of the complexity of the neural network and the latter because of the basic engineering principle engineers refer to as the "black box" constraint on system analysis.

Another important conceptual issue should also be considered. We are working within the context of a specific computational and mathematical environment. The analytic mathematical techniques we use are embodied in discrete mathematical or locally interactive algorithms developed on a conventional serial computer system. There is no certainty, and perhaps not even a good likelihood, that the choice of mathematics we use is appropriate. Indeed, there is increasing evidence that the integral equations and forms of analysis that we use and that were developed primarily to deal with continuous systems are quite inappropriate for modeling the logic of the brain or comparable information processing systems. Nevertheless, that is all that is available, and we must work within that context. Future mathematical developments will, no doubt, permit other steps to be taken.

---

[3]This is a somewhat different interpretation of Marr's approach than is usually given. However, we feel strongly that the neurophysiological accouterments of Marr's theory are really irrelevant to the kind of modeling he championed. From our perspective, Marr was only *describing* the functions of vision with available, appropriate, and relevant mathematical apparatuses and was not searching for a truly valid reductive explanation of the mechanisms of vision. If he did not say this explicitly, the nature of his models suggests that this was his theoretical philosophy. The mathematics he utilized to perform the necessary image transformations could model virtually any analogous mechanism and are indeterminate with regard to the actual physiological action of that mechanism.

On the positive side, our choice of mathematics is not completely inappropriate. While it may not be either reductionalistically realistic or maximally efficient, it is likely to be as good an analog as any other of the infinite number of mathematical alternatives for describing the involved processes and transformations. Indeed, just as mathematics is neutral with regard to the internal mechanisms, so too can any kind of mathematics be represented on any information processing mechanism (including the trivial and inefficient one consisting only of a sign inverter, an OR unit, and a long tape, to cite one of the most famous simple computational systems—that of Turing, 1936.)

On a more mundane level, our modeling experiments are carried out on a local area network of Apollo workstations and often do not run in real time. However frustrating this may be to us in our day-to-day computer experiments, this is not a serious conceptual matter. All of our programs could easily be accelerated (and probably will be in the near future) by the development of novel fast transforms or by transferring the algorithms to equivalent programs on a higher speed supercomputer or to an even more unconventional parallel processing computer. Improvements in speed of program execution based on novel kinds of parallelization are imminent. New computers capable of vector processing and exploiting fine- or coarse-grain parallel organization will shortly be available and will be able to accelerate the execution of our library of algorithms. The important point is that they may do so without introducing any changes in the conceptual structure of any model, including our own.

What is conceptually disconcerting is that the analogs we (as well as many of our colleagues in this field) are developing may be totally incorrect in terms of the implications they make about biocognitive information processing simply because of the limited array of mathematical tools available. For example, where both the available mathematics and current computer technology compel us toward local feature processing, the biological truth may lie in a kind of logic that is completely different—one that depends on broadly distributed, global, or holistic processes not well modeled by current mathematics or computer technology. We make no apology about this possible misdirection nor look forward to a major conceptual breakthrough in this regard from others in the field in the near future. Valid or not, there is no alternative to using what is available now.

With these preliminary matters out of the way, we can now turn to the substantive content of this monograph.

2 An Integrated Model: The Philosophy

While there is still some controversy concerning the acceptability of the idea of a serial sequence of processing stages in human information processing as opposed to a holistic, integrated, unified process, few viable alternative theories have been forthcoming to the *sequence-of-stages* approach. Even those scholars who appreciate some of the problems associated with serial processes (e.g., van de Grind, 1984) and who cite in passing such alternatives as the direct, ecological perception approach of Gibson (1966, 1979), usually revert to a model that is implicitly serial when they become specific about the details of their own cognitive theories. While this may be due to the limits of contemporary theorizing, it is, however, also true that the anatomy and physiology of the nervous system, as we currently understand it, is strongly suggestive of a series of anatomical, if not functional, stages. Whether they deal with "observers" or "primal sketches" and no matter how parallel the mechanism underlying an individual stage may be, some of the most up-to-date models (e.g., Bennett, Hoffman, & Prakash, 1989; Marr, 1982) still consider the visual system to function as a series of processing stages conceptually comparable to the anatomic stages of neural information processing. Observers pass information sequentially to other observers; the primal sketch passes the outputs of its transformation to other, more central, levels for further processing and subsequent transformation into a $2\frac{1}{2}$D and then 3D representation.

As a specific example, van de Grind (1984) presented a flowchart-type model of the anatomy of the visual system (reproduced in Figure 2.1) that strongly implies serial organization. Other serial or sequential-type models of visual

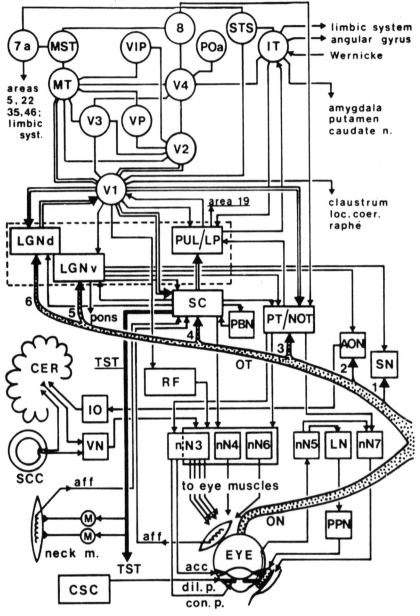

FIG. 2.1. A flowchart model of the anatomy of the visual processing system presented by van den Grind (1984), showing the emphasis on serial processes. The abbreviations are the usual ones, but are not relevant to the point being made here—the linearity of almost all contemporary theories of vision.

processing have been presented by Ratliff (1976) and Landy and Bergen (1991) and are shown in Figures 2.2 and 2.3 respectively.[1]

Interestingly the newest developments in computer visualization also follow this kind of organization. The automatic languages for encoding image processing programs, such as apE (developed by The Ohio Supercomputer Center in Columbus), are serial systems allowing local parallel operations. This is, as we shall see in chapter 5, also true of the menu-based operating system we developed for this project.

Even the so-called parallel distributed processing models (McClelland, Rumelhart, et al., 1986; Rumelhart, McClelland, & The PDP Research Group, 1986) are essentially serial systems with multiple levels of processing, local parallelicity, and feedback, all of which are certainly containable within the philosophy expressed here.

Given this Zeitgeist of practical and theoretical constraints driving our perspective toward serial organization, our integrated model should, almost necessarily, be conceptualized in the form of a sequence of processing stages. Thus, both in general and in particular, the specific series of stages we propose becomes a metamodel that defines our groups's view of the overall framework of the information flow in an entire simulated organism—the SWIMMER.

Fortunately, this general theoretical approach is likely to be relatively uncontroversial as a model of human perception, cognition, and performance because it embodies much of contemporary thinking in psychology, neuroanatomy, and computer science. This overall framework probably will not change much as the model evolves over the years. On the other hand, the individual steps, currently programmed as more or less conventional serial algorithms, are specific and detailed enough that their realism is likely to be constantly challenged, not only by others but by us as well. Indeed, one of our project requirements is that each component of our overall system must be subject to change and modification as we pass to successive stages of development and as we approach more realistic analogies with human cognitive processes.

Thus, this book offers a conceptually global, but algorithmically serial, model of a set of cognitive functions in which the component subprograms are executed using our estimate of what is the best of the currently available set of computational tools. The component algorithms simulate and describe stages in organic cognition but are not intended to explain them in any mechanistic or reductionistic sense. We repeat: We make no claim that each step is carried out in the brain in the same way as it is in our model, but that the general framework is made up of a number of stages of transformation that we believe must be included if the system is to perform in a comparable way to an organism.

---

[1]To our knowledge no equivalent structural or process-oriented model has been forthcoming from workers interested in the entire perceptual-motor complex.

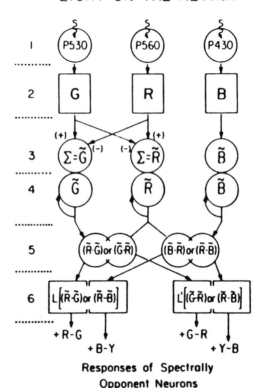

FIG. 2.2. A flowchart model of visual processing presented by Ratliff (1976), also illustrating the emphasis on serial processing.

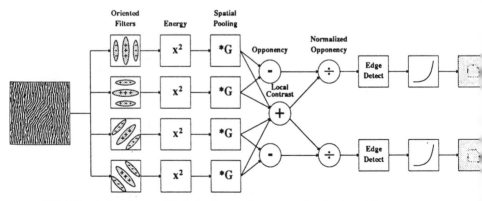

FIG. 2.3. A flowchart model of visual processing presented by Landy and Bergen (1991), also showing the emphasis on serial processing.

Specifically, we see the following correspondences as some examples of the relations between our program components and the processes of the visual system:

Computer	Human
Image acquisition	Receptor transduction
Pixel sampling	Retinal mosaic sampling
Image smoothing and noise redution	Local retinal averaging
Edge detection	Lateral inhibition
Object segmentation	
from attributes of form	Figure ground segregation
from attributes of motion	Common motion grouping
from attributes of depth	Stereopsis
from attributes of color	Color discrimination
from attributes of texture	Texture disrimination
from attributes of lightness	Lightness discrimination
Object reconstruction	Closure and completion
Object classification	Naming, recognizing
Object discrimination	Organic discrimination
Navigation	Locomotion

Our version of a sequential stage model is directly linked to a theoretical taxonomy (Uttal, 1981, 1988) that attempted to classify the various stages of visual perception in a manner that would allow their individual assay by appropriate empirical tests of such phenomena as detection, discrimination, and recognition.

The recent flurry of activity in parallel distributed processing or connectionist models is not in any way antithetical to the point of view that an overall theory must be currently formulated in terms of a series of stages. The parallel approach to modeling perceptual and other cognitive processes typically operates at a level comparable to only a single stage in the integrated serial model we are developing. Several of the individual stages in the model described have been programmed into algorithms that are parallel. As we shall see when we discuss the perceptual components of the model, parallel transformations are implicit throughout. When we discuss *convergence* or the *integration of multiple attributes,* in reality we are discussing what are parallel processes. It is the overall structure of the model we propose that is a serial or stage model, not the individual stages that are more realistically conceptualized as parallel processes.

As we mentioned earlier, the computational model presented here is not intended to represent a universal perceiver and responder. Thus, our computer programs are constrained to carry out only a circumscribed kind of visual and motor information processing. The SWIMMER's regular "food" objects must be segmented from their background, their shapes reconstructed from noisy and partial information, and discriminated from irregular "nonfood" objects. The spatial locations of the SWIMMER and the "food" are then analyzed to establish the three-dimensional world map of the environment. These simulated perceptual processes are then integrated with a navigational program that simulates the motor behavior that the SWIMMER must emit as it moves and orients itself with regard to the detected and recognized objects.

Working algorithms, sometimes in several different versions, were developed or adopted for all of the individual stages of this model. The concepts behind some of these algorithms were often drawn from the traditional literature of computer science research and in some cases do not represent a major technological step forward, nor are they presented as such. Our major technological or programming aim, it must be remembered, is to integrate these components into a broadly based model of perceptual-motor processing rather than to fine-tune the individual algorithms. Increasingly, as the project has matured, we found ourselves inventing new algorithms to accomplish a given transformation more efficiently, more realistically, or more biologically.

We are particularly satisfied with our accomplishments in developing new approaches to the integration of some novel texture segmenters, to the reconstructions of two- and three-dimensional surfaces from sparse samples, and to two- and three-dimensional form recognizers. These topics will be discussed extensively in the next chapter.

In our psychological and theoretical mode, we do want, to allow to the maximum extent possible, the design of the system of algorithms to be influenced by what is known about the nervous system and human cognition. One particular relevant aspect, and another way in which the collection of program modules is integrated in a biologically realistic manner, involves the use of multiple attributes of the image to carry out a transformation. Considerable recent interest is directed at the use of converging information to carry out visual functions. In particular, Livingstone and Hubel (1988) and Livingstone (1988) have shown that information about chromaticity, luminosity, and motion seems to be carried by separate *channels* of the visual nervous system. The information coming along these separate channels is, they assume, mixed at some higher-level stage to give a more precise representation of the external stimulus world. Poggio, Gamble, and Little (1988) carried this idea forward into the image processing domain and showed that it is possible to produce a better segmented image with multiple cues than with only one using Geman and Geman's (1984) Markov Random Field (MRF) procedure.

We carried out similar kinds of integrations within our model. Early segmentation routines that were based on single-channel (i.e., monochromatic) images were replaced by segmentation routines based on trichromatic analyses as well as on texture. We now have texture analysis systems of programs that merge the output of a half-dozen texture-sensitive filters to produce a pooled estimate of area boundaries with a sensitivity that is vastly superior to the output of any one.

When combined with the output of the color segmenters, this multiple filter produces superb image segmentation.

Thus, the model presented here draws from the technology of computer vision, from the results of psychophysical experiments, from various theoretical sources in cognitive psychology, and from the neurosciences. It is, as noted earlier, a hierarchical stage model that explicitly assumes a sequential series of transformations of information as that information is transmitted through the system, but incorporating parallel processing within many of these serial transformations. Within the context of these assumptions, it must continually be kept in mind that the model is intended to provide only descriptive simulations, and we are not proposing that any algorithm invoked in this model is actually present in the nervous system—only that the *transformation* carried out by that algorithm is more likely than not to also be performed by an analogous (though not homologous) neural mechanism of unknown nature.

To clarify this point, we cite the following example. In one of our algorithms for a particular stage of information processing, we require that the image be enhanced by a process that increases the signal-to-noise ratio. This kind of image cleaning is almost certainly carried out by the nervous system, since we are able to detect signals in dense noise levels and see objects that are obscured and occluded by a wide variety of interfering, occluding, degrading, or masking stimuli. We usually accomplish this image enhancement in this model by using a particular algorithm, namely local averaging. But the reader must be wary in interpreting our reports regarding this point. There are actually three separate levels of explanation in a discussion of this process: the process of image enhancement, the concept of local averaging as a means of carrying out that process, and the specific algorithm that carries out the local averaging. It is entirely appropriate, in our opinion, to assume that there is something akin to image enhancement by means of noise reduction occurring in the organic visual system. It is possible that this image enhancement is instantiated by some kind of local averaging process. However, because of the complexity of the visual system, we argue that there is no way in which the particular algorithm used in the computer simulation can be verified as a true explanation of the mechanism actually at work in the organic nervous system other than in terms of some secondary cue, such as goodness of fit, or some subjective criterion of elegance. As Moore (1956) has shown, there are always many more (possibly infinitely more) possible alternative algorithmic mechanisms than can ever be tested. The specific neural logic or computational process occurring within the nervous system is, therefore, not specifiable; simulation models of the kind presented here are necessarily descriptive rather than reductively explanatory in the manner often suggested.

Moore is a mathematician who has worked in the field of finite automata theory. A *finite automaton* is a device that is deterministic (as opposed to probabilistic, random, or stochastic) and has a finite number of internal states, a finite number of possible input "symbols," and a finite number of output "symbols."

Moore's (1956) Theorem 2 is directly related to the argument made here that the reductive (as opposed to descriptive) aspects of models such as the one presented in this book cannot, in principle, be tested, verified, or validated.

> *Theorem* 2: Given any machine S and any multiple experiment performed on S, there exist other machines experimentally distinguishable from S for which the original experiment would have had the same outcome (p. 140).

Moore goes on to assert:

> This result means that it will never be possible to perform experiments on a completely unknown machine that will suffice to identify it from among a class of all sequential machines (p. 140).

It is certainly debatable whether Moore's theorem is applicable to the modeling of human cognitive processes. But since the brain meets all of the definitional criteria mentioned previously, it seems that the mind-brain can be considered to be a finite automaton (even if very large numbers of states and neurons are involved, the number is finite). His argument strongly influenced us and we are constrained by its meaning for the type of work we report here.

Now that these conceptual and philosophical matters have been considered, we turn to the specific accomplishments of our group in implementing our model of perceptual-motor behavior.

3

Perceptual Processes

The computational model of the predatory behavior of a simple swimming pseudo-organism—the SWIMMER—presented here is divided into three major divisions: the perceptual process, the response processes, and the system support work created to carry out the simulation. This chapter deals mainly with the simulated perceptual algorithms that we developed, using computer image processing ideas and technology.

The ability to acquire visual information and then interpret it in what ultimately will be a behaviorally appropriate manner is an outstanding accomplishment of organic evolution. In spite of the enormous progress in the neurosciences, it must be accepted that the brain carries out these functions by means of logical processes that, in the main, remain as mysterious to us as they were to the philosophers who first confronted the problem of "How do we see?" The act of defining a simulation program, however, provides a powerful impetus to specifying precisely hypotheses concerning putative steps in the visual processing sequence. If you leave out a step, the simulation fails. It is powerfully self-tutoring!

Our computational model simulating the perceptual processes of a SWIMMER requires that we develop computational apparatuses and algorithms capable of executing the following transformational processes. Steps 1–3 collectively correspond to the perceptual process we call object detection.

1. Image acquisition
2. Image preprocessing
   a. Image smoothing and noise reduction
   b. Contrast enhancement and thresholding

    c. Contour enhancement
    d. Contour completion
    e. Quantifiaction
3. Object segmentation
    a. Of linear components—the Hough transform
    b. Of objects with closed contours
    c. Based on binocular disparities
    d. Based on multiple attributes of color
    e. Based on multiple attributes of texture
4. Object reconstruction
5. Object recognition

The following sections describe the visual processes that we simulated, make a few comments about the mechanisms by means of which organisms carry out these functions, and consider the nature of the computational algorithms generated to instantiate the simulation.

3.1. IMAGE ACQUISITION

The essential first step in image processing is the acquisition of a representation or image of an object in a form that is suitable for further computational transformation and manipulation. This process is analogous to photoreceptor transduction and the initiation of the electrochemical events that make up the transmitted neural codes by the physiological retina. Although the emphasis in visual physiology is usually on the organic photochemical processes involved in the conversion of photic to neuroelectric energy, our emphasis in this simulated transductive process is mainly on the spatial representation of the information in the scene rather than the energetics of the process. The physical act of transducing photic information into electronic signals is handled almost trivially, as far as we are concerned, by the video camera in our system.

A two-dimensional representation of the image painted by the optics of the eye on the eye's (or video camera's) photoreceptor array must be converted into a machine-readable form. In the eye, this process is carried out by a very fine grained array of exquisitely sensitive photoreceptors—the rods and cones in the retina. The cross-sectional size of these photoreceptors defines the basic acuity of the eye, although interactions among photoreceptors allow an even greater spatial acuity—the process we call *hyperacuity* (Westheimer & McKee, 1977)—than would be predicted on the basis of the receptor size, density, and distribution alone. The spatial relationships of the receptors produce a natural retinotopic map that is preserved in the visual pathway up to what are now believed to be relatively high levels of the visual cortex. The analog of this retinotopic mapping of the stimulus scene in the computer is the regular way in which information is stored in arrays in the memory of the computer. Such a retinotopic or topologically constant mapping is not a sine qua non of efficient processing in the organic or the computer vision system, however; if the rules by which an image are scrambled are known, appropriate decoding algorithms can do a respectable job of providing adaptive information to response mechanisms. This is exactly what seems to happen in the wildly scrambled peripheral visual system in the Siamese cat and albino tiger.

In a classic study of receptor numerosity and distribution, Østerberg (1935) reported that there are about 120 million rods and 6.5 million cones in the human retina. This number is at least two orders of magnitude above the number of pixels (picture elements) available in current image-capturing equipment where even a relatively fine grained image array may consist of only about 1000 by 1000 elements. The impact of these numbers is that any foreseeable computer vision system must necessarily display less spatial and depth acuity than does the human eye. Even though the perceptual effect of this difference is hardly noticeable on a moderately high definition television screen, pixel counts have an explosive impact on computer processing time that increases at least with the square of the linear density of pixels. As we shall see in our discussion of the stereo image processing algorithms, it is in this domain—computational load— that the number of pixels can produce severe computational barriers to the production of good measures of depth from binocular (or dual camera) disparity.

The difference in the raw information content of the eye and a computer vision system would be of much less import in our simulation if the computer used the same kind of parallel logic as does the eye. However, with the exception of a few very modern, massively parallel computer systems, most simulations of visual processes (even those that model parallel processes) are carried out in a serial manner rather than in the truly parallel manner of the retina. The impact of this difference in processing strategies is (usually) a vast discrepancy in the time it takes to carry out the operation in the eye and in the computer, respectively. The inability of most computer systems to simulate the visual processes in real time is an often unacknowledged limitation in contemporary reports of otherwise very exciting computational models.

Perceptual processing in the present model is, acknowledgedly, *not* operating in real time. Indeed, in some cases the model is very slow, taking more than a half hour to produce, for example, depth from stereopsis or image segmentation from multiple aspects of texture. The parallel processing system of the human visual system, on the other hand, may take only 50 ms (Julesz, 1964; Uttal, 1983) to generate depth or even less to respond to textural differences. Obviously, the larger the number of pixels, the slower the computer program will be executed. Furthermore, it must not be forgotten that even systems with relatively small numbers of pixels can require an enormous number of computer operations if intricate interactions among the pixels are processed. The reader is directed to the work of Bremermann (1977), Stockmeyer and Chandra (1979), and Tsotsos (1990) for an elaboration and clarification of this "complexity" problem.

The image acquisition apparatus used to convert images into the machine-readable form required by our simulation is an Imaging Technology Inc. (ITI) IP512 system connected to an Apollo DSP-90 computer through a multibus interface. Three analog video signals (coded as R, G, and B, respectively, to indicate the long-, medium-, and short-wavelength-sensitive outputs of the camera system, respectively) were converted on-the-fly to digital codes by a three-channel analog-to-digital (A-D) converter in the IP512. These three digitally coded images were then stored in the three color planes of digital memory of the IP512. All scenes were transformed into a stored digital image that typically was 256 × 256 pixels wide and high, but in some instances ranged up to 512 × 512 pixels and down to 128 × 128 pixels. (The 256 × 256 pixel size is but one quarter of the image storing capacity of the ITI-Apollo imaging system, but these and even lower pixel densities were more than adequate for most of our purposes. In this manner, we were able to reduce the processing time and storage requirements to more manageable levels without losing the impact of our computer experiments.) Each pixel was encoded by 8 bits, thus allowing 256 different distinguishable levels of any variable (e.g., color, brightness, texture values, etc.) to be encoded.

In those cases in which only a monochromatic image was required, the G image from the trichromatic (R-G-B) television camera (a JVC HZ-C6-11AF-U) was used as input to the processing algorithm. In those situations in which trichromatic information was required, the coded representation of all three image planes were utilized to produce a more complete (i.e., a 24 bit) and, as we shall see, a less-color-blind analysis.

Once acquired within the memory of the Apollo DSP-90, the images and all of their subsequent transformations were displayed on either a standard video monitor connected directly to the ISI unit or on the displays of the other Apollo computers connected in the local communication ring with the DSP-90.

Far more important to the goals of this project than the initial display of the captured raw image, however, was the availability of the stored, machine-readable image in the computer's memory for subsequent processing. Once the image had been transduced into a stored representation, it could be processed by the various stages of the simulated perceptual system.

Though the acquisition of the image and its subsequent storage in the computer memory is currently a technologically straightforward task, a considerable effort was required to organize the image into the most easily processed arrangement and to create compatibility between successive processing stages. Because our simulation was developed by a group of programmers, each of whom coded only a small portion of the whole process, it became necessary to specify a standard image format that could be written and read by all program segments. The format we selected was designed to be size independent; that is, any size array of pixels could be stored by a single, common "store image" program, and any size stored array could be recalled by a single, common "read image" program. This standard format included a region that specified the size of the image. The input-output routines were also designed to accept this information in a way that efficiently used memory storage space and execution time, two factors that quickly become very important in image processing applications.

The simplest possible file structure turned out to be the best. The size of the array was defined in the first four bytes ($1-2 = x$, $3-4 = y$) of a file. The total file size in bytes, therefore, was simply the number of pixels (the product of the x and y extent of the image) defined in these 4 bytes plus these 4 bytes. This simple, standard coding scheme allowed all programs to read and write standard image files.

3.2.   IMAGE PREPROCESSING

In the mammalian retina, as in simpler invertebrate eyes, a considerable amount of local image preprocessing occurs prior to higher and more complex perceptual tasks. Typically these initial, peripheral processes transform the image in ways that improve its quality or simplify the image for later transforming stages. The information in the image may be substantially reduced by paring redundant information (such as those bytes representing adjacent regions with identical luminosity), leaving only those parts of the image that contain high-information-content signals (such as the boundaries delineating the redundant areas). This reduction may be accomplished by different algorithms that produce only lines or boundaries by distinguishing between some other salient spatio-temporal-qualitative feature of the stimulus scene such as regional differences in texture, movement, or color.

Another important preprocessing task is reducing the amount of spatial *noise* in the image. Various methods, most of which involve some kind of averaging, can be used. Noise within a local region of an image can be reduced by averaging the values of a cluster of nearby pixels. Such spatial averaging reduces the acuity of the system, because averaging is functionally equivalent to introducing some degree of blur into the stored image. Nevertheless, random-amplitude fluctuations in adjacent areas may be greatly reduced, contours smoothed, and local noise reduced. It is also possible to reduce fluctuations between sequential samples by averaging the values of a given pixel across several images acquired at different times.

Automatic gain controls may also be invoked that raise the contrast of low-contrast images. The human eye's automatic dynamic intensity ranging system is extremely useful in allowing us to see small differences in luminosity or contrast at low luminances while still maintaining the ability to function in bright lights. In our computational model, this process is simulated by manipulations of the intensity histogram of the acquired image.

Preprocessing of this kind is essential to image interpretation both in the human and computational models in order to reduce overloading of the computational and transmission capabilities of the processing system. Therefore, we programmed several general-purpose algorithms to carry out these kinds of function in our SWIMMER. One analogous process in our system is *binary thresholding,* an extreme form of brightness or contrast stretching, which will be discussed in detail.

Another very important contribution of preprocessing for the computer vision system is the transformation of some qualitative property of the shape or form of an image into an equivalent quantitative attribute. The qualitative attributes of an image (such as shape) cannot be dealt with directly by the computer. It is necessary to apply an appropriate transformation method to provide a numerical representation of such a geometrical attribute. A very important step in the segmentation of an object from its background is the definition of its extent—in other words, its boundary or edge. Edge or boundary definition or enhancement can be based on a wide variety of stimulus attributes, including color, brightness, and texture (all of which are represented in the computer memory by numerical values). We also, therefore, describe the powerful role edge enhancers play in the segmentation routines.

In the following sections we deal with image smoothing and noise reduction, contrast enhancement and thresholding, edge or contour enhancements, contour completion, and quantification of images in turn.

3.2.1. Image Smoothing and Noise Reduction

The classic means of reducing random noise in any signal is to average it out of existence. Averaging is the procedure of choice in the processing of one-dimensional signals like radio waves, acoustic signals, and electroencephalograms. Signal averaging can also be applied to two- and three-dimensional signals (images) in computer vision. Indeed, noise reduction by spatial averaging of some kind is also very likely to be a major mechanism used by the visual nervous system.

Averaging is available in our library of algorithms in several different forms. It may be carried out locally (i.e., around each pixel) to remove local noise, or it may be applied to a sequence of images to reduce the random variations between successive versions of the same scene. In each case, the process depends on the respective qualities of the salient information (the signal) and the noise, respectively: Noise is unstable and varies from point to point or time to time, whereas a signal, by definition, remains constant from instance to instance. Thus, it is likely that noise will cancel itself just as a signal will reinforce itself if the repeated samples are simply averaged on a pixel-by-pixel basis. In this manner local irregularities within a single image can be eliminated as can irregularities among a series of images.

3.2.2. Contrast Manipulation and Thresholding

The manipulation of the contrast of an image and the choice of a contrast threshold below which image information is ignored is, as noted, a critical aspect of any computer image processing or perceptual simulator. Biological systems have a powerful ability to distinguish between different levels of luminance; and, most interestingly, there exist mechanisms that have variable sensitivity to accommodate different levels of illumination. The discovery of the variation of sensitivity with stimulus intensity was perhaps the first modern psychophysical fact: It is, of course, well known as Weber's Law ($K = \Delta I/I$). Computers being far more linear and far less well evolved systems than are organisms, it is necessary to provide algorithms for varying the contrast of the image rather than depending on the kind of automatic sensitivity variations found in the eye.

Contrast manipulation is a powerful tool that can be used in several ways. One useful procedure is simply to increase the range of absolute contrast in an image so that, whatever the discriminability of our algorithms is, they will have a wider range of gray levels with which to work. Contrast stretching is a simple algorithmic process: First, a histogram is made of the luminosity values (typically in our system in an 8-bit code) of all of the pixels in the image. That is, a graph that indicates the number of times each pixel gray-level value occurred in the image.

Second, all values in the histogram are multiplied either by a constant greater than 1, to linearly expand, or by some selected function to nonlinearly expand the originally measured pixel values to cover more fully the maximum possible range of the coding system used. In this manner, the contrast of an image can be enhanced. Of course, image contrast can also be reduced by using a constant less than 1 or a compressive, rather than expansive, function.

Thresholding is an equally simple, and ubiquitously used, computational tool in our programs. It is extremely useful in removing from the scene those parts of the images in which the individual pixels do not have a high enough gray-scale value (before or after contrast stretching) to be of interest. All values below some threshold value (which may be determined by either arbitrary or programmed decision rules) are simply eliminated from the calculation by setting them to a zero value. The amount of processing that has to be carried out on a thresholded image is greatly reduced compared to one that was not subject to this simple transformation.

Binary images are also regularly generated throughout our simulation system by using a concept similar to thresholding. To produce a binary image (the ultimate high-contrast version of an image), all values below the threshold are given a minimum value (zero) and all pixel gray-level values above the threshold are given a maximum value (typically 256). Thus, a given pixel would be considered to be either on or off, and the portion of the displayed image associated with that pixel will be all black or all white. This process has the effect of also increasing the contrast of the image to its extreme and thus accentuates white regions on a black background, or vice versa. Many of our programs are designed to operate on binary images of this kind.

The concept of an intensity or gray-level threshold is, therefore, very important in any image processing program. Nevertheless, the situation is not totally without complications. There is a compensatory trade-off between the completeness of the transformed image and the reduction of irrelevant noise or low-priority information. Except in those situations in which there is initially very high contrast, a low threshold will inevitably lead to the introduction of large amounts of noise and the incorporation of unimportant pixels into the transformed image. This can produce a computational explosion. A high threshold, on the other hand, may ignore some portions of the image that actually should be of interest in the analysis. Restricting the range of pixel amplitudes for which algorithms are applied gives a much lower probability that extraneous noise from the original image will be injected into subsequent transformations of the image. Similarly, following some algorithmic transformations, even a relatively low level threshold can lead to additional selectivity since the salient regions of the transformed image may be distinguishable from those of unimportant regions simply on the basis of amplitude.

One of the truly critical problems we confronted early in this project was how to automate the determination of an appropriate threshold value for *any* image that might be produced as the output of a given algorithm. Variations in image contrast, color, and other properties could lead to substantial differences in the histogram of gray levels of a transformed image. Thus, it was imperative that we utilize some conventional techniques or develop some new ones to standardize the range of gray levels as generally as possible.

The first step in our proposed solution to this problem was to produce a pixel-by-pixel, gray-level histogram of each output image. This procedure usually produced one of two types of histogram. The first type was characterized by a simple monomodal or monotonic decay of gray levels with a slope that depended on the nature of the image. For positive images of light objects on a dark background, the histogram was characterized by many low gray-level values and a decline to a smaller number of high gray-level values. A typical curve of this kind is displayed in Figure 3.1. For negative images or images in which dark images were present on a light background, the course of the histogram was reversed.

When dealing with monotonic or monomodal histograms of this kind, our goal was to set a threshold value below which all pixels would be assigned a constant value of zero and above which all pixels would be assigned a constant value of unity. The image would thus be transformed into what we have already referred to as a binary image—a high-contrast image in which all pixels are either black or white. Images of this kind are eminently suitable for further

FIG. 3.1. A typical monomodal pixel intensity histogram. Since the leading edge of the distribution is so steep, we considered this to be an example of a monotonic decline from the peak value.

processing. However, as we have noted in the case of low-contrast original images, such a transformation could lead to a loss of important information. Nevertheless, it also has the effect of substantially reducing the subsequent image processing requirements.[1] These two compensatory criteria must be balanced against each other. Whatever threshold value is chosen has to be arbitrarily defined for these monotonic histograms, there being no simple criterion that could be used to specify precisely the gray value at which the pixels mainly associated with the background could be demarcated from those associated with the objects in a scene.

The other kind of pixel gray-level histogram—the bimodal type illustrated in

---

[1]In some instances, especially with low contrast images, we also normalized a narrow-range histogram to span the entire gray-level intensity range prior to establishing a demarcating threshold between the black-and-white regions, respectively.

FIG. 3.2. A typical bimodal pixel intensity histogram.

Figure 3.2—was often found when a contour enhanced image was processed. In most cases the larger of the two modes represented the low gray-level values associated with background, noise, and other non-contour-enhanced regions; the smaller node represented the bright pixels associated with the enhanced edges or contours. In this case, a specific criterion could be utilized that was not available for the monotonic-type histogram to distinguish between the salient contours and the irrelevant background or noise pixels. We simply placed the threshold value midway between the two peaks of the bimodal histogram. This technique would work on either positive or negative images.

As important as it is to the automation of the sequence of image processing stages, it must be acknowledged that threshold determination will always be an arbitrary process with the crucial criteria varying from situation to situation. We expect that in its final form the automation of this aspect of the image processing problem will always involve several criteria interacting with each other and may represent one of the most difficult challenges in the entire project.

3.2.3. Edge and Contour Enhancement

One of the most valuable and frequently used techniques for preprocessing an image, and one that removes considerable redundancy (thus substantially reducing computational demands during image processing) is edge or contour enhancement. Algorithms of this genre can be created that are sensitive to the transitions between regions of different texture, hue, or brightness (among other possible attributes), all of which are represented as nothing more than numbers in the computer's memory. Edge or contour enhancing algorithms transform continuous images into line drawings, with the lines being especially significant because they represent informationally significant transitions. The interior regions of constant texture, hue, or brightness are suppressed; they are redundant. The advantage is an enormous reduction in the computational load on the information processor, whether it be a computer or the human visual system. Visual edge enhancement, or the Mach band phenomenon (as described in Ratliff, 1965), as it is denoted in perception circles, is a well-known and well-studied visual phenomenon. Many other visual effects (e.g., the Ganzfeld phenomenon and the Hermann grid) also seem to reflect a transformational capacity of the visual system that is analogous to algorithmic contour enhancement in computational models.

As we developed our simulation of the perceiving SWIMMER, we programmed several different edge enhancers, each of which has certain useful properties. A Soble transform was initially used and then replaced by a Roberts (1965) algorithm. We then moved on to develop a modification of the Canny edge detector that was particularly effective in enhancing continuous edges and in filtering out short segments typically associated with noise. This improved version of the Canny detector utilized two stages of image processing. First, the image was convolved with a Gaussian function to reduce noise. This smoothed image was then processed by taking the partial derivatives in both the x and y directions; this transformation is actually responsible for the enhancement of the edges.[2]

Recently, we added two edge enhancers to our library of algorithms. The first, the Kirsch transform (1974) examines the region of 8 pixels around each pixel and computes simple differences. If there is no change, the difference values, of course, will be zero. Thus, a contour is defined by a large pixel-to-pixel differ-

---

[2]Canny originally suggested using directional operators to enhance the contours even more. We tried to do this, but were unsuccessful in improving the quality of the images, that is, as perceived by the human eye. The horizontal and vertical operators seemed to do as competent a job as the more elaborate form of his transformation.

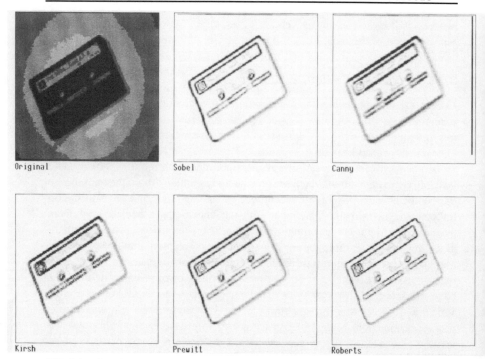

FIG. 3.3.   Samples of the outputs of several edge enhancing (i.e., edge detecting) algorithms. Though all do a fair job of detecting edges in this simple image, differences exist between the various algorithms that can be important in later stages of processing.

ence. The advantage of the Kirsch enhancer is that it considers edges in all directions, unlike, for example, the Sobel transform, which is sensitive only to the horizontal and vertical discontinuities, the Roberts, which is sensitive only to diagonal edges, or our version of the Canny.

The second new enhancer is the Prewitt (1970) transform, very much like the Sobel except that it does not weigh the horizontally and vertically connected pixels disproportionately. Both of these new transforms have an advantage over the Roberts algorithm in that they are less sensitive to noise. Figure 3.3 shows an image and a comparison of the outputs from the several contour enhanced algorithms that we have described so far.

The previously mentioned algorithms do not produce complete contours in situations in which the contrast of the original image is poor. This poor performance was drastically improved in some cases by using a combination of variable threshold and edge enhancement programs. First, an edge enhancing transform was applied to an image, but only to pixel gray-level values above a high threshold. Then the threshold was reduced, and the edge enhancer algorithm reapplied to the same image only at the ends of existing edges. The process is repeated several times until the contrast is so low that no distinction can be made between the edges and areas of constant luminance. The effect of this iterative process is that the enhanced contours are considerably more complete than those produced by a detector operating only at a single fixed and relatively high level of contrast. This is a preliminary means of closing an incomplete contour, a topic to be discussed in greater detail later in this section.

Many other important auxiliary steps in the edge enhancement process can accentuate the discontinuities defined by the standard algorithms. One important follow-up process is the elimination of any line segment below a certain size. This size filtering removes the many small segments corresponding to noise that are likely to be found in the edge enhanced output of virtually any acquired image other than a very high contrast one. This technique is particularly useful in dealing with images that have been processed in conjunction with thresholding operations. Such procedures tend to introduce messy images with many short-length artifacts.

Following size filtering we usually employed a variety of additional programming steps to further improve the quality of the lines or edges extracted from the original scene. One of them, line closure or contour completion, is discussed in the next section. Another, the pooling of information from several different edge enhancers, each of which is based on a different attribute of the image, is a major goal of our project and will also be considered in detail later. Others included dilation (which swells an edge), erosion or skeletonizing (which thin an edge to a width of a single pixel), and detwigging (which removes dead end branches) routines. We will return to these topics shortly.

3.2.4. Contour Completion

As we shall see when we discuss segmentation, contour continuity is a very powerful attribute in visually isolating or segmenting a figure from its surround. Unfortunately, completely continuous contours are not always present. For example, in underwater scenes, poor image contrast conditions can lead to substantial breaks in the outlined edges of an object following contour enhancement transformations. As we saw in the previous section, the Canny edge enhancer procedure was able to close up some slightly broken contours by a process in which images with successively lower thresholds were sequentially transformed. The portions of an edge that are enhanced at high contrast levels thus became clues to those edges that are just dimly present in the image at low luminance levels or low contrast levels. However, such a procedure works only on contours actually present, at least to some degree, in the poorer contrast levels. If a portion of a contour is not physically present or if the signal-to-noise ratios are too low, then other techniques must be used to recreate or *impute* their existence.

The human visual system has powerful abilities to complete or close discontinuous figures. Gestalt Theory of the 1920s and 1930s was, in large part, based on the repeated demonstration of this profound human visual ability to group, as

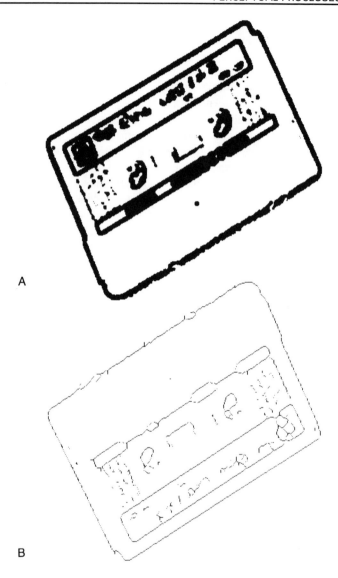

A

B

FIG. 3.4.   Diagram of the effects of the line-skeletonizing process: (a) before and (b) after.

well as to close, incomplete figures. It is also known that there is a special visual sensitivity to figures that exhibited some kind of proclivity to be completed—the elusive property denoted as *Pragnanz,* but connoted to almost no one's satisfaction.

The task we faced, both as a practical necessity and as a theoretical goal, was to impute figural continuity across actual breaks in a discontinuous contour. The mechanisms by which the human performs this task are still unknown, even though we know quite a bit about the course of the process and the factors that influence it. Nevertheless, we have developed some computer algorithms that do a fair job of closing incomplete contours when they are not retrievable from the original image by any other means.

The first procedure was a simple algorithm for connecting line segments broken by short artifactual gaps. This procedure consisted of sequential dilation and erosion of the enhanced, but discontinuous, edges. Each pixel above a threshold value was dilated by simply raising the immediately surrounding pixels to the gray-level value of the central pixel out to a predetermined distance. This process has the effect of swelling all lines consisting of suprathreshold pixels so that slightly discontinuous segments of a putative edge would then touch and become continuous. The thick dilated edges are then eroded by a skeletonizing algorithm in a way that preserves the new connections that had been made during dilation, but thinned down the line representing the edge to a width of only a single pixel. Sequential dilation and thinning, skeletonizing, or erosion has the happy outcome of also reducing the amount of salient information (i.e., the number of pixels) that must be processed to a very small portion of those in the original image. The results of this process are illustrated in Figure 3.4.

The second procedure for connecting broken line or edge segments that we used was effective for larger discontinuities or gaps than could be encompassed by the dilation and skeletonizing algorithm. This line closure algorithm was based on a selection procedure that operated on relatively long line segments that were already isolated by the contour enhancement procedures and was carried out, necessarily, prior to detwigging. (Detwigging is the process of removing lines connected at only one end from a contour.) This second procedure is essentially a statistical process in which the computer program looked for line terminations that might be connected with varying degrees of probability. Depending on the nature of the scene, this alternative contour completion algorithm performed with varying degrees of competence. If there were few lines in the scene, the algorithm would work well over relatively large breaks. If the scene was cluttered, spurious connections would be made and it would be much less competent in connecting the ends of lines that should be connected.

We now consider this second line completion algorithm in detail. This algorithm is founded on the idea that lines are more likely to continue in the direction in which they are proceeding than to make abrupt directional changes the closer the putative segments are to each other. Essentially, this premise embodies the simple extrapolation hypothesis that the probability of a line going off in a direction other than the one in which it is heading is progressively larger the further away one is from the present end point. To embody this probabilistic hypothesis, a symmetrical teardrop-shaped search region was extended along a tangent to a given line segment from its terminal point as shown in Figure 3.5. If the end of another sufficiently long (i.e., if a criterion line length was exceeded) line segment was found inside the teardrop-shaped search region, it was pre-

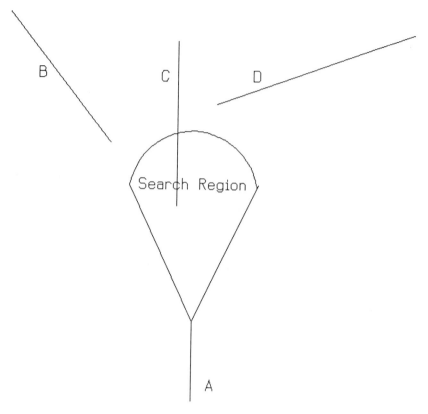

FIG. 3.5. Diagram of the teardrop-shaped search region used in the contour-closing routines. Only line C, which terminates in the search region, will be connected to line A.

sumed that line represented a continuation of the first segment and the gap was filled in the memory map of the image.

The shape of the teardrop thus represented a probabilistic or statistical theory of edge continuity. Specifically, two distant line segments might be relatively far apart and still be parts of the same line. When the two line segments were closer together, a more stringent propinquity criterion is applied. This is the primary source of the teardrop-shaped search region; the distal portion could be broader than the nearer regions. The probability that two segments should be connected was also progressively reduced as the difference between the tangents of the two line segments increased.[3]

---

[3]This hypothesis is also a characteristic of human visual perception. Gestalt psychology told us that one of the most important factors in establishing a sense of closure was the good continuation of the line. This algorithm models that process.

Next, to test whether two line segments should be connected, the line terminations discovered inside the teardrop-shaped region were extended by a linear extrapolation procedure. If the extrapolated line approached the line termination from which the search was initiated, it was assumed to be a continuation of that line. The intervening points were then filled in with an imputed straight-line segment.

This line completion algorithm contains several approximations that are comparable to the moveable criterion built into the Signal Detection Theory test of the presence or absence of a signal in a noisy background. Thus, there are linked probabilities of a detected false connection and a missed true connection that will depend on arbitrary decisions made of the criterion angle of intersection and the exact shape of the teardrop-shaped search region.

Our program adjusted the size and exact shape of the search region to match the characteristics of the processed image. A sample of the effectiveness of the algorithm is shown in Figure 3.6. In the first part of this figure we show a sample discontinuous image. The second part shows the figure completed by the procedure just discussed. Contour completion of this kind plays an important role in providing higher quality representations to the segmentation routines (to be described later) than the raw edge enhanced image mapped from the camera.

A third, more elaborate but conceptually very similar, contour closure algorithm was based on a system of multiple rules. This algorithm works by exploring the context of a given line as it appears among other lines. Three interdependent criterion, applied in order, must be satisfied to determine whether line segments in a scene should be connected together. The first criterion states that very small gaps (no greater than 4 pixels) can immediately be closed between a line segment end point and any part of another line that is in the path of the continuation of the line segment. The second criterion asserts that the end points of two closely spaced line segments should be connected if they have similar slopes (within 20°) and their end points are close (separated by no more than 8 pixels.) The third criterion permits two more widely separated long line segments to be connected if an end point of one line segment points directly to the end point of the other, even though there is a very large difference between the two, and if the separation is no greater than 40 pixels.

The three criteria must be applied in the order just presented because each one depends on previous ones to fill higher priority gaps. Priority is defined in terms of the likelihood that two line segments should be combined. For example, the closure of small gaps is of a higher priority than the closure of a long gap. As each line segment is combined with another, the coordinates of its end points are removed from the list of end points that remain to be connected.

To implement these rules, we must determine each line segment's slope, length, and position of its end points. (The input image to this algorithm is an edge enhanced version made up of 1-pixel-wide skeletonized lines. Thus, the lines in this type of image contain pixels that can have only one or two neighbors

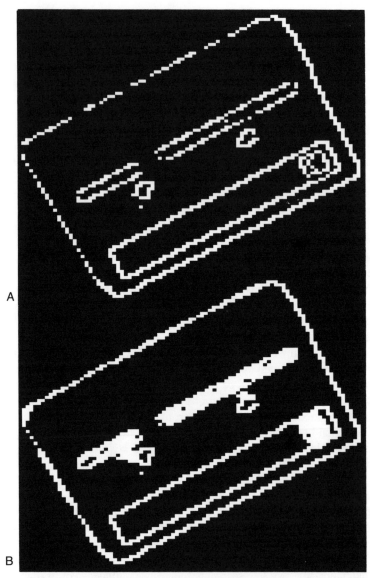

FIG. 3.6. An example of the contour-closing process using the teardrop-shaped search region: (a) discontinuous image; (b) improved version with many of the breaks closed up. Note the introduced errors, however. Compare with Fig. 3.8.

in their 4-connected neighborhood.) Once this information is available, the end points of each line segment can be compared with all others to determine whether any of the criteria apply. When a criterion indicates that two end points should be connected, a line is drawn between them in a transformed image. Both straight and moderately curved lines can be connected with this procedure.

An end point is defined as a pixel that occurs at the end of a series of pixels that are connected in a line. An end point is considered to be either any pixel with only one neighbor in the eight spaces around it or, ambiguously, with two neighbors connected to each other. In either case, there is an input path into the 3 × 3 pixel area but no exit from it. Figure 3.7 depicts these two possibilities.

Once an end point is identified, a second point in the interior of the line must be obtained. This second point is used to determine the length and orientation of the section of the line that contains the end point. The interior point is found either by tracing, from the end point, along the line a specified distance, or until the other end of the line is reached, whichever comes first. If the line's length is less than a specified threshold, it is not tested with the gap-filling rules. If the other end of the line is not reached within the criterion distance, the point at the criterion distance is used. Another pair of points is then found to define the line containing the other end point.

Contour tracing is accomplished by searching the 8-connected neighborhoods (first around an end point and then around successive points) for pixels that were not traversed by the tracing algorithm. The untraversed nonzero, pixel becomes the next pixel in the edge. This procedure permits both curved and straight-line segments to be traced, but may introduce mistakes at the point of intersection of two or more lines. Whichever branch exiting an intersection is first encountered becomes the continuation of the line being traced. The length of the line segment is defined as the number of pixels between the end point and the corresponding interior point. The orientation of the line segment is defined as the slope of the line defined by the end point and the interior point. Angles below the horizontal are negative and vary from $0°$ to $-180°$; angles above are positive and vary from $0°$ to $180°$.

Figure 3.8 shows the results of an application of this alternative contour-closing procedure. When this original image is edge enhanced, many of the contour lines are incomplete because of the poor contrast conditions. After the application of the three criteria, many of the lines that a human observer would see as closed are also closed by this algorithm. In some cases, however, incorrect closures were made. Further development of the algorithm to prevent spurious connections of interior points may alleviate this type of problem and further improve the quality of the image created by the closure procedure. It is unlikely, however, that any such procedure will ever be totally error-free.

We plan to develop other closure procedures. One such method applies an autocorrelation transform to a discretely dotted version of any straight-line segments in the edge enhanced image. Autocorrelation produces a transformed

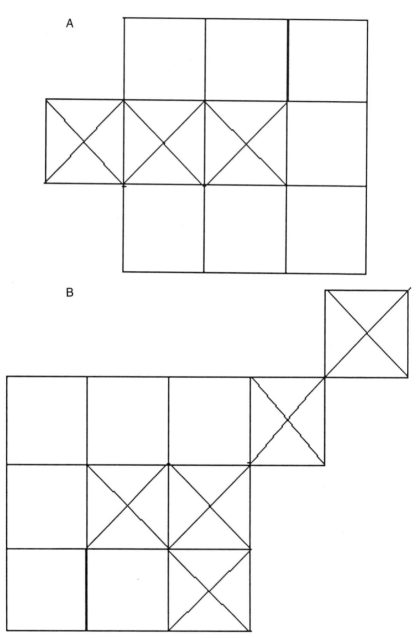

FIG. 3.7. Two ways in which a pixel (represented by an x in a 3 × 3 array of otherwise empty pixel locations) may be defined as an "end point" of a line. (a) An end point with only one neighbor in the eight spaces surrounding it. (b) An end point with two connected neighbors. The situation in (b) is ambiguous, however, and only suggests an end point.

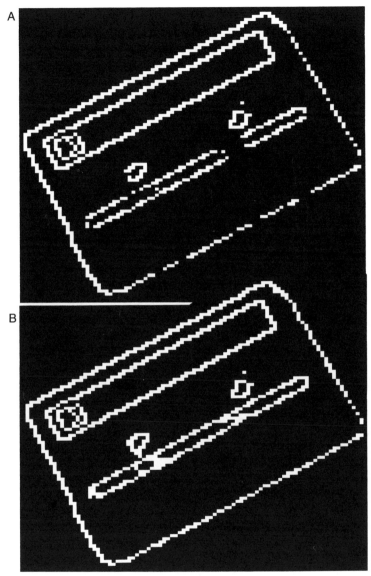

FIG. 3.8. The results of the improved contour-closing routine. (a) Shows the incomplete input image and (b) the output image with fewer false closures and line thickenings than indicated in Figure 3.6.

image of a straight line that is also a straight line but is longer than the original. Thus, two collinear straight lines separated by a suitably small gap would tend to be completed. Curved lines produce more complex autocorrelations, but the use of such an artifice as autocorrelating the terminal tangents of the discontinuous curve (rather than the curve itself) would allow this process to be carried out even in that case. This process has already been shown to be a good model of human form detection (Uttal, 1975).

3.2.5. Quantification

Another essential aspect of preprocessing is the conversion of the global, geometric, qualitative, or pictorial aspects of an image into numerical values that can be processed by a computer. The shape of an object, for example, is a configural property that cannot be directly analyzed computationally even though the visual system seems to deal with it effortlessly. The geometrical attributes of a form or shape must be quantified in some way so that a computer can deal with a property such as *triangularity* just as it might deal with the numerical gray-level values assigned to a given pixel. Transforms are required that convert such qualitative geometrical aspects of an image into computer-manipulable values. Two traditional ways in which quantification has been carried out are Fourier Analysis and Autocorrelation.

Two-dimensional Fourier analysis converts shapes in the xy domain into spectral plots in the $\omega_x \, \omega_y$ frequency domain in which the respective amplitudes—a numerical value—of a set of orthogonal sinusoidal functions becomes the collective numerical code for the spatial properties of the original image.[4] The spatial Fourier components $\mathscr{F}(\omega_x, \omega_y)$ of an image $F(x, y)$ are defined by the expression

$$\mathscr{F}(\omega_x, \omega_y) = \int\!\!\!\int_{-\infty}^{\infty} F(x, y) \, exp \, \{-i(\omega_x x + \omega_y y)\} \, dx \, dy, \quad (3.1)$$

where $i = \sqrt{-1}$.

When the analysis is carried out in a manner in which phase and amplitude information are preserved, the original shape of the object is fully represented and can be reconstructed from the numerical values by Inverse Fourier Analysis. The expression for the inverse transform is:

---

[4]When the set of orthogonal functions (i.e., functions that cannot be transformed into each other by simple linear operators) is a set of sinusoids, the analysis is referred to as Fourier Analysis. However, a wide variety of alternative sets of orthogonal functions can be substituted for sinusoids. The Walsh and Hadamard transforms utilize an orthogonal set of square and rectangular waves, the difference between the two simply being the way in which the respective sets of orthogonal waves are organized.

$$F(x, y) = \frac{1}{4\pi^2} \int\limits_{-\infty}^{\infty}\!\!\!\int \mathscr{F}(\omega_x, \omega_y) \; exp \; \{i(\omega_x x + \omega_y y)\} \; d\omega_x \, d\omega_y. \qquad (3.2)$$

A related procedure uses a set of orthogonal functions defined over a much narrower region than are the infinitely extending sinusoidal components of a Fourier Analysis. For example, computational requirements can be reduced by applying a set of orthogonal Gabor operators (shown in Figure 3.9) to limited areas of the image. Each Gabor operator is the product of a sinusoid and a range-limited Gaussian function and varies from the other members of the set in the spatial frequency and orientation of the constituent sinusoid as well as in the extent of the Gaussian. Gabor operators $h(x, y)$ are defined by the equation

$$h(x, y) = g(x, y) \; exp \; \{2\pi i[u_0 x + v_0 y]\}, \qquad (3.3)$$

where

$$g(x, y) = exp \; \{-\tfrac{1}{2}[(-x/\sigma_x)^2 + (y/\sigma_y)^2]\} \qquad (3.4)$$

where σ_x and σ_y define the limits (i.e., size) of the two-dimensional Gaussian function g(x, y) and μ_0 and γ_0 are the two spatial frequency components of the modulating sinusoid. That is, the modulating sinusoid's spatial frequency is equal to $\sqrt{u_0^2 + v_0^2}$. An important psychobiological aspect of this approach is that the Gabor operator simulates much of what is known of the center-surround receptive field of visual neurons at several levels of the nervous system and, therefore, has a certain biological face validity. We shall discuss this function in greater detail later.

An alternative technique of representing forms by means of a transformation from the image space to another space also utilizes the Autocorrelation Transformation. Autocorrelations typically produce a system of numbers in a space that is one dimension greater than the original image space. Thus, for example, a two-dimensional picture in the (x, y) space is transformed into a three-dimensional plot in the $(\Delta x, \Delta y)$ space, where Δx and Δy are the amplitude of the shifts in position of the image and A_c is the value of the autocorrelation integral at $(\Delta x, \Delta y)$. Autocorrelation is defined by

$$A_c(\Delta x, \Delta y) = \iint f(x,y) \cdot f(x + \Delta x, y + \Delta y) \; dy \; dx. \qquad (3.5)$$

The numerical value of A_c at each point in this new space is determined by the shape of the object in the original image space. These numbers are then suitable for further analysis, for example, by the construction of a figure of merit of detectability. (See Uttal, 1975, for a full discussion of this algorithm.)

These forms of quantification are of interest because they represent a means of manipulating the qualitative attributes of an image mathematically. For example, an image that has been transformed into a set of Fourier components can be

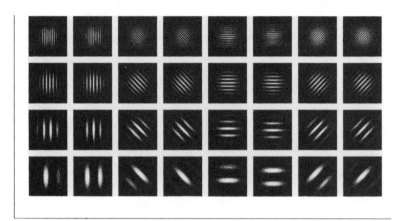

Frequency

Orientation

Filter size : 65x65 pixels

Orientation : 0, 45, 90, 135 degrees

Frequency wavelength : 32, 16, 8, 4 pixels

Phase : 0, 90 degrees

Standard deviation : 12.5 pixels

FIG. 3.9.   A partial set of Gabor operators that can be convolved with an image
to represent that image in a manner similar to Fourier Analysis with spatial sinusoids.

filtered by removing a subset of components from the Fourier spectrum before
reconstructing the image by the Inverse Fourier Transform. Removal of high-
frequency components may blur the reconstructed image, and removal of the
low-frequency components is equivalent to the kinds of edge enhancement procedures we already considered. This kind of selective filtering depends on the
fact that Fourier Analysis is a linear process. Therefore, the different frequencies
can be linearly superimposed (added or subtracted) on and from each other.

There is a common concept—the idea of a *vector*—underlying all of these
filter-based procedures. Each such transformation results in a table or set of
numbers representing the proportion or quantity of a standard component—a
frequency in a Fourier Analysis or an operator in a Gabor-type transform, for
example. Collectively, the tables of numbers or vectors describe a unique form
that can be reconstructed by adding the appropriate amounts of each of the
components. The number of values in each vector is a priori unlimited, though
practice usually limits the set to some relatively small number. Furthermore,
there is no reason why all of the components in a vector need come from the
same set. Mixing different orthogonal sets is a novel approach to form processing

that offers considerable promise in enhancing the outcome of computer vision, especially with regard to object segmentation and recognition, the topics to which we now turn.

3.3.   OBJECT SEGMENTATION

Images, once acquired, preprocessed, and quantified in the manner described in the previous sections, we now move on to the main part of the image detection process. In our simulation, detection is defined in a highly circumscribed manner (as are all tasks in all computer image processing tasks.) That is, detection is the process that answers the questions: Are there any objects present in the scene that are delimited by closed (or closable) contours? If so, what are the coordinates of the points on these contours? The determination of the extent or contour of an object is operationalized by the program's ability to segment or isolate the representations of individual objects from the background of an acquired scene and from other objects in that scene. The human perceptual analog of the segmentation problem is the segregation of figures from grounds, or in a more general sense, image understanding.

Within the context of the present model-building exercise we are remember that we are not considering *energy* detection. That is, we assume that the energy of the stimulus is sufficiently high to produce a nonzero response in at least a portion of the array of pixels representing an object (or objects) in an image. We are also assuming that the signal-to-noise ratio is sufficiently high so that at least a part of a putative image can be extracted from its background by appropriate algorithms. A challenging aspect of this part of the problem is to simulate the extraordinary ability of the human visual system to detect objects that may overlap or be occluded by other objects and to distinguish the boundaries between objects in complex juxtaposition with each other. As we shall see, we made considerable progress in this regard in the recognition phase of the simulation.

At the outset of this project, we appreciated that the development of a powerful detection ability generalizable to many different kinds of scenes was a formidable challenge. Therefore, we had to define a highly constrained microworld in which the objects to be manipulated and the tasks to be performed were precisely defined. If there is any fundamental truth in the image processing world toward which we were guided by our experiences so far, it is that no computer system is yet (and in the future may not be) capable of the unconstrained, generalizable, and adaptive kind of visual processing exhibited by the human visual system. Perhaps at some later time we will have a sufficiently complete understanding of the logic that allows such magnificent generalization across visual domains by human observers. However, for now this simulation, like all others of its genre, is limited to a set of precisely defined processes in an equally precisely circumscribed microworld. Neither our group nor any other has yet developed a computer vision system that generalizes across microworld boundaries; all are designed to work only within a narrowly circumscribed context. Workers in this field find that when such models are extended to other microworlds, they are extended by a process of accreting new algorithms rather than by the generalization of old ones. The conceptual issue confronted here is that computer vision, like all other forms of artificial intelligence, has far to go in its attempts to simulate the full power of organic vision.

We already defined the boundaries of our perceptual microworld. To reiterate, it is one inhabited by a simulated SWIMMER confronted by only two kinds of objects—salient or food objects and irrelevant objects to be avoided. The food objects sought by our SWIMMER are defined as regular two- or three-dimensional forms. Irrelevant objects are defined as being irregular in form. As noted, the simulated detection task consists of locating in space (i.e., detecting) either of these two kinds of objects and segmenting or separating them from the other objects in the scene and the scene's background. Subsequent programs in the sequence are called upon to distinguish between the regular and the irregular objects (discrimination) and to attach classifications (recognition) to them. As also noted, the main criterion for a segmentable object in the current version of our program is that it be enclosed within a closed or nearly closed contour. In addition, we also implemented a version of the Hough algorithm (1962) to detect narrow linear structures stretching across major portions of the image field. The detection of these open-ended lines and of closed-contour structures are discussed in this section.

Several types of attributes can be used to segment forms from their background once the preprocessing has made the amount of information (for us, this is nearly always defined in terms of the number of pixels) in the image computationally manageable and quantitatively available. In the following sections we consider only five of the many types of segmentation cues. One method is appropriate for the segmentation of solid objects, since it is based on the interpretation of stereoscopically generated disparities. Another uses color, or, more correctly, the intensity relationships among the three electronic receptors in the image-capturing camera—the R, G, and B image planes—as the cue. The third depends on the textural attributes of the image, and the fourth examines edge information searching for closed contours. We begin our discussion with an image segmenter that isolates lines from an image, the Hough transform.

3.3.1. The Isolation of Linelike Structures— The Hough Transform

The detection of lines of arbitrary orientation was accomplished in our system by a modification of the Hough (1962) transform, the now nearly standard line detector (as opposed to edge enhancer) used throughout the computer vision community. The version of the Hough transform we developed was capable of providing a good estimate of the best-fitting straight-line approximation even to lines with modest degrees of curvature.

The successful application of the algorithm depends on an automatic thresholding procedure. The acquired image is scanned with a relatively high criterion so that only the small set of the brightest pixels is present in the initial transformed image. These bright pixels are then arranged into all possible pairwise combinations. Each pair of pixels thus defines a straight, but fictitious, line. These fictitious lines are then tabulated by the program on the basis of their intersection with the boundaries of the image space. A line might cross, for example, the bottom and top of the image, the left side and the right side, or the bottom and the right side. If a string of pixels lays along a nearly straight line, they would all be likely to cross the boundary at or near the same point on the boundary and create a cluster of intersections there.

The line detection algorithm's task is to determine which of these clusters is dense enough to characterize a real line in the image. To the degree that the line is curved, the cluster of points on the boundary would be more or less broadly distributed—the more curved, the broader the cluster of dots. Therefore, a simple statistical analysis (the computation of the standard deviation) of the distribution of the clusters on the boundary can be used as a measure of curvature.

The final step in the line detector algorithm is the reconstruction and selection of the strongest line in the image. This was done by looking for the densest and narrowest cluster of intersections on the boundary and its mate on the other side of the display. We usually superimposed this line on the original image in color as a means of highlighting the final outcome of the process. Figure 3.10 is an example showing the application of this modified Hough routine to an image of a pipeline obtained from a side-scanning sonar system.

The Hough line detector was not a main goal of our current work. Nevertheless, it possesses some interesting psychological implications. The Hough transform is a means of detecting line segments on the basis of statistical considerations that requires no special sensitivity to straight lines per se. Thus, it exists as an alternative theoretical heuristic to the notion of *tuned line detectors* popularized by the distinguished neurophysiological work of Hubel and Wiesel (1962). As our simulation continues to mature, the Hough line detector may prove to be of more direct interest.

3.3.2. The Isolation of Objects with Closed Contours

Unlike the Hough line detector just described, the identification of forms that are enclosed by continuous contours is a major goal of this project. We described how contour or edge enhancement is accomplished with any of several alternative procedures. In this section we consider how an enhanced contour is evaluated to determine if it is closed and continuous.

Following the contour enhancement process, we invoke a series of programs

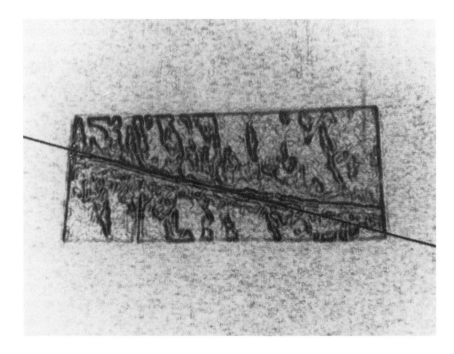

FIG. 3.10.   An example of the output of a Hough line-detecting routine to lo-
calizing a pipeline in an underwater scene produced by a side scan sonar. (Side
scanning sonar courtesy of Naval Ocean Systems Center, Hawaii Laboratory.)

designed to locate and identify continuous boundaries or closed contours. Two
techniques are used. One technique worked on contours that are actually completely closed. The other worked on contours that might have some breaks in
them, a not uncommon situation when photographs of natural scenes with wide
ranges of contrast are used as the input.

The first technique for determining whether a boundary is closed depends on
the availability of extensively preprocessed and enhanced contours or edges. As
described on page 33, contours fed into this algorithm are skeletonized or thinned
so that they are only 1 pixel wide. This thinning altered the lines representing the
edges so that there could be only two neighbors of the 8 possible pixels that
surrounded each ("eight connected") pixel in the rectangular coordinate system
world of the computer image.

The algorithm actually tracks the perimeter of the form. The execution of this
technique is, therefore, straightforward. The computer samples the edge enhanced image space until it finds a pixel with a suprathreshold value (*one* if the
image had been made into a binary image). The neighbors of the pixel are then
examined to determine if only two of them have suprathreshold values. If so,

then the program tracks one of the two neighbors to determine if it has only one additional neighbor. The process is iterated in the same direction until one of the new neighbors turns out to be either the first one sampled or a pixel with only one neighbor—an end point. If the former condition exists, return to the starting point, the contour is designated as closed. If the iterative tracking of the chain of pixels ends on a value other than the initial pixel, it indicates that the contour was not closed.

This first technique only works on completely closed contours. While this may seem to be a rather rigid and drastic restriction, it proved to be surprisingly useful in a wide variety of tests of our algorithms. The preprocessing steps, particularly the dilation and contraction or skeletonizing algorithms, themselves have a tendency to fill in minor breaks in contours and, therefore, to correct many of the minor defects in the original edge enhanced image.

The second technique for determining if a contour is closed (and, therefore, represents a segmentable object) utilized a process of radius or ray casting. This technique is especially useful for contours that almost completely enclose a two-dimensional space. In the first step of this algorithm, the center of gravity of a putative two-dimensional form is determined. This point then becomes the origin for a system of radii that is cast out toward the putative contour. Depending on how complete the contour is, a certain proportion of the radii intersects it, an occurrence signaled by one of the pixels of the cast radii intersecting one of the pixels on the contour. If the proportion of radii that intersects the contour exceeds a manipulable threshold, the contour is assumed to be closed.

Of course, there are many arbitrary decisions in the application of this algorithm. The contour intersected must be at least partially present on both sides of the center of gravity. A test that identifies the two intersections as samples of the same contour is a prerequisite for its use. The process also requires that a decision be made concerning what proportion of hits are necessary to accept a contour as closed. In our system, we arbitrarily choose 75% as an appropriate threshold. The system was very successful in removing from our images many contours that were not closed, particularly long, isolated lines that did not represent closed and, therefore, segmentable objects.

We were reminded of something especially important by our work on this part of our integrated model: No single algorithm is likely to successfully segment all kinds of objects in even a simple scene. Each algorithm that we programmed was inadequate in one context or another. However, the concatenation of a group of algorithms into an integrated and interacting system now seems to be a major step towards successfully simulating visual processes. The theoretical and practical programming implications of this conjecture will be discussed later.

The conclusion that integrated systems of algorithms, as opposed to single transformations, are necessary for efficient and satisfactory image processing also emerged in other contexts. A closely related idea is that of *pyramiding* programs of varying levels of resolution in tasks such as segmentation or stereomatching. Work of this genre has been carried out by Uhr (1974) and Rosen-feld (1980) and is a basic part of the stereomatching algorithms of Grimson (1981) and Marr and Poggio (1979).

Pyramiding is becoming increasingly important in visual theory. An entire symposium was dedicated to it in a recent meeting of the European Conference on Visual Perception, a major meeting in this field held each year.

The general philosophy behind pyramiding is that it is uneconomical to apply the most detailed, high-resolution algorithm that happens to be available to all parts of a newly encountered scene. The amount of computation required is enormous. The pyramid approach suggests that first a very low resolution image processing technique should be applied to a scene to determine regions with a reasonable probability of being of interest. Then additional programs of increas-ingly high levels of resolution should be applied to progressively increase the probability of the estimates that a segmentable object is present or to establish, for example, an increasingly precise registration of two stereoimages.

It seems evident from this study and from decades of psychological research that the human possesses an extraordinarily powerful visual system that utilizes an integrated ensemble of many different mutually interacting mechanisms. Con-trary to much recent myth in psychology and curiously irrelevant results in neurophysiology, we believe that the idea that the action of a single and simple neuron can account for or even represent something as complex as face recogni-tion is almost certainly unsupported.

Similarly, the general approach taken in our work and much of the other recent work in computer image processing suggests that a search for single algorithms capable of such powerful processing would be futile indeed. For example, much of the controversy concerning local feature versus global visual processing is clouded by what is known and not known of human vision. For example, Navon's (1977) seminal paper was criticized by Miller (1981) in terms of what it is that is being attended to at any moment. Miller's point is that either local or global attributes may take precedence, depending on what we ask the observer to do. According to Miller, there is no global precedence per se. Most likely, both processes are available (a first glance global form of vision followed by a more careful scrutiny of details). Much of the rest of the argument revolving around this issue is probably nothing more than a mass of technical trivialities.

We shall discuss later the details of our progress in integrating multiple al-gorithms to achieve high performance in a vision system.

3.3.3. Isolation of Three-Dimensional Form
Based on Binocular Disparities

In the previous section, we considered how the two-dimensional attributes of a form can be used to identify an object surrounded by a closed contour and to isolate it from its background. Other kinds of information are available, however, in many situations that may allow a visual system to distinguish between figural objects and ground or between different objects. Among the most salient of these are the three-dimensional attributes of the scene. Objects situated at different depths in a volume can be distinguished from each other on the basis of those depth differences if relative depths are measured; portions of an image that are situated at different distances or in front of a distant background are likely to be demarcatable objects. Discontinuities in depth are as strong clues to object segmentation as discontinuities in the two-dimensional representation. The rate of change of depth of the surface of an object is also a strong cue to its shape; continuity of depth is a cue to the closure of solids just as continuity of a contour is a cue to the closure of a two-dimensional object.

Determining the depth of an object or its parts can be accomplished in many ways. Sonar, radar, and even some newer infrared ranging techniques all depend on the transmission of energy and a measurement of the time it takes for a radio, acoustic, or optical echo to return to the transmitter. However, information about depth or range is obtainable on the basis of the simple geometry of the viewing situation that can be utilized in a purely passive manner. That is, depth can be obtained in situations in which no signal need be transmitted, but only the image of the object is analyzed. For example, information can be obtained from the changes that occur in an image when a solid object moves from one position to another or is rotated about an axis, that is, from the cues associated with motion parallax. We did not pursue this line of analysis, but the work of Lappin, Doner, and Kottas (1980), Braunstein, Hoffman, Anderson, Shapiro, and Bennett (1987), and Ullman (1979), among others, is germane to any discussion of object detection or the extraction of shape from motion cues.

The three-dimensional shape of an object can also be obtained from monocular views if it is textured or has differences in shading or contour lines. The projective geometry of static and dynamic viewing conditions produces attributes that can be summed up by the term *perspective*. Works by Stevens (1981, 1986) and Koenderink (1990) are examples of an approach that concentrates on these results forthcoming from the trigonometric definition of the viewing angle and the fundamental nature of the viewed space.

The initial effort of determining the three-dimensional shape of an object in the present research program utilizes a very different approach, however. We concentrated on the determination of binocular (or, more properly, bicameral) disparity from image differences in the views of two horizontally separated cameras. Specifically, we simulated the stereoscopic process that occurs in human vision as a result of the slightly different viewpoints of the two eyes by recording two images of the same solid object from two camera positions. The stereoscopic technique is important to computer vision specialists and is supported by one of the most highly developed computer simulation technologies. Work by Marr and Nishihara (1978), Marr and Poggio (1979), and Grimson (1981), all suggested that this approach would be one of the most useful for our studies.

There is, however, a major difficulty with stereoscopic analysis. Fundamental constraints are at work in any practical computational stereoscopic system that are not present in the human visual system, prohibiting fine resolution of depth differences. In brief, this means that it will be difficult for contemporary computer technology to provide rigorous estimates of depth to a precision comparable to human vision until much faster computers and finer grain image representations become available. It must be understood that these constraints do not depend on the theory behind shape from disparity algorithms. In principle, given a suitably powerful computer and a suitably fine receptor grain (e.g., as is found in the human eye or in a camera with an ultra-fine pixel density), a high degree of depth precision (i.e., depth acuity) can be obtained. Rather, these constraints depend on the practical computability of the stereoscopic algorithms in real-world situations with available technology.

The problem arises because of the trade-off between the resolution of the image of the three-dimensional scene that is stored, the amount of computer time required to execute certain parts of the process, and the size of the computer memory required to store intermediate images. The essence of the problem is that there is an inherent contradiction built into the process. To achieve good depth resolution one must have an adequate pixel density, yet to achieve good depth resolution using all available pixels requires inordinate amounts of computer processing time. For current stereoscopic analysis algorithms, the image resolution in the xy plane that is required for adequate depth resolution is astonishingly high. The human being is able to accomplish the remarkable process of reconstructing depth from retinal disparities only because the retinal receptors are so small and so densely packed *and* the processing is done in parallel—all local operations occur concurrently. Computer vision systems will undoubtedly face great difficulty with such analyses for the foreseeable future until resolutions much greater than those currently at hand become available and until computer speeds or parallel processing technology become sufficiently powerful to handle the enormous number of pixels involved in these image analyses.

To be more specific, the practical, computational obstacle is that, as the resolution of the image is increased, the computational requirements imposed on any computer (but accentuated in contemporary serial devices) go up at least as fast as the square of the improved resolution. It can be shown that the maximum ability to discriminate between depths (z resolution) is a fixed proportion of the xy resolution. For practical resolutions (for example, 256×256 pixels or 512×512 pixels) that do not overload the computer and, thus, extend the processing time beyond acceptable limits, the depth resolution is only about 2% (256×256) and about 1% (512×512) of a total depth range of 500 cm with a full depth range of 500 cm, a viewing angle of 30 deg, and a sensor width of 1.27 cm. These rather poor depth resolutions compare extremely unfavorably to that of the human eye, which typically is assumed to be 2 s of arc out of a total range estimated to be about 100 m, a depth acuity approximately 0.00048% of the total range.

This severe constraint on the depth resolution of computer vision systems is not usually made explicit in most presentations of new stereoscopic processing algorithms. The fact that even those algorithms that have been successful in achieving this limited degree of resolution run exceedingly slow on even the fastest available processors is usually glossed over in theoretical presentations. The end result of this obfuscation is that the practical utility of any currently available stereoscopic image processing system is severely limited and will be until major improvements in high-speed, parallel processing computers occur.

Nevertheless, the development of an algorithm to simulate stereoscopic vision is of considerable theoretical interest. Such an exercise was extremely valuable in defining the transformations that "must" be carried out to transform two two-dimensional images into a single three-dimensional representation even though the system may not operate in real time. Furthermore, even modest depth resolution may be useful in our work. For these theoretical and practical reasons we implemented one version of such an algorithm, and, acknowledging its limitations, we learned a considerable amount about what will ultimately be necessary to make it a practical part of a working simulated vision system. The following paragraphs describe our implementation of this algorithm.

Stereoscopic analysis is fundamentally a two-step procedure. The first step is to determine which parts of the two two-dimensional images are equivalent. This part of the procedure is a search for the solution of the *correspondence* problem. The second step determines the horizontal shift (if the two cameras are, like the human's eyes, displaced from each other horizontally) of the parts of the image identified as corresponding. This shift, or *disparity*, is the critical factor in calculating the distance from that part of the scene to the camera—the depth. However, this second step is essentially a trivial piece of computational trigonometry: The solution to the correspondence problem, on the other hand, is the source of most of the difficulties and time-consuming calculations in the computational modeling of stereoscopically defined depth.

The correspondence problem is so difficult because it requires a very subtle judgment by a computer, which must determine whether two parts of two views of an image are identical. In essence, this requires understanding the scene in a way that goes far beyond simple tasks such as; for example, contour enhancement, a more or less straightforward application of a relatively simple algorithm. In our judgment the formalisms and artifices for identifying correspondence between parts of two two-dimensional images in a computer vision system probably are less likely to truly represent the neural processes underlying human stereopsis than are the ones representing contour enhancement.

The difficulties in establishing correspondences arise at the outset of the process and illustrate likely differences between algorithmic and organic stereopsis. In general, computer algorithms that attempt to achieve stereopsis do not work well on the global attributes of an image. Objects that show little local detail are enormously difficult to process; the identification of correspondences in this approach must be made on the basis of what are often very local cues. Thus, a frequent artifice is to cover the object with a random pattern of curved lines, short fragments, or even dots. These local regions then provide the required detail needed by the algorithm to compare the two pictures. (Remember that this local texture must be random and not periodic both for computer processing and human vision. Otherwise, false correspondences will result.)

Several mechanisms have been suggested for making the comparison as the program seeks to identify two image components as different views of the same part of the object. Cross-correlation of each part with all of the other parts can work in some instances, but such a brute-force, hammer-and-tongs procedure is often cumbersome and ineffective. Such a method may also degrade drastically, due to shape distortions of the two putatively corresponding images. Other comparison procedures involve a search for a part of an object (or, more formally, an interest operator) that can be identified in both images. However, the distortions produced by the differing points of view of the two cameras (or eyes) can also make this approach uncertain or inefficient.

The algorithm we developed for stereoscopic image processing follows closely the one proposed by Grimson (1981), which in turn is based on the idea of "zero-crossing" analysis originally proposed and formalized by Marr and Hildreth (1980). The correspondence problem is solved in an ingenious manner. The features used as interest operators are the zero crossings of a gray-scale image (i.e., the specific boundaries or contours between regions of different brightness at the point where the Laplacian of the image, $F(x, y)$, equals zero). That is, where

$$\frac{\partial^2 F(x, y)}{\partial x^2} + \frac{\partial^2 F(x, y)}{\partial y^2} = 0. \tag{3.6}$$

Usually, the Laplace Transform is carried out on a preprocessed version of the image that was smoothed by the application of a two-dimensional Gaussian transform to reduce noise and the effect of small image irregularities. Application of the Laplace Transform to such an image produces an edge enhanced representation as exemplified in Figure 3.11. These edges, the interest features, extracted by the Laplace Transform are brought into correspondence at this stage of this procedure for extracting depth.

An important characteristic of the Laplacian of the Gaussian transform is that each zero-crossing point has certain properties that derive from the nature of the original image, namely, sign, orientation, and location. The sign is $+1$ if the image brightness is changing from negative to positive, and -1 if it is changing from positive to negative. It location is that (x, y) coordinate value in the image space. Orientation is a measure of the slope of the original image at the point of the zero crossing. These characteristics give a sufficient number of independent degrees of freedom so that individual lines can be compared with a reasonable degree of immunity to ambiguity to determine whether they are alternative representations of the same object in the original two images.

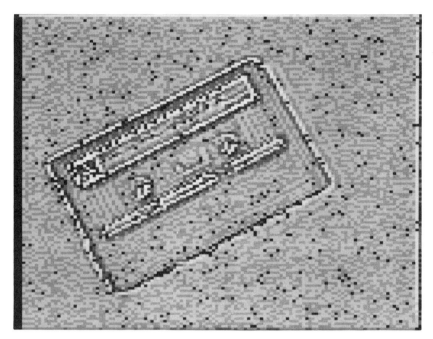

FIG. 3.11. A sample image to which has been applied the Laplace Transform to extract the zero-crossing or edge information. Black spots indicate zero crossings in the negative direction, and white spots indicate zero crossings in the positive direction.

As easy as it is to describe these comparisons with words, it proved to be extremely challenging to implement them in a computer program. As noted, in the context of stereopsis, relatively low resolution images (128×128 and 320×320 pixels) were used to avoid a computational explosion in terms of running time and memory requirements, which accentuated the problem alluded to earlier concerning the poor depth resolution of these algorithms.

Once the zero crossings have been determined by application of the Marr-Hildreth version of the Laplace Transform for the left and right camera images, respectively, and their characteristics cataloged, the next task was to compare the two processed images so that corresponding interest features in the two images (i.e., the zero crossings) could be identified. Our adaptation of Grimson's matching (correspondence detection) algorithm utilizes a procedure in which interest feature matching is carried out at four levels of resolution: This is an important example of a pyramidal approach to image processing. At each level, horizontal lines of pixels on the left camera image are examined to determine if there is a zero crossing present. If there is, an area (varying in size with the resolution factor being used) is searched in the right camera image to determine whether there is a pixel with the same characteristics (i.e., sign, orientation, and location) present. The zero crossings in the two images must have the same sign and a slope within 30% of each other's value to be considered to be corresponding interest features. Their (x, y) coordinate values must also vary by no more than half of the size of the search region. Once this correspondence is established, it is easy to specify disparity, since it is only necessary to measure the difference in the horizontal separation between the two pixels that were declared to be corresponding components of the image.

Many false correspondences will be generated by this search procedure, particularly at the coarsest resolutions, along with the true correspondences. If less than 70% of the zero crossings in the left image are matched, then everything is rejected as false. If more than 70% of the putative interest features are matched, then the correspondences are accepted and the process repeated at the three finer levels of resolution.

The four progressively finer resolutions of matching produce four correspondence maps. The findings at each level are then used to help resolve any ambiguities that may still exist at the higher levels. In cases in which that threshold value was not achieved different offsets of the search regions are utilized that help raise the number of matches at the higher levels above the 70% threshold.

The end product of this iterative process is a final map showing the correspondences of the many zero crossings. As noted, transforming these disparities into the depth values for each corresponding interest feature in the original image is easy. Once a fixation region is identified at which the corresponding components are in the same (x, y) location, only simple trigonometry is required to compute the depths associated with various disparities.

This zero-crossing approach throws away an enormous amount of information. Only at the positions of the zero crossings can depth be determined. This means that depth is indeterminate at other portions of the image, and that other procedures (including either mathematical interpolation by a computer or subjective filling by a human) must be used to specify the depth of a continuous surface at all points.

Because of nonzero crossing information lost in the transformational process, some structured texture is usually applied to any surface that is to be stereoscopically examined for depth by computer algorithms. Without zero-crossing information from fairly dense sets of boundaries, or some other natural or artificially added texture within the boundaries there may be too little information to bring into correspondence either to define depth or to reconstruct the surface.

These facts also argue, as already suggested, that the algorithm used in the Marr-Hildreth-Grimson procedure is unlikely to be the same as the one used in human vision. Human vision is much more capable than computer vision of dealing with simple untextured figures. What this model provides is a statement of the general processes and transformations that must be carried out, such as interest feature designation, correspondence detection, and disparity measurement. While analogs of these processes must be carried out by the nervous system, our intuition is that the specific instantiating algorithms, such as the zero-crossing filter or the search process, used by our computer are not actually the ones carried out in brain. The algorithmic approach that Marr, Hildreth, and Grimson invented and that we modified is characterized by a more or less local, but totally deterministic analysis of the relationship of the interest features. It is purely a bottom-up procedure in which only the local characteristics of the image are used to achieve the desired depth estimates. Human stereopsis seems, on the other hand, to involve much higher level, top-down, cognitive, global functions that do not depend to any great degree on the local pictorial attributes of an image, but are mainly influenced by the global pictorial attributes of the scene. For example, we can perceive depth in two-dimensional images that only suggest the shape of the solid object.

Obviously, additional levels of processing are activated in the human brain that go far beyond (or implement in other manners) the transforms executed by the present version of the computer vision–stereopsis model we have developed for this project. At the very least, the model is incomplete as a theory of the details of human vision; at the very worst it may be completely misleading in terms of the actual biological mechanisms underlying the perceptual transformations. In other words, it is very likely that it carries out the salient processes (e.g., interest feature specification, correspondence determination, and disparity-to-depth conversion) by totally different internal mechanisms than those in the human brain. The model of stereopsis presented here, in terms of the details of its constituent algorithms, may be more a description of the power of computers to compute depth than a reductive theory of a biological stereoscopic process. Indeed, given this analysis, one wonders how the visual system could possibly carry out a depth discrimination purely on the basis of retinal disparity. The answer must be framed in terms of several factors: (1) the much higher resolving power of the eye; (2) the fact that the sheer computational power of the parallel processing brain is so much greater than that of any contemporary computer system; and (3) the ability of the brain to utilize top-down, globally oriented, heuristics to solve the correspondence problem.

Some other practical limitations of the Marr-Hildreth-Grimson approach transcend these theoretical, indeed almost philosophical, speculations. Obviously the requirements for computer processing are enormous in the correspondence determination process. In some versions of our programs, it took from 10 to 30 to 120 min for our dedicated graphic workstations (Apollo DN3000 and DN3500 models) to perform a single step of the four-stage solution to the correspondence problem. The image's pixel count was greatly reduced to make some of the algorithms work at all, and shortcuts were continually required to allow computational experimentation to go forward. Some convolutions thought to be essential for the Marr-Hildreth transform required as much as 6 Mbytes of memory and a 480 × 480 pixel image. Even with fast transforms these demanding programs took as long as 2 h to run.

Therefore we were forced to invent some novel shortcut procedures. Rather than calculate the Gaussian transform directly (a process initially required to smooth the original image), a much simpler and less computationally demanding local averaging process was substituted. Rather than attempting to calculate the Laplacian directly, a Difference of Gaussians (DOG) approximation was used. While there are some advantages to such approximations (e.g., computational speed in this case depends only on the size of the image and the process can be speedily conducted in the spatial domain) these short cuts do not exactly reproduce the specific procedure described by the formal Marr-Poggio-Grimson mathematics.

The difficulties encountered because of memory and computational speed requirements would be greatly reduced with a faster computer. But, beyond these basic computational difficulties, there are other fundamental problems with any approach that uses this most famous of published stereoscopic vision algorithms. The Marr-Poggio-Grimson procedure is very sensitive to any vertical misalignments of the two cameras because it ignores vertical disparities. A small vertical misalignment of even 1 pixel can produce wild fluctuations in the final depth estimates by destroying the ability of the computer to specify correspondences that may be well registered horizontally. Periodic patterns such as found in a regular texture can pose insurmountable problems for the procedure, since many false correspondences will be detected at each cycle of repetition. Therefore, irregular or even random textures are more desirable as the interest features than regular patterns in this kind of image processing. Of course, if the zero-crossing edges are purely horizontal, the process will not work at all.

Another problem alluded to earlier is the inability of this stereo analysis system to finely resolve depth given the relatively coarse pixel counts we were forced to use. This poor resolution suggested that we try to interpolate between the pixel values in order to simulate a higher two-dimensional resolution and thereby obtain a finer delineation of the object's three-dimensional structure. This is the direction that our exploration of a model of stereoscopic depth has now taken.

Given these difficulties and, in particular, the resolution problem discussed at the beginning of this section, neither the Marr-Poggio-Grimson algorithm nor our modifications of that method are good models of the exquisitely sensitive human stereoscopic capability. The practical implication of these difficulties is that for us to insert a stereoscopic capability into our current model will require a different level of computer power, one that has just now become available.

In sum, while no theoretical model of vision would be complete without some effort to understand and simulate stereopsis, current theoretical and practical criteria suggest that it would not be a good judgment to insert a stereoscopic algorithm into the present version of the computational model of the SWIMMER. (Note added in proof: since writing this, we have accomplished this formidable task.)

3.3.4.   Transformations Based on Multiple Attributes of the Stimulus: Color

One of the most interesting contemporary developments in perceptual psychology, neurophysiology, and computer science is the increasing awareness that visual perception is almost certainly based on the integration of separate representations or attributes of the visual image. Coded representations of various attributes of the stimulus are now know to be transmitted through relatively independent channels (Livingstone, 1988; Livingstone and Hubel, 1988; Van Essen, 1985; Zeki, 1978) of the visual pathways. Form, color, orientation, spatial information, movement, and depth are typical of the parameters that seem to be independently conveyed from the periphery to the central nervous system. In neurophysiological laboratories neurons are regularly found at the several different levels of the visual pathway that are selectively sensitive to only one, or at most a few, of this gamut of possible stimulus attributes. Yet, somehow the end product of all of this independent processing is a unified experience of an object, once again perceptually displaying the ensemble of attributes that was present in the distal object.

If one denies the nervous system the information carried by any of these channels, or any of its subchannels, some relevant perceptual blindness will eventuate. This phenomenal *attribute-specific blindness* is most familiar in color vision anomalies; a deficiency in the information conveyed by any of the three color channels results in a predictable form of color insensitivity. Similarly, when

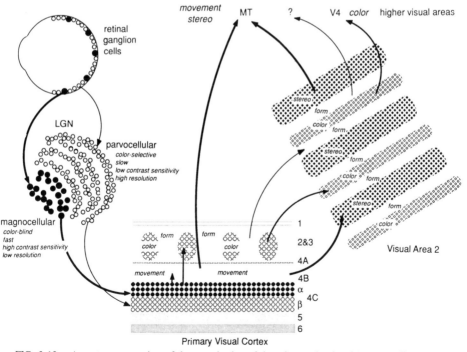

FIG. 3.12.   A contemporary view of the organization of the primate visual pathway according to Livingstone and Hubel (1988). (Copyright 1988 by the AAAS.)

information is blocked in a putative form, orientation, contrast, or movement channel, then some analogous form of attribute insensitivity should be anticipated. For example, if a channel conveying orientation information were interrupted, an observer might be able to discriminate color but not some salient textural attribute.

Among others in recent years, Livingstone and Hubel (1988), traced the anatomical pathways that are responsible for the coded representation and transmission of information associated with the various stimulus attributes. Figure 3.12 summarizes their thinking about the anatomical pathways along which contrast, color, form, movement, and stereoscopic depth are conveyed. An important aspect of their work is the inference that, given that these parallel channels are actually anatomically separate, then the information they carry must be integrated into a single unified perceptual experience at some higher level of the nervous system. It is not certain whether this information must actually converge anatomically or that a complete experience can emerge when the activities of the separate centers and regions occur synchronously. It is possible that the activities in separate regions collectively determine the percept because of the temporal overlap of these activities, but without actual physical convergence.

In an experiment that is relevant to this issue, Nawrot and Blake (1989) showed that information about depth from two cues, stereopsis and motion, can mutually influence each other in a way that modifies the combined depth experience. Since stereopsis (depth from disparity) depends on images that are disparate in space and depth from motion cues depends on images that are disparate in time, Nawrot and Blake's result suggests that the two *channels* may convey these two kinds of information to a common locale where the adaptive interactions occur.[5]

Unfortunately, these data do not provide an unequivocal answer to the question of functional (i.e., temporal synchrony) versus anatomical (i.e., spatial congruity) integration. What is clear is that integration of the *information* contained in the separate channels must be carried out in some manner by a wide variety of perceptual processes. The inference drawn from the physiological evidence and psychophysical data is that a marked improvement (in terms of the practice of computer vision and in terms of a theory of vision embodied in computational models) will occur if a variety of separate representations or attributes of the image are integrated into a composite representation.

Suggestions that computer image processing should proceed in this direction were foreshadowed by Geman and Geman (1984), Terzopoulos (1986), and by Poggio, Gamble, and Little (1988). These workers emphasized the importance of combining multiple versions of transformed images, each transformation repre-

---

[5]The specifics of the experiment are not germane to the present discussion. But, briefly, the effect is that the experience of depth generated from ambiguous motion is influenced substantially by adaptation to unambiguous depth from stereoscopic displays.

senting the output of a process that depended on a different stimulus attribute. The general goal of this work was to produce a higher quality image segmentation, by merging multiple sources of information, than could be achieved with only one attribute.

A need for some statistical consideration arises because all of the algorithms may not produce exactly corresponding (i.e., spatially congruent) results. For example, there is usually some uncertainty about where the different boundaries of an object will be placed when different edge determination criteria are used.

One of the statistical approaches initially suggested by Geman and Geman (1984) is designated as the Markov Random Field (MRF). Poggio et al. (1988) applied the MRF procedure to the reconstruction of a surface from a sampled set of randomly positioned depth measures on that surface. To achieve this reconstruction (one that people do remarkably well; see Uttal et al., 1988) a priori probabilities were assumed that the random depth estimates represented samples from any one of a set of possible surfaces. To converge on which surface was actually being sampled, they noted that the depth at any point was constrained more by the depths of its neighbors than by more distant points. The statistics of the variation in the depth measurements were then evaluated, and a Monte Carlo technique was used to match the a priori estimates of the possible surfaces, the estimates of the noise (i.e., variability in the depth measurements), and the few available sampled depth measurements. The MRF was then extended to incorporate other information from additional aspects of the stimulus, such as color, motion, and texture to model the reconstruction of visual depth processes.

Beyond the procedure's mathematical details, the most germane aspect of this work is that the Geman and Poggio groups (as well as other pioneers) have developed a technique that emphasizes the importance of integrating various measures or attributes of the stimulus rather than using only a single attribute of the original scene. The exact details and success of their procedure are less relevant than the general philosophy of multiattribute integration, an approach to visual image processing that seems to hold the promise of providing the most effective and plausible way for either a computer or an organism to proceed with the task of image analysis and understanding.

Other approaches to the integration of multiple sources of information were described and compared by Massaro and Friedman (1990). They were concerned with the purely psychological aspects of the problem and eschewed reductive neurophysiologizing. The methods they described (Bayesian Integration, Fuzzy Logic models, Theory of Signal Detection, Multidimensional Scaling, and a Two-Level Connectionist Model) are all descriptive mathematical approaches to this problem with many commonalities and often, as they point out, with formal equivalences.

Similarly, in our simulation of the SWIMMER we made extensive efforts to integrate several measures of the stimulus into our segmentation procedures. At the present stage of our work we are concentrating on two-dimensional image processing. The attributes available to us for the segmentation of image components from each other and from the background are incorporated in the three brightness maps represented by the information stored in the three color planes of the DSP-90/ITI image capturing system. As our initial effort in integrating multi-attribute information to enhance the quality of the segregation of components of the image, we concentrated on giving our model a sensitivity equivalent to human trichromatic vision and the human ability to discriminate texture. We now discuss segmentation algorithms that are based on color, and in the next section, present a discussion of the integrated texture-based segmentation routines.

The differential action spectra of the organic R, G, and B cones are modeled in our computer vision system by the R, G, and B sensitivities of the charge-coupled detector (CCD) camera. The three sets of data stored in the three color planes of the image-capturing apparatus individually represent three mono-chrome brightness images. Because, there are the three type of receptors in the human color vision system, each plane is individually color-blind. An interesting, although certainly not unexpected, aspect of this computer color blindness is that the three planes of information each exhibit a different kind of color weakness. For example, the medium-wavelength (G) image does not distinguish between two wavelengths that are quite discriminable by the normal human trichromat. The two wavelengths may produce the same degree of image intensity in the camera's output signal because they are at equal response levels on opposite sides of the peak of the respective spectral sensitivity curve. Thus, an object that is reflecting a considerably different spectrum of light than its background may be quite indistinguishable from that background to the green color plane and may be perfectly camouflaged. Obviously, many other color combinations are equivalently camouflaged to the view of the other two color planes yet appear quite different in hue to the normal trichromatic vision system.

To create the full range of color sensitivity, the human visual system mixes the information from the three channels to allow discrimination based on relative differences among the three receptor types. In this manner, a much richer and more complete representation of the external world is maintained. For the human it is not just a matter of aesthetics; it is a practical matter of image segregation that could sometimes affect the survival of the organism. An object that may be invisible to one receptor may be made visible by a mechanism that integrates information from three channels that are differentially sensitive to wavelength.

This highly adaptive evolutionary outcome—a system with hue sensitivity as well as brightness sensitivity—in the organic eye is simulated in our computer model by a simple algorithm. We performed a brightness edge extraction process on all three of the monochrome images stored in the three color planes of the image-capturing equipment and then integrated (i.e., combined) the edge enhanced outputs of the three parallel transformations by means of a simple OR operation. Although the image of an object might be missing from one or two of the three image planes, this simple operator allows the partial images passed from all three planes to be pooled to give a complete representation of all objects in the scene. Any specific color attributes that led the object to be missed by one plane will be compensated for by the sensitivity of another plane.

This process is illustrated in Figure 3.13. Note the absence of some parts of the object images that were present in the original scene in all three planes in Figure 3.13a. These omissions result, as noted, from the different color sensitivities of the three color planes of the video camera. Figure 3.13b shows what happens when the three images of Figure 3.13a are simply ORed together; a robustly complete, edge-transformed image of the entire scene has been salvaged from the three incomplete images. Figures 3.13c,d show the rest of the segmentation process.

In this case, the registration of the three edge enhanced images from the three color planes was sufficiently good that a simple OR operation was satisfactory. As we shall see, in situations in which the registration is not as good (e.g., when attempts are made to pool the outputs of different algorithms to segment texture, for example), more elaborate approaches to attribute integration are required.

3.3.5. Transformations Based on Multiple Attributes of the Stimulus: Texture

Not all objects exhibit color differences. In optically restricted environments (e.g., underwater), the spectrum of colors reflected from a scene may be highly constrained to a narrow band of wavelengths. In such situations the lack of chromatic differences and accompanying poor contrast conditions prevent segmentation of objects from each other or from their backgrounds when chromaticity is used as the distinguishing attribute. Therefore, we wanted to consider alternative approaches to color or pixel gray-level intensity that would allow segmentation even under poor conditions of visibility.

In a visually restricted environment, *texture* becomes an important alternative cue for the segmentation of objects. The word *texture* refers mainly to the arrangement of a wide variety of patterns, shapes, and other components that can make up a surface. Therefore, regions that differ in texture consist of component units that differ in some global, spatial, or organizational way even though they may be alike in average intensity, color, or even local form. Texture is a global spatial attribute of a region that is not evident or measurable in the data associated with a single pixel. Multi-pixel regions must be examined to define the local component units of larger textured surface. Following Julesz's (1981) invention of the terminology these component units have come to be known as *textons* in both engineering and psychological circles.

No single technique can segment regions characterized by all types of textural differences. Even when dealing with a single, relatively successful algorithm that works well on one class of textures under one set of conditions, it is not likely that the parameters of that algorithm can be set so that it will work under all

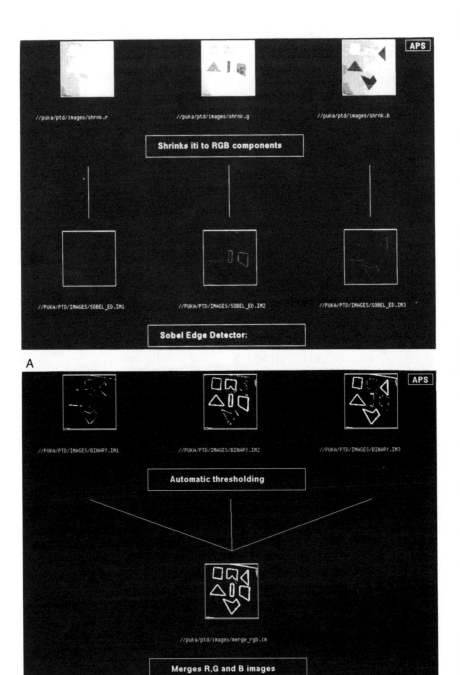

FIG. 3.13. A demonstration of the trichromatic visual system capability coded into our model presented as a flowchart of the steps involved. (a) Three mono-chromatic images captured in the R, G, and B planes of the video camera, respectively, and the first stage of edge enhancement by a Sobel operator. Note the missing components in each of the images due to the inability of the stored image representations to discriminate between certain colors. (b) Automatic thresholding

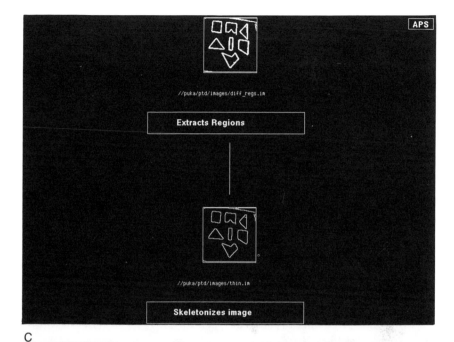

APS

//puka/ptd/images/diff_regs.im

Extracts Regions

//puka/ptd/images/thin.im

Skeletonizes image

C

APS

//puka/ptd/images/no_branches.im

Removes twigs

NOT
AN
IMAGE FILE

//puka/ptd/images/pointers.dat

Traces contours

D

stages and the essential step—the pooling of the three outputs to produce a complete set of edge enhanced objects in a single image. (c) Step in which closed contours are identified and their contours skeletonized. (d) Removes twigs and transforms the information into an image file in which shapes are represented by tables of numbers rather than a pixel-by-pixel map.

conditions or for other classes of textures. Hence, we believe that to develop a broadly competent texture segmenting process, we must program a variety of algorithms with different sensitivities and combine their results.

Although the integration of the output of several texture algorithms is a major goal of this project, two major obstacles obstruct this goal. First, if several algorithms produce different estimates of boundaries between regions of different texture, how can the computer know which boundaries are correct and which are incorrect? Second, the volume of information obtained from the initial analysis may be so large that it produces an unacceptable load on available computational power.

We believe that some kind of spatial statistics offers the best solution to the first problem. In this section we report the development of a boundary averaging program that does an excellent job of combining several texture boundary estimates to produce an improved texture segmentation. The second problem, we have come to believe, is probably going to be ameliorated by faster computers, but will never be completely solved. Multiple attribute texture analysis is always going to be a computationally demanding process.

A large amount of work has been done in texture segmentation and classification. Previous workers have used many techniques, including Gabor filters (Clark, Bovik, & Geisler, 1987; Turner, 1986) frequency-based transforms (Bajesy & Lieberman, 1974; Gramenopoulos, 1973; Jernigan & D'Astous, 1984; Kirvida & Johnson, 1973; Maurer, 1974; Unser, 1986), textural edginess (Kartikeyen & Sarkar, 1989; Rosenfeld & Thurston, 1971; Rosenfeld & Troy, 1970; Sutton & Hall, 1972; Triendl, 1972), the Co-occurrence Matrix (Carlucci, 1972; Darling & Joseph, 1968; Haralick, 1971; Haralick & Shanmugam, 1973; Haralick, Shanmugam, & Dinstein, 1972, 1973; Julesz, 1962; Lu & Fu, 1978), probabilistic spatial dependence (McCormick & Jayaramamurthy, 1975; Read & Jayaramamurthy, 1972), eigenfilters (Ade, 1983), the autocorrelation function (Kaizer, 1955) relative extrema (Enrich & Foith, 1976; Mitchell, Myers, & Boyne, 1977), run length (Galloway, 1974), texture units (Wang & He, 1990), weak texture measures (Tomita, Yachida, & Tsuji, 1973; Tsuji & Tomita, 1973), and fractal dimensions (Ait-Kheddache & Rajala, 1988; Heeger & Pentland, 1986; Peleg, Naor, Hartley, & Avnir, 1984). Two comprehensive reviews of the field are also available (duBuf, Kardan, & Spann, 1990; Haralick, 1979).

Texture segmentation methods are classified as either statistical or structural analyses. Statistical analysis demarcates a textured region based on the common statistical properties of the arrangement of the textons. The density or the variability of the spaces between textons are typical measures used by this type of analysis. Structural analysis, on the other hand, is typified by grouping processes that identify the component geometric elements (textons) of a texture and then defining a region by grouping elements that are geometrically similar. We consider filtering methods such as Fourier Analysis or similar methods that use sets of special orthogonal functions such as the product of Gaussians and sinusoids (i.e., Gabor functions) to be structural in nature because they are sensitive to texton shape. Depending on the "graininess" or spatial frequency of repetition, such methods may be influenced by the statistical arrangement of the textons. Similarly, we consider convolutional methods, in which a mask is compared to the individual textons, to be structural in the context of this dichotomy.[6] The statistical and structural categories are not completely exclusive, but this dichotomy does emphasize the differences between the two main general approaches to texture segmentation. At some level of analysis, they are likely to be mathematically interchangeable or even formally equivalent.

Both statistical and structural methods are intended to define regions differing in texture and produce, as an output, boundary information suitable for pooling with the boundary information from other similar algorithms. Both approaches may be necessary to achieve this goal. We now consider the two approaches in detail.

Statistical Segmentation

Algorithms relevant to the texture segmentation problem that are primarily statistical include:

Presegmentation image transformations

Statistical grouping

Region extraction

Presegmentation Image Transforms.   The presegmentation image transforming algorithms that we used are specially designed to enhance particular attributes of the image and to improve the input to the statistical texture analyzers per se. We already considered some procedures of this class, and we now discuss some that are especially relevant to the texture analysis problem.

A particularly useful preliminary enhancement of the image can be accomplished by applying a z- or standard score transformations. A z score is a measure of the number of standard deviations a score is away from the mean rather than the value of the raw score itself. Therefore, the z-score transformation, minimizes intensity effects and emphasizes the structural differences in an image. It emphasizes how the properties of an image vary relatively rather than absolutely.

Another useful preliminary transformation is obtained with the Kirsh edge detector. The Kirsh algorithm works by examining the eight possible neighbors

---

[6]Some methods used by Julesz to describe the attributes of dotted textons are themselves statistical. But, within the context of this dichotomy, we would consider them to actually be alternative ways of describing the shape of a texton and thus *structural.*

around a pixel and choosing the maximum gradient value. Specifically, if the pixels in a 3 × 3 neighborhood are labeled a through i as follows:

```
----------------------------------
|   a   |   b   |   c   |
----------------------------------
|   d   |   e   |   f   |
----------------------------------
|   g   |   h   |   i   |
----------------------------------
```

then the eight edge gradients from which a maximum is chosen are

$$val1 = |a\text{-}e| + |b\text{-}e| + |c\text{-}e|,$$

$$val2 = |b\text{-}e| + |c\text{-}e| + |f\text{-}e|,$$

$$val3 = |c\text{-}e| + |f\text{-}e| + |i\text{-}e|,$$

$$val4 = |f\text{-}e| + |i\text{-}e| + |h\text{-}e|,$$

$$val5 = |i\text{-}e| + |h\text{-}e| + |g\text{-}e|,$$

$$val6 = |h\text{-}e| + |g\text{-}e| + |d\text{-}e|,$$

$$val7 = |g\text{-}e| + |d\text{-}e| + |a\text{-}e|,$$

$$val8 = |d\text{-}e| + |a\text{-}e| + |b\text{-}e|.$$

The result is a transformed image enhancing the strongest edges in the original scene without any biasing that may result from the orientation selectivity that is typical of other edge enhancing algorithms. (See page 29 for a more thorough consideration.) Using the Kirsh transform as a preliminary step, we construct a new image that contains information only about the orientation of the strongest edges. For convenient visualization, this image is usually plotted in eight false colors, where each color represents one of eight edge orientations.

The orientation image produced by the Kirsh edge enhancer is especially useful as a precursor to segmenting textured patterns where the strongest edges all have the same orientation or in situations where the edges lie in a constant pattern of orientations such as a set of L-shaped textons. In these cases, homogeneous regions are formed by simply establishing those areas within which the textons are identical. This method is often applied before applying Co-occurrence Matrices to the image.

Statistical Grouping: Our first attempt at texture segmentation using statistical grouping involved an examination of the properties of local areas in the raw gray-level data that represented the original image. The usual descriptive statistical measures were implemented: mean, median, minimums, and maximums, all of which are first-order statistics, and the standard deviation and variance, both of which are second-order statistics. Each measure is obtained by applying the appropriate transformation to a local area around each point in the image, the size of the local region depending on the specific situation. For example, the mean of a 3×3 region is calculated by adding all of the pixel intensity values in that region and dividing by 9.

The mean, median, minimum, and maximum operators distinguish regions that differ in brightness (i.e., average gray-level intensity). These statistics can only define the regions by establishing an average brightness value for those regions and, therefore, can be insensitive to regions of equal average brightness, but different spatial distributions.

Nevertheless, the mean and median transforms do have different effects in computer vision just as they do in ordinary descriptive statistics. The median, in particular, has special properties that make it especially interesting. Its effect depends on the shape of the region examined. With a square mask, the median transform removes thin lines and clips off corners. (The mean filter only makes these object attributes fainter by blurring them.) The shape of the median filter can be modified to obtain different and improved results. When the region examined (as determined by the shape of a mask) is cross-shaped, the median filter will keep the corners of objects intact, remove single-pixel effects, and remove single-pixel-wide nonvertical and nonhorizontal lines while not affecting vertical and horizontal lines.

The maximum and minimum operators are both sensitive to the overall brightness of an image, but they can also perform another useful and distinct function. In regions that contain large background sections with only a few small areas of greater or lesser intensity, applying the minimum or maximum operator makes such regions more homogeneous than in the raw image. These operators can also separate regions in which one of the extreme values (the minimum or maximum) has different properties. For example, cases in which the maxima may all be nearly constant and the minima more variable (or vice versa) allow one to define a boundary by tracing the boundary of the more constant region.

Obviously, the mean, median, minimum, and maximum statistics all share a common flaw, as do all other first-order statistical operators—they are not able to distinguish regions that have higher order statistical differences. Furthermore, if the average brightness slowly fluctuates over an area, the image resulting after the transformation typically contains those same overall intensity fluctuations. In such cases, without abrupt discontinuities in the intensities of the involved regions, the choice of a threshold will be very difficult and regions cannot be demarcated.

Second-order statistical transformations, such as the variance and standard deviation of local areas are sensitive to fluctuations in image intensity. Thus, these measures differentiate between regions with different intensity distributions or different texton spacings even when the average brightnesses do not differ. Second-order statistical operators or filters are especially powerful texture discriminators in our work. Among others, we used transforms closely related to Rosenfeld and Kak's (1976) Co-occurence Matrix. This matrix is a second-order gray-level statistic that measures the frequency with which pairs of gray levels occur in certain spatial relationships. They describe the prototypical Co-occurrence Matrix:

> Let $\Delta_{i,j}$ [an element of (Δ_x, Δ_y)] be a displacement, and let M_d be the k by k matrix whose (i, j) element is the number of times that a point having gray level z_i occurs in position $\Delta_{i,j}$ relative to a point having gray level z_j, $1 \leq i, j \leq k$. For example, if f [the original image] is:
>
>   1 1 2 2
>   0 2 2 1
>   0 0 2 1
>   1 0 0 1
> and $\Delta_{i,j}$ is (1,0) then M_d is:
>
>   2 1 2
>   1 1 1
>   0 2 2
> Note that the size of M_d depends only on the number of gray levels, not on the size of f. Elements near the main diagonal of M_d correspond to pairs of gray levels that are nearly equal, while elements far from the diagonal correspond to pairs that are very unequal (pp. 295–296).

A Co-occurrence Matrix is defined as the matrix $\mathbf{P}_d$ produced by dividing the matrix $\mathbf{M}_d$ by the matrix $\mathbf{N}_d$ (the number of point pairs in the original image in relative position $\Delta_{i,j}$. The matrix $\mathbf{P}_d$ describes the texture in terms of the spatial relations of individual pixel gray levels. A Co-occurrence Matrix with a heavy concentration of values on its diagonal implies that the region represented by the matrix is homogeneous. That is, similar gray levels are situated next to similar gray levels. Values in areas outside of the diagonal represent nonhomogeneous textured regions. Rosenfeld and Kak (1976) pointed out that "the arrangements of values in the co-occurrence matrices depend not only on the coarseness or busyness of the given picture, but also on its lightness and contrast" (p. 299).

It is important to appreciate that there may be many Co-occurrence Matrices computed for each pixel defined for particular distances and orientations. For example, the following expressions describe four Co-occurrence Matrices computed for four orientations:

$$\mathbf{P}^d_{0°}(m, n) = \sum_{\substack{i=x-a \\ k=i}}^{x+a} \sum_{\substack{j=y-b \\ l=j+d}}^{y+b} \begin{cases} 1, & \text{if } m = f(i, j) \text{ and } n = f(k, l), \\ 0, & \text{otherwise.} \end{cases} \tag{3.7}$$

$$\mathbf{P}^d_{45°}(m, n) = \sum_{\substack{i=x-a \\ k=i-d}}^{x+a} \sum_{\substack{j=y-b \\ l=j+d}}^{y+b} \begin{cases} 1, & \text{if } m = f(i, j) \text{ and } n = f(k, l), \\ 0, & \text{otherwise.} \end{cases} \tag{3.8}$$

$$\mathbf{P}^d_{90°}(m,\ n) = \sum_{\substack{i=x-a \\ k=i-d}}^{x+a} \sum_{\substack{j=y-b \\ l=j}}^{y+b} \begin{cases} 1, & \text{if } m = f(i,\ j) \text{ and } n = f(k,\ l), \\ 0, & \text{otherwise.} \end{cases} \tag{3.9}$$

$$\mathbf{P}^d_{135°}(m,\ n) = \sum_{\substack{i=x-a \\ k=i-d}}^{x+a} \sum_{\substack{j=y-b \\ l=j-d}}^{y+b} \begin{cases} 1, & \text{if } m = f(i,\ j) \text{ and } n = f(k,\ l), \\ 0, & \text{otherwise.} \end{cases} \tag{3.10}$$

where $\mathbf{P}^d_\tau(m,\ n)$ is a Co-occurrence Matrix and d and θ are the distance and orientation of the matrix.

Rosenfeld and Kak go on to describe four measures (originally suggested by Haralick, 1979) that can be applied to a Co-occurrence Matrix, namely contrast, inverse difference moments, angular second moment (or energy), and entropy. The measures can be defined as:

$$\text{Contrast} = \sum_i \sum_j (i - j)^2\ \mathbf{P}^2_d(i,\ j), \tag{3.11}$$

$$\text{Inverse difference moment} = \sum_i \sum_j \frac{\mathbf{P}^2_d(i,\ j)}{1 + (i - j)^2} \tag{3.12}$$

$$\text{Angular second moment} = \sum_i \sum_j \mathbf{P}^2_d(i,\ j), \tag{3.13}$$

$$\text{Entropy} = \sum_i \sum_j \mathbf{P}_d(i,\ j)\ log_d\ (i,\ j). \tag{3.14}$$

Contrast is the moment of inertia of the Co-occurrence Matrix about the diagonal. It is low when values are grouped around the diagonal and is high when they are scattered about the matrix. The inverse difference moment is the inverse of the contrast. The angular second moment or energy is lowest when all the matrix values are equal and is high when the matrix values vary. It tends to be high when the matrix consists of a high diagonal concentration. The entropy is highest when all values of the matrix are equal.

Several parameters of the Co-occurrence Matrix can be manipulated to sensitize it to detect certain features of a texture. These parameters are Δ_x and Δ_y, the number of gray levels and the local area over which the matrix is formed to calculate the entropy (or another measure). Together Δ_x and Δ_y designate (by their polar equivalents) the orientation and distance by which pixels in the Co-occurrence Matrix are separated. Differences in the variances in particular orientations and at particular separations can be used to distinguish different textures. The number of gray levels represents the number of bins into which the range of gray levels is placed, and represents another manipulable program parameter. This parameter makes the Co-occurrence Matrix less sensitive to brightness differences and more sensitive to texture element differences by reducing the gray-level resolution. A final parameter, the local area over which the matrix is formed, determines the area over which the co-occurrence measure (energy, contrast, etc.) is calculated.

One new transformation closely related to the Co-occurence Matrix depends on what we call *area effects*. Like the Co-occurence Matrix area effect operators perform operations on or between local areas in the image rather than on individual pixels. One such area effect operator measures *area differentials*—the pixel-by-pixel difference between two local areas when they are superimposed or when they are shifted in any direction. Execution of this algorithm tends to produce high-value boundaries between regions of different texture but lower values for regions that share the same texture.

Structural Segmentation

The second major approach to texture segmentation does not depend directly on statistical measures of pixel distribution, but on the shape, form, geometry, arrangement, or structure of the component textural elements or textons. In general, the goal is to define the shapes of these constituent units and then group all that have the same shape. Of course, not all textures have demarcatable textons and, just as the statistical methods cannot be applied to all kinds of textures, texton shape analysis cannot be universally applied.

Textons of similar shape are identified in a number of ways. Convolution with a prototype computed over the entire image space extracts the shapes that correspond to that prototype. The forms used for the comparison process need not be known in advance.

Texture is defined in terms of the arrangement of component parts or textons. These textons may themselves have their own microstructure that can influence or even determine the overall texture. A novel method we developed—sample-and-match—allows the nature of the texton itself to act as the guide to texture segmentation. This technique samples an arbitrary texton and then matches it with other textons in the image.

The idea behind the sample-and-match approach is to extract a relatively small, but randomly selected, area from the image and compare it with the remaining areas of the image. This comparison may be performed by convolving, differencing, or statistical matching. The outcome of the sample-and-match operation is the identification of all local regions that share similar structural properties.

An obvious problem exists with this method, namely how does the computer know where to sample the image to get good matches so that the various textured regions can be grouped appropriately? One solution is to sample numerous areas in the image and compare them with all areas in the image. This results in many new images, each the size of the original image. The new images display high values where a match has occurred between the sample and the compared region, and low values where there was no match. High-value regions are likely to be regions of similar texture.

This approach is very inefficient, and there are many alternative means of more selectively sampling a textured surface. For example, an image containing relatively large shapes or blobs can be converted into a binary image of white blobs on a black background. Each white object is identified by determining the set of connected white pixels, and then a shape of that white blob is represented by a tabulation of the boundary pixels. The shape is then made invariant by normalizing the position of all of the pixels around its center of gravity. As each new shape is encountered and represented, it is compared to the previously recorded shapes by a simple template matching procedure. If the match is good, the newly encountered shape is ignored. Only if there is a significant mismatch is the new shape added to the library of previously encountered forms.

This procedure generates only a small set of prototypes, and each one is checked against all of the white areas in the original image. Those regions that compare well with the same prototype are considered to be uniformly textured regions. A sample-and-match procedure that operates on smaller units more comparable to the texton is possible and was included in our model.

The next step with either of these sample-and-match techniques is to edge-enhance all of the new images. Transformed in this way they now become outline images that can be added or averaged together. The sum (more correctly, the scaled average) values are highest at the edges, and these high values represent the highest probability of boundaries between regions of different texture.

We developed novel procedures to compare a sampled patch and an equivalently sized image region. The first simply finds the sum of the differences in intensity between the pixels in the sampled patch and pixels in another image region. This way of comparing the patches is sensitive to the cumulative intensity in the patch as well as its texture.

A second class of matching procedures includes some that are sensitive only to the texture (i.e., the spatial distribution of intensities), but ignores the cumulative intensity. Two algorithms achieve this goal. The first converts the regions to be compared to their z-score representations and calculates the sum of the pixel-by-pixel differences. The other determines the sum of the standard deviations of the differences of the two patches.

A third variation is sensitive only to the cumulative intensity. In this case, the pixels in each region are sorted by intensity. The sum of the pixel-by-pixel differences in the sorted data is then computed.

These various sample-and-match methods were implemented and tested. Each program produces a transformed image where the value at each pixel represents how closely the surrounding areas match the sampled area. After this trans-

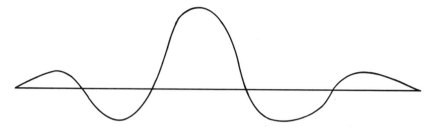

FIG. 3.14.   A projective drawing of a single Gabor filter suggesting its essentially three-dimensional form.

formed comparison image is produced, several steps are carried out to extract the boundaries between regions of different texture. However, first a threshold must be chosen that specifies what degree of similarity is considered to represent identity.

Convolution with a known image and the automatic generation of large- or small-shape prototypes, as just described, operate in the spatial domain. There is no reason why this must occur. The convolution need not be carried out on the raw image itself, but may be carried out on a coded form of the image, specifically the frequency components of a Fourier, or similar, Analysis.

One of the most important texture segmenting algorithms characterized within the structural category and yet not operating in the spatial domain is based on a set of linear Gabor filters; the application of this procedure to model human vision was originally suggested by Watson (1983). This technique provides an image map that distinguishes objects on the basis of their local spatial frequencies and the orientation of the textural components.

The set of Gabor filters we used is shown in Figure 3.9. In this type of display, color (not shown in this black and white figure) acts as a surrogate for the third dimension, the amplitude of the filter, at each point. Figure 3.14 shows a cross-sectional drawing of one Gabor filter. The filters function very much like the set of orthogonal sinusoids in a one-dimensional Fourier transform or the set of gratings in a two-dimensional one. The main differences between the Gabor filters and the conventional Fourier set of sinusoids is that they are localized in space and are sensitive to more orientations than just horizontal and vertical. The property of having a region of sensitivity that is localized in space is shared by neurons, and, thus, the Gabor filters are more biologically realistic than the Fourier spatial frequency filters. The set of Gabor linear filters we used is a selection from among many possible ones and is represented by Equation 3.3. A Gabor filter can be interpreted to be a three-dimensional sinusoid constrained within a Gaussian envelope. Each filter in the set represents a different combination of spatial frequency, spatial phase, and orientation. A full set, therefore, can be very large, and our set is necessarily a smaller selection of all possible Gabor filters.

An excellent modern discussion of Gabor filters can be found in Chapter 2 of Graham's (1989) treatise on visual pattern analyzers. She points out that Gabor filters have many more degrees of freedom than the three (frequency, phase, and orientation) that we used. In fact, she observes seven spatial degrees of freedom, five temporal ones, and also notes that a Gabor filter may vary in contrast, luminosity, and, finally, with regard to the different positions of the two eyes. Obviously, contemporary computer vision researchers have only begun to exploit the full range of sensitivity of Gabor filters. At present the computational load created by using all degrees of freedom would be prohibitive. In any event, no foreseeable computer could do as well as the massively parallel processing organic visual system should this mechanism be instantiated there.

To process an image, the set of orientated Gabor linear filters is convolved with the image at regularly spaced locales just as if it was a set of prototypical templates. The result is a vector defined at each locale consisting of an amplitude score for each filter of the set. The amplitude score of each filter at each locale corresponds to how well the textural properties (in this case, orientation and frequency) at that locale exhibit the same properties as each filter. The complete scene is defined by a vector consisting of the values for each filter in the set for every locale. In this manner, the qualitative spatial attribute of texture is converted to a set of numbers comparable to the spectrum of sinusoids in a conventional Fourier transform.

We are continuing with our implementation of Gabor filters. Several improvements were made to the original program, some of which dealt with the pixel density. Our original implementation convolved 65×65 pixel Gabor filters with a 128×128 pixel image, skipping every 16 pixels. In this case, the filter was half the size of the image. This produced an extremely low resolution (8×8) representation of the image. In the work of others (e.g., Turner, 1986) 512×512 pixel images were used. In that case a 65×65 pixel mask was one eighth of the size of the image. The convolution of the image with each Gabor filter thus resulted in a 32×32 representation of the original image. Taking these ratios as a desirable starting point, we reduced the size of the Gabor filter to about one eighth of our 128×128 pixel image. This simple computation suggested that we use a 17×17 Gabor filter. We then chose to skip every four pixels when applying the Gabor transformation, thus producing a 32×32 transformed image.

The Gabor filter has properties that make it a plausible model of the operation of the human visual system. The most important one is that it utilizes filters that are localized in a circumscribed region of the visual field. This property corresponds closely to the concept of the receptive field in the organic visual system and mitigates against the complaint raised against imagewide gratings in a more conventional kind of spatial frequency analysis, namely, that the width of each member of the set of orthogonal functions was much too broad to be physiologically plausible.

Integration of Textural Segmenters

Let us now consider some specific algorithms used to extract the boundaries between texture regions and the way in which the outputs of these algorithms were combined to produce a superior segmentation based on texture alone. In the example we present now, we used as many as six textural segmenters, some of which we introduced previously and some of which are newly introduced here. We then combined their outputs, using a novel method that provides a demarcation of differently textured regions better than any similar process. We also describe the textural segmenters we used. The important point is that each segmenting algorithm is relatively frail and unlikely to produce the correct boundaries between regions of different texture as a reliable basis for a variety of different textures. Our goal is to combine their outputs in a way that makes the final estimate of the intertexture boundaries superior to that obtainable by using any one alone.

Three new analyzers were invented in the course of the present exploration of texture segmentation: the area differential, the sample-and-match, and the redundancy of neighborhoods.

Method 1: The Area Differential. The area differential is the sum of the differences between the values of corresponding pixels of two neighboring local areas. It is calculated for every pixel in the image and represents the cumulative difference in the intensities between neighboring local areas. The relative position of the two differenced areas is defined in terms of the distance between and the orientation of the pixels at each area's center of gravity. The distance between the areas is usually chosen to be half the width of the area, and the orientation is usually one of four alternatives: $0°$, $45°$, $90°$, or $135°$. The size of the local area is usually 11×11 pixels.

After the initial computation of the area differential, the standard deviation of local areas surrounding each pixel is computed so that regions of similar variance can be grouped. The variance measures the amount of fluctuation in intensity that occurs across a local area. After the variance computation, the transformed image contains a certain amount of introduced noise that must be filtered out, by applying a median filter over 7×7 pixel square areas. Next, 8-connected pixels of similar intensity are grouped to define the distinctively textured regions of the image. These regions are then combined by joining those that have common weak boundaries. Weak boundaries are defined as those for which the regions on either side contain pixels that are less than 16 gray levels apart over 50% of their boundary's length.

Boundaries are then extracted from the resulting image by eroding the boundaries of regions and XORing the resulting image with the original one. The final result is an image in which each pixel value represents a region label. Boundaries are composed of two lines of different values: one line from the region on one side of the boundary and the other line from the region on the other side. Each

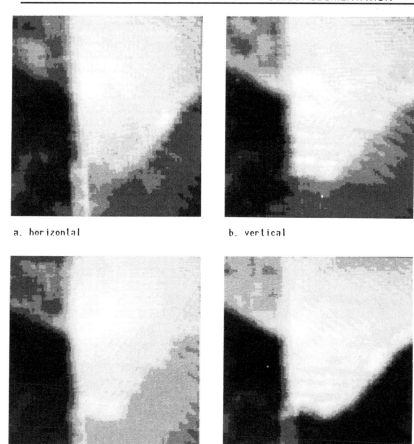

a. horizontal

b. vertical

c. left diagonal

d. right diagonal

FIG. 3.15.   Four sample output images produced by the area differential algorithm for the four directions of sensitivity (i.e., horizontal, vertical, left diagonal, and right diagonal).

line is 4-connected and 1 pixel wide along its entire length, and both lines are used in the subsequent statistical integration. Figure 3.15 depicts the four output images of this area differential algorithm, one for each of the directions of sensitivity (i.e., horizontal, vertical, left diagonal, and right diagonal.)

Method 2: Sample and Match.   The sample-and-match procedure was applied as one of the six texture segmenters in the integration exercise. Several methods can be used to compare a sampled patch and another area of the image. Each method differentiates some textures better than others. The first variation of the comparison algorithm simply finds the sum of the differences in intensity between comparable pixels in the sample and the pixels of the other local area as denoted by

$$\sum_{i=x-k}^{x+k} \sum_{j=y-k}^{y+k} |f(i, j) - f(i + dx, j + dy)|, \qquad (3.15)$$

where $f(i, j)$ is the sample and $f(i + dx, j + dy)$ is the area it is being compared with. Since this method is a pixel-by-pixel comparison, it is coarsely sensitive to the average brightness and the arrangement of the pixels. Low values indicate a good match, high values a poor match.

A second approach to making the comparison between the sample local area and the local areas of the rest of the image essentially ignores the gray-level differences and is mainly sensitive to form. There are two ways to accomplish this. The first is to transform the image into a z-score representation

$$f(i, j) = \frac{f(i, j) - \mu_0}{\sigma_0} \sigma_n + \mu_n, \qquad (3.16)$$

where μ_0 and ρ_0 are the mean and standard deviations of the local area around the point (i, j) and μ_n and σ_n are an equalizing mean and standard deviation, and then find the sum of the differences between the pixels in the sample and those in all of the other local areas by using Equation 3.15. The second technique is to find the sum of the standard deviations of the differences between the two local areas as expressed in Equation 3.17:

$$\sum_{i=x-k}^{x+k} \sum_{j=y-k}^{y+k} \frac{(\Delta(i, j) - \mu\Delta)^2}{2k + 1}, \qquad (3.17)$$

where

$$\Delta(i, j) = f(i, j) - f(i + dx, j + dy) \quad \text{and} \quad \mu\Delta = \frac{\displaystyle\sum_{i=x-k}^{x+k} \sum_{j=y-k}^{y+k} \Delta(k, j)}{2k + 1}.$$

Here, $\Delta(i, j)$ is the difference between a sample pixel and a pixel in the compared local area, μ_Δ is the mean of the differences of the two areas, and $2k + 1$ is the size of the local areas.

A third way to carry out the comparison is sensitive only to gray-level intensity differences between the sample and all other local areas in the image. Our algorithms do this by sorting the pixels in each local area and in the sample and then summing the differences between what are essentially intensity histograms.

However, in this case, we used a fourth comparison or matching process, namely a convolution $[F_s(x, y)]$ of the sampled area $[s(x, y)]$ and the original image $[F(x, y)]$, as expressed by

$$F_s(x, y) = \iint F(x - a, y - b)s(a, b)da\,db \qquad (3.18)$$

The area sampled in this case was a 7×7 region located at the center of gravity of diffuse blobs defined by a preliminary stage of processing in which a standard deviation filter was applied to the original image. The blobs were specified as regions of common intensity differing by no more than one standard deviation unit. This method is a poor way of distinguishing textured regions, but it is used only to locate the sample and has no further purpose.

The samples so produced are then convolved with the entire image on a piece-by-piece basis to identify the specific regions of common texture. Then the boundaries are determined by using the relaxation threshold procedure in which the sequence of steps is (1) intensity slice, (2) merge areas with weak boundaries, (3) erode boundary of combined regions, and (4) XOR this transformed image with the original image to recover the boundaries and remove inner portions of the regions. The boundaries are now ready for the integration procedure described later in this section. Figure 3.16 shows a few of the many possible outputs of this sample-and-compare algorithm, the exact number depending on the complexity (i.e., the number of regions) of the image.

Method 3: Redundancy of Neighborhoods.   Texture segmentation based on redundancy involves four primary stages of processing: labeling, spatial averaging, thresholding, and boundary extraction. The labeling of textured regions is accomplished by sampling all possible local regions of a predetermined size and shape and comparing each one with all others in the same row or column of the image. The row or column is defined by the position of the center pixel of the sampled local region. Then the central pixel of each local region is assigned a value indicating the number of times the same pattern of intensities found in the sample occurred in that same row or column. This assigned value is the measure of redundancy among the pixels, and the image can now be replotted as a function of that value at each pixel. The comparison process is the same as used in computing the area differential.

A certain amount of noise is inherent in the resulting labeled image. As a result, this image must also be filtered to reduce the amount of noise present. After the labeled image is filtered, a statistical intensity threshold of 0.5 standard deviation unit is applied to differentiate irregularly textured regions from homogeneously textured regions.

At this point, boundaries are extracted from the image. The result is an image showing 10-pixel-wide boundaries between regularly textured region and irregularly textured region. (This technique does not distinguish between regularly textured, i.e., redundant, regions, or between irregularly textured regions.) These boundaries are then skeletonized to produce a set of 1-pixel-wide boundaries separating the textured regions that were present in the original image. Figure 3.17 depicts the output resulting from a sample application of the redundancy algorithm.

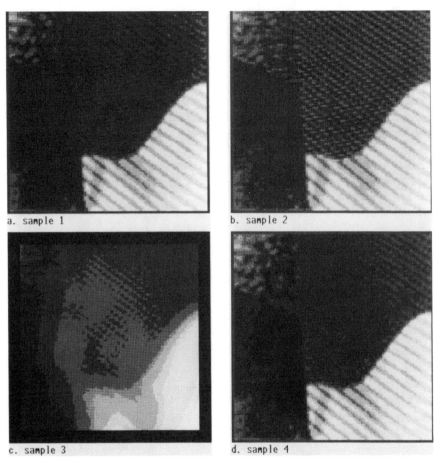

a. sample 1   b. sample 2

c. sample 3   d. sample 4

FIG. 3.16.   Four sample output images produced by the sample-and-compare algorithm. Each image was generated with a different sample.

The following three methods, Laws's Microtexture Masks, the Co-occurence Matrix, and the Fractal Method are well-known texture analyzers that we modified for our use.

Method 4: Laws's Microtexture Masks.   Four incomplete output images are produced by convolving the image with the four standard *Microtexture Masks* suggested by Laws (1980). The four images are transformed by computing the standard deviation over 11×11 local areas in accord with a method suggested by Hsiao and Sawchuck (1989) and Coleman & Andrews (1979). This operation separates regions of similar variance by measuring the amount of fluctuation in intensity that occurs across a local area. After the variance computation, these images, like those produced by the other texture segmenters, contain a certain

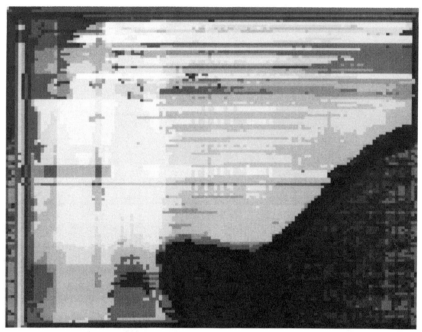

FIG. 3.17.   A sample output image from the redundancy algorithm showing the
horizontal and vertical rows and columns of similarity.

amount of noise. Noise reduction is accomplished by applying a median filter
over square areas of 11 × 11 pixels.

Next, connecting pixels of similar intensity (no more than 16 gray levels
apart) are grouped or merged into separate regions. These regions are then
combined by joining those regions that have common weak boundaries. To
repeat, weak boundaries are defined as those for which the regions on either side
contain pixels that are less than 16 gray levels apart over more than 50% of their
common boundary's length. As before, boundaries are then extracted from the
resulting image by eroding the outermost areas of the labeled regions and XOR-
ing the resulting image with the original. The final result is a set of images in
which each pixel value represents a region label. This process is diagrammed in
Figure 3.18.

In this case, boundaries are also composed of two lines of different values:
one line from the region on one side of the boundary and the other line from the
region on the other side. Each line is 4-connected and 1 pixel wide along its
entire length; both lines are passed on to the statistical integration phase of our
segmentation algorithms. Figure 3.19 depicts the four output images produced
by Laws's microtexture algorithm corresponding to the four standard masks.

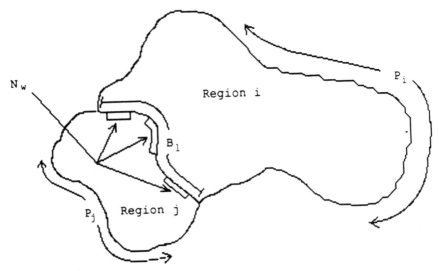

FIG. 3.18.   Diagram of the process by which regions of similar intensity are merged into single regions. Region merging is accomplished as a multistep procedure. First, regions are merged based on the weakness of intervening boundaries. A weak boundary is defined as follows: A boundary length is calculated (B_1) and the number of weak pixels (N_w) is determined by using some threshold T_1. If the boundary between the regions is long enough, that is, the ratio of the boundary length to the perimeter length of one region is large enough $(B_1/P_i > T_2$ or $B_1/P_j > T_2)$, and if there are numerous weak pixels along the boundary $(N_w/B_1 > T_3)$, then the regions are combined. In subsequent steps, only the average intensities of each region are compared until no more regions can be merged.

Method 5: Co-occurrence Matrix.   As already described, every pixel in an image can be assigned an angular second moment value (along with three other values) calculated from the co-occurrence matrices computed for local areas. In the present case, for each local area, four co-occurrence matrices are formed as indicated in Equations 3.7 through 3.10. The matrices are formed by using a large 20×20 pixel area centered on each pixel. Each matrix represents the adjacency of pixels of a particular gray level to pixels of another gray level at a particular orientation and distance. Each of the four matrices represents the relationship of gray levels at one of four orientations: $0°$, $45°$, $90°$, and $135°$. Only pixels that are at a city-block distance of 1 pixel at orientations of $0°$ and $90°$ and 2 pixels at $45°$ and $135°$ are used. (This is, of course, another way to define 8-connected adjacency.) The size of each Co-occurrence Matrix depends on the number of intensity values in the image's histogram.

In our modification of this algorithm, the number of intensity values in the image is reduced so that the image's histogram contains only 64 levels of gray instead of 256. This range compression (necessary because of the enormous

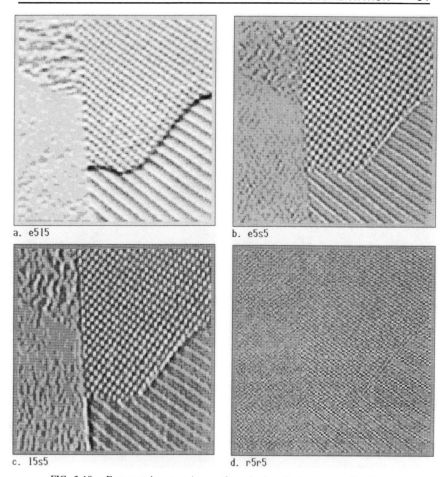

a. e5l5

b. e5s5

c. l5s5

d. r5r5

FIG. 3.19. Four sample output images from the Laws' microtexture algorithm corresponding to the four standard masks: e5l5, e5s5, l5s5, and r5r5.

memory and computational load generated by the large number of pixels) is accomplished by multiplying each pixel's value by 0.25 and rounding fractional values into the nearest whole number value. For each pixel, the total value of the four matrices is calculated by summing the squares of each value (i.e., computing the angular second moment with Equation 3.13) of the leading (i.e., upper left to lower right) diagonal of all of the matrices. This value is then assigned to the pixel around which the matrices were calculated.

The resulting image, now normalized back to 256 gray levels, is then spatially averaged by applying a median filter over each 7 × 7 pixel area. The areas of similar values are then grouped by a two-stage process. First, subregions in the resulting image are defined by grouping 8-connected pixels of similar intensity.

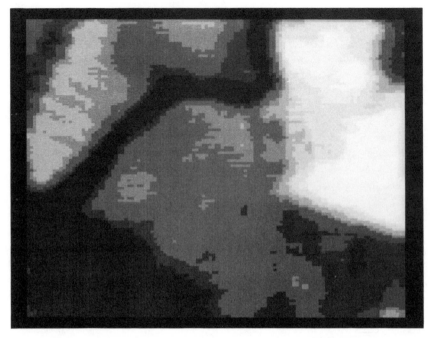

FIG. 3.20.   A sample output image from the Co-occurrence Matrix algorithm based on the four selected matrices in Equations 3.7 through 3.10. A single image described by the expression for the angular second moment in Equation 3.13 is generated by this procedure.

Second, these subregions are combined with surrounding subregions by again joining those whose common boundaries have more than 60% weak boundary points (of the total number of perimeter boundary points). This is done to avoid linking subregions that have in common only a small portion of their total perimeters.

Boundaries are then extracted from the resulting image by applying a mask over all 3 × 3 areas in the image so that areas in which there is a value change (i.e., a boundary) are deleted and those in which there is no change are included. This effectively places zeros along the boundaries. This image is then XORed with the image existing prior to the application of the mask, to produce an image consisting of only the boundaries.

These newly defined boundaries are composed of two lines of different values: one from the region on one side of the boundary and the other from the region on the other side. Each line is 4-connected and 1 pixel wide along its entire length. Both lines are used in the subsequent statistical integration. Figure 3.20 depicts the output image—a plot of the angular second moments—from one sample application of the Co-occurrence Algorithm.

Method 6: The Fractal Method. The Fractal Model for surfaces (Mandelbrot, 1982) provides a metric for texture by supplying a link between the concept of the fractal dimension (a numerical quantity) and other measures of surface roughness. Using this dimension to characterize parts of a surface, we can distinguish surfaces of different texture within a scene.

Our technique uses an important measure of fractal-dimension-defined surfaces, the *true surface area*. The true surface area takes into account the areas of the faces on any "hills" and "valleys". Thus, anything other than a flat surface will have a larger value than a simple width times length estimate of surface area. By a "blanket" technique (Peleg, Naor, Hartley, Avnir, 1984), the true surface area of a surface is measured over different scales, by mathematically "draping" blankets of increasing "thickness" over the surface and measuring the area touched by the blanket. The area of the blanketed surface decreases as the thickness of the blanket increases, since thick blankets will not mathematically fill in valleys of the surface as well as thin ones. In other words, the level of detail contributing to the computation of the true surface area decreases with blanket thickness.

The critical fact is that the true surface area is a function of the fractal dimension (Mandelbrot, 1982) of the surface. The fractal dimension can thus be estimated from the graph of the measured area versus blanket thickness. In this manner, each pixel in the image is assigned a fractal dimension value describing the local area in which it is centered. Pixels with common fractal dimension values are then grouped into regions that are assumed to have common texture.

Integration of Segmentation Images—The Approach

The six texture segmenting algorithms described are each actually elaborate systems of programs that may produce several outputs. We have indicated that some of these programs produce separate suggested boundaries for each of four directions: horizontal, vertical, leading diagonal, and trailing diagonal. In addition, we described several intermediate steps carried out prior to the combination process that will shortly be discussed. The end result of this multiple texture segmenting process is some 20 or 30 separate images that may be available to the integration routines to produce the final estimate of the texture boundaries. Figure 3.21 is a general, but incomplete flowchart of the entire system. Figure 3.22 is an enlarged and more detailed version of the transformations applied just to the four outputs from the area differential analyzer. Because of the flexibility of our system and its ability to generate many versions of the vision system, these figures are only examples of the network of parallel and serial processes that have been implemented in different instantiations of our model.

In general, texture algorithms operate by performing operations over local areas. Texture, by definition, is a regional property that cannot be distinguished at the level of individual pixels. The location of a texture boundary is not

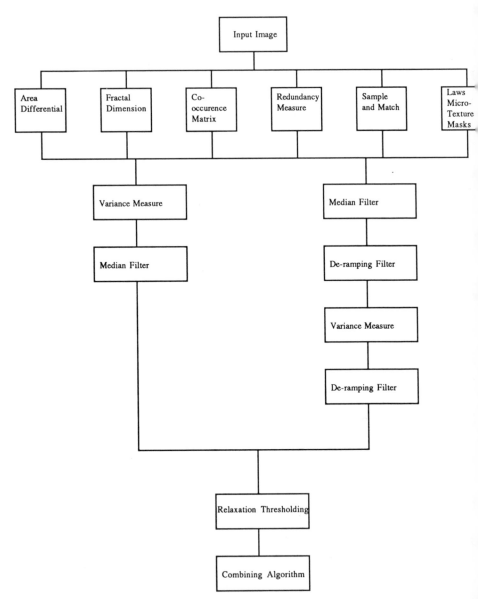

FIG. 3.21. An incomplete flowchart of the texture combining algorithm. Each line on this chart may represent a complex series of processes as exemplified by Figure 3.22.

84

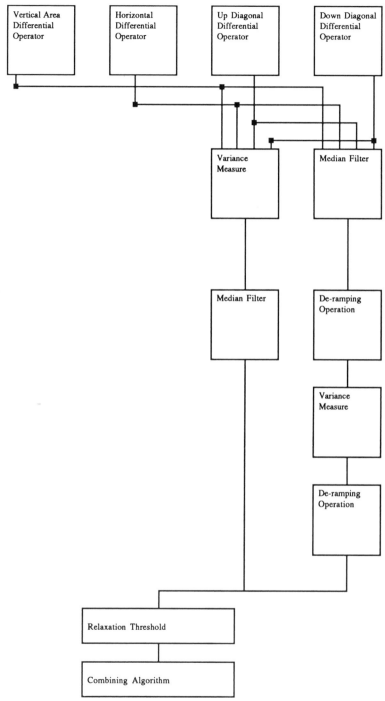

FIG. 3.22. A flowchart of the area differential portion of the texture combining algorithm.

available simply as a difference between two adjacent pixels. Rather, it be must be computed from the statistical effects of the surrounding pixels (statistical segmentation) or from a comparison of texton shapes in their raw form or as transformed by some structural segmentation algorithm that identifies shapes with numerical quantities. As a result, all texture segmenting algorithms discussed so far produce boundaries that are inherently noisy and potentially inaccurate. The possible location of a boundary can be as uncertain as the size of the local area within which the algorithm functions.

In addition, each texture segmenting algorithm is likely to perform differently in different situations. At best, it will only produce approximate estimates of the location of the image's texture boundaries. In any image some boundaries will be found by all methods, some will be found by only a few methods, some will be missed entirely, and occasionally a false or spurious boundary will be identified.

Furthermore, the image from each texture segmenting algorithm often contains small errors in the location of the boundaries it does suggest. These errors may be due to factors such as image ambiguities, local area size over which operators are applied, image noise, and/or threshold sensitivities. The errors are of two kinds: errors mispositioning true boundaries and errors that suggest that boundaries exist where they actually do not. The integration of information from several algorithms tends to reduce both kinds of error. First, it is unlikely that all of the segmentation algorithms will make the same kind of misposition error. We suggested as one working rule that boundaries identified by only one algorithm are to be considered erroneous and discarded. For mispositioning errors, the combining algorithm must be insensitive enough to allow for small deviations of the position of lines but still demanding enough to accept nearby boundaries as samples of the same real texture boundary. All of these factors suggest a statistical approach to the essentially geometric problem of combining the outputs of the multiple analyzer used in this procedure.

Our goal is to combine the sometimes fallible and often idiosyncratic results of the individual texture segmentation methods into a composite image that represents a much better estimate of the, texture boundaries than is obtainable by using only a single method.

Let us first consider how we compute the suggested boundaries from the initial stage of texture analysis. Each of the six texture analyzers produces one or more output images in which the regions of different texture are numerically distinguished. Next, the boundaries between these regions are extracted. As a preliminary step, all of the output images (with the exception of the fractal dimension algorithm where the regions are extracted directly) are processed by applying a standard deviation transform that evaluates the image's variability.

For the variability computation, the standard deviation $\rho(i, j)$ is computed over an 11-pixel square window. The following expression is used:

$$\rho(i, j) = \sqrt{\mathscr{E}(f(i, j) - \mu)^2}, \tag{3.19}$$

where $f(i, j)$ is the central pixel of a local area, μ is the mean intensity of the local area, and $\mathcal{E}(f(i, j) - \mu)$ is the expected value of the central pixel $f(i, j)$. Given the distribution of pixel intensities in its local area this expands to

$$\rho(i, j) = \sqrt{\sum_{i=x-k}^{x+k} \sum_{j=y-k}^{y+k} (f(i, j) - \mu)^2 P(f(i, j))}, \qquad (3.20)$$

where $P(f(i, j))$ is the probability of intensity level $f(i, j)$ occurring. For $P(f(i, j))$, the histogram is used as the probability measure.

After these preliminary steps toward boundary extraction and image smoothing are finished, the next step is image thresholding. Thresholding is accomplished through an initial partitioning of the image and a subsequent iterative procedure in which similar regions are merged together with a relaxation method. Partitioning is accomplished by grouping 8-connected pixels of similar intensity (typically 48 gray levels apart) into separate regions by collectively tagging them with the same numerical label. If another group of pixels with a similar intensity range, but not connected to the first, is located elsewhere in the image, it is given its own distinct label.

Partitioning is followed by the iterative region merging relaxation procedure described in Figure 3.18. Unlike regions are merged by joining those regions with common weak boundaries. Initially, a weak boundary between two areas is defined by the ratio of the number of weak pixels to the total number of pixels in the common boundary between adjacent regions. In the initial merging, three thresholds are specified that determine whether regions are separated by weak boundaries and should be merged: (1) T_1, the intensity at which a boundary pixel will be considered to be weak; (2) T_2, the ratio of the common boundary length (B_1) to either region's total perimeter length (P_i or P_j) of the two regions, B_1/P_i or B_1/P_j; and (3) T_3, the ratio of the number of weak boundary pixels (N_w) to the common boundary length, N_w/B_1. The algorithm is most sensitive to T_1, the absolute intensity difference between the two regions, which is set relatively high so that adjacent regions with relatively large intensity differences will be merged. Two other threshold parameters ensure that short, weak boundary segments will not lead to adjacent regions being incorrectly merged. In subsequent mergings only the average intensity of neighboring regions is tested against T_1 to determine whether the regions should be merged. This is an iterative process that continues until no more regions can be merged.

Intertexture boundaries are then extracted from the resulting image by eroding the boundaries of all regions in the image to a width of 1 pixel and XORing the resulting image with the pre-XOR image. The final result is an image where the remaining pixels represent intertextural boundaries. These boundaries are composed of two lines of different values: one representing the region on one side of the boundary, and the other representing the region on the other side. Each line is 4-connected and 1 pixel wide along its entire length. Both lines are passed to the statistical integration phase of segmentation. The resulting boundaries are now referred to as suggested boundaries.

The suggested boundary images that the six segmentation algorithms produce are the inputs to the statistical combining or integrating algorithms that we developed. The different texture segmenting algorithms may produce either one or two suggested boundaries for each real boundary in each output images. Each boundary in each image is 1 pixel wide and 4-connected. For segmenting algorithms that suggest two boundaries, they are always adjacent along their entire length and never cross or intersect. These two boundaries are therefore redundant and could conceivably be combined. However, we decided not to do so because their positions represent the limits of our knowledge of the true boundary location. In any event, it is not necessary to combine them at this point because the combining algorithm will fuse them during the process of combining the many segmentation images. For display purposes, each boundary in a segmented image is labeled a different color than the others.

All of the suggested boundaries from all of the texture segmenters are read in by the combining algorithm and transformed into a new image called the *contour string image*. The contour string image thus consists of all suggested boundaries represented as a series of connected adjacent pixels. These contours may now actually cross over each other, but they are independently coded so that they preserve their identity in the contour string image. To maintain their identity, each pixel in the new image contains a pointer to a list of contour strings that pass through it. Each entry in that list represents 1 pixel of a boundary and contains pointers to the next pixel and previous boundary pixels.

Our experience with texture segmenting algorithms demonstrates that these algorithms produce all of the types of segmentation errors already mentioned. The goal of the integration process is to combine and adjust the locations of (or remove) each suggested boundary based on the statistics of the other boundaries in the string image. To do this, each contour string (i.e., the representation of the suggested boundary in the contour string image) is traced pixel by pixel, and the location of each pixel is redetermined based on the statistics of the locations of the pixels in nearby contours. A contour string pixel is considered to be "nearby" if it is within an arbitrarily sized local area around the string pixel being examined at the moment, the current pixel. (In the current version of this algorithm, the local area is usually specified to be 19×19 pixels.) The new location of the current string pixel is specified as the center of gravity of all of the pixels in adjacent contour strings within this local area.

The overall result of computing a new location for each pixel in a contour string is that the string's location is adjusted toward other strings in the local area. As the algorithm is iteratively applied, contour strings within a local area move toward each other and the adjusted strings eventually become collinear. The ultimate result is a better estimate of the location of a texture boundary than is possible with only one algorithm.

Not all sections of a contour string may move in the sense we desire. There are two types of nonmoving sections. The first consists of strings already at the center of gravity of their neighbors; this represents no problem. The second type consists of isolated string segments. Isolated segments generated by idiosyncratic texture segmenters are removed simply because of the high likelihood that they represent a mistaken segmentation; only one segmentation algorithm suggested the boundary.

In some instances a contour string is broken by this adjustment procedure, leaving large distances along its length between certain pairs of pixels. This distortion typically occurs when a string perpendicularly (or nearly so) crosses an empty area between nearly parallel strings. The parallel strings tend to reposition the pixels of the string crossing the gap in opposite directions. To overcome this difficulty, we adopted the following *Large-Gap Rule:* If the distance between adjoining pixels is greater than a specified threshold, the pixels are not considered to be connected, and the line representing the contour string is broken into two lines. If the lengths of the resulting fragments do not meet a minimum length criterion, those fragments are deleted from the list of contour strings.

Many other procedures have been suggested for combining multiple estimates of image properties. Two recent books have come to our attention (Aloimonos & Shulman, 1989; Clark & Yuille, 1990) that describe elaborate and sophisticated advanced statistical methods of image combination. These methods are, in the main, based on Bayesian statistical procedures. We have already mentioned the work of Poggio, Gamble and Little (1988) and that of Geman and Geman (1984) using Markov Random Fields for this same application.

Throughout these works, however, there is an undertone that simple statistical averaging of the kind that we have chosen to use may be as practically effective as any of the much more computationally demanding Bayesian procedures. Poggio and his colleagues (1988) assert that "Marroquin (1985) has shown that the average surface f under the posterior distribution is often a better estimate, which can be obtained more efficiently simply by finding the average value of f at each lattice point." (p. 437). Aloimonos and Shulman (1989) also acknowledge the existence of "robust, simple methods of combining information" (pp. 207–208) including weighted least squares or weighted medians. It is certainly the case that these simple approaches do not provide information about the constraints that may be required for full characterization of the combining process. Nor do they analyze the special statistical properties of images. Both kinds of information may be necessary for a deep understanding of the combination process. However, as will be shown, simple statistical averaging does work very well, indeed, and serves our needs adequately. Although more rigorous mathematicians may not be satisfied with this approach, it is effective and relatively efficient computationally.

Details of the Integration Algorithm

The boundary integrating algorithm is implemented as a four-step process. (1) Suggested boundaries from the segmented images are traced and transferred to the composite contour string image; (2) small contour strings are removed; (3) contours strings are integrated by statistically repositioning the individual pixels in each string image until all of the strings in a local area converge; and (4) a list is prepared of the remaining strings.

Each contour string is a file with information about a series of pixels; the data for each pixel contain pointers to its adjacent neighbors. There is also a master file for every pixel in the image space, which consists of a list of labels or designators, each of which represents the contours that pass through that pixel. Thus, several contour strings can intersect at a single image pixel location without losing their identities.

To transfer the suggested boundary images produced by the several texture segmenters to the contour string image format, we must trace the boundaries and develop lists of the involved pixels. This task is not without its difficulties. Initially, boundaries are 4-connected and must be continuous. Furthermore, the overall shape of the boundary is unpredictable and can contain multiple 3- or 4-exit intersections. Therefore, a region around an individual pixel can have more than two end points, or none. Depending on the number of intersections and end points in a suggested boundary, it may have to be decomposed into several contour strings to accurately represent the texture boundaries. In our boundary tracing algorithm, new contours are created at each intersection, and the one being currently traced is continued. The longest branch out of an intersection is considered to be the continuation of the contour currently being traced.

The procedure we developed for tracing suggested boundaries is repeated as necessary. Each time an intersection is encountered, the algorithm is applied to each exit from the intersection to determine the longest boundary. The longest boundary is then connected with the current contour string. All other boundaries that exit the intersection become new contour strings. Tracing of boundaries is accomplished by looking within the 8-connected neighborhood of a boundary pixel for pixels that were not traversed. As each pixel is inserted into the contour string, it is marked as "visited" and a pointer to the previous string pixel is assigned.

After the suggested boundary image produced by a texture segmenting algorithm has been converted to a contour string image, all contour segments shorter than an arbitrary threshold are deleted. This action removes some of the effects of noise introduced during the segmentation process. This deletion process is based on a simple idea. As each pixel in a contour string is visited, a counter is incremented. If this counter is less than the threshold at the end of the string, the string is considered to be noise and is removed. (Currently this threshold is set at 50 pixels.)

The next step is to combine the remaining contour strings from all segmenters into a unified image. This key element in the process—statistical integration—is accomplished by adjusting the location of each pixel in each contour string by the method described earlier. Any pixel within the local area that has contours passing through it contributes to the calculation of the center of gravity, that is, the new location of the pixel being position adjusted. The center of gravity is determined by evaluating the expression

$$(c_x, c_y) = \left(\frac{\Sigma(x)}{N}, \frac{\Sigma(y)}{N} \right), \tag{3.21}$$

where N is the number of pixels within the local area and $\Sigma(x)$ and $\Sigma(y)$ are the sums of their x and y coordinates, respectively. The location (c_x, c_y) becomes the new position of the pixel in what is now an adjusted contour string. This pixel location adjustment is performed recursively three times for all contour strings. Each iteration creates a new image with the pixels in all of the contour strings adjusted progressively closer to the center of gravity of all the contours within a local area each time.

This statistical manipulation of the geometry of the image is the key step in the integration process. After three iterations all of the involved contour strings (those that traverse the local area) converge to approximately the same position. All of their constituent pixel locations need only be listed (or plotted on a graphic display) to provide a single new string that is the integrated combination of all suggested boundaries. In general, we find that this procedure results in a very narrow, but not single-pixel-wide, trace. Standard skeletonizing routines are then applied (if the trace is more than 1 pixel wide) to produce the final single-pixel-wide contour string. This is considered to be the best available estimate of the texture boundary.

We find that after three iterations the contour strings start to degenerate as the individual pixels of the contour string move apart within and along the axis of the suggested boundary. Increasingly large gaps form along the contour string, depending on the number of strings in the local area. With many iterations, corners become rounded and intersections become distorted.

Experimental Results

The procedure using multiple weak texture analyzers and spatial statistical averaging discussed so far was tested on a variety of natural and synthetic images. The results of four of these computer experiments are now presented.

The first representative test image (Tex2.im), shown in Figure 3.23, is a real image consisting of a chair seat cover, carpet, and two types of wrapping paper digitized directly from a video camera image. The image appears as two random textures and two patterned textures that are easily discernible by the human eye.

The second test image (Csub.im), shown in Figure 3.24, is a real photograph of a submersible remote-controlled vehicle in an underwater environment. Textured areas of the image, as visually defined, consist of the water, the top of the vehicle, and the other vehicle surfaces.

The third test image (Wowapig.im), shown in Figure 3.25, is a synthetic

FIG. 3.23.   The sample input test image Tex2.im.

FIG. 3.24.   The sample input test image Csub.im.

FIG. 3.25. The sample input test image Wowapig.im.

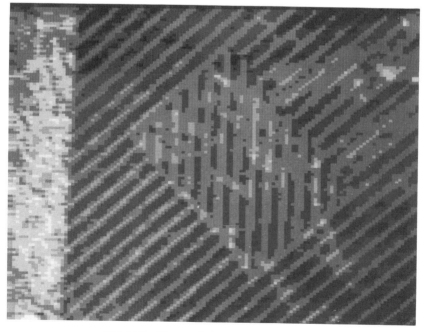

FIG. 3.26. The sample input test image Stripes.im.

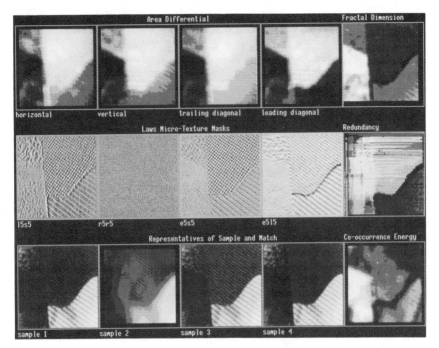

FIG. 3.27. A collection of the output images resulting from applying the first stage of transformation of several of the texture analyzers to the input image Tex2.im. Each image in this figure shows the effect of applying a particular case of an analyzer.

image consisting of the three Brodatz textures: wood, water, and pigskin (Brodatz, 1966). This image was artificially constructed within the computer by combining three digitized images of the three textures.

The fourth test image (Stripes.im), shown in Figure 3.26, is a real photograph of two sections of striped paper at different orientations on a dotted background.

To test the integrated texture segmenting procedure, we created a script file to execute all six texture segmenting algorithms and the combining algorithm as one extended program. The script also contained threshold values and other parameters that had to be passed to the individual algorithms as needed at each processing step. During all test trials, all of the parameters passed from the script to the component algorithms were kept constant at values that were empirically determined by pilot studies.

Figures 3.27 through 3.30 show the results of the several stages of processing on one of the four test images (Tex2.im). Figure 3.27 shows the results of the first stage of processing after the initial operator from each texture segmenting algorithm was applied. This transformation stage is specific to each segmenting algorithm and consists of a variable number of outputs, depending on the al-

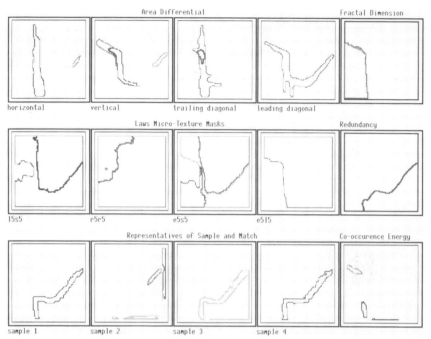

FIG. 3.28. A collection of some (but not all) outputs from the next stage of transformation following Figure 3.27. Here the suggested boundaries have been extracted (by a variety of algorithms). It is clear that there is a great deal of variation in the accuracy of the various texture analyzers. It is not so evident, but should be appreciated nevertheless, that a very different pattern of successes and failures will result with other images.

gorithm, as described earlier. Figure 3.28 shows the next stage of transformation after suggested boundary extraction. The first picture in Figure 3.29 shows all of the texture boundaries plotted superimposed on a single image for each of the four images and a few of the intermediate images produced by the combining algorithm. The last picture in Figure 3.29 shows the final estimate of the texture boundaries produced by the entire integrated system. Figure 3.30 presents the final results of the segmentation process with the boundaries superimposed on the original image to show the competence of the entire procedure. Figure 3.31, 3.32, and 3.33 present the final estimates of the three other input images (Figure 3.24, 3.25, and 3.26), respectively.

The results of these experiments demonstrate both the need for and the power of combining the outputs of different texture segmenting algorithms. Each of the six texture operators used is effective for different kinds of texture. Every operator except for one of the Laws Microtexture Masks (e5s5 in Figure 3.28) failed on at least one of the four test images. Furthermore, for several images, some

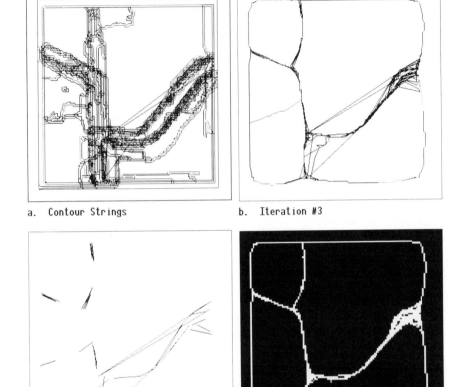

a. Contour Strings   b. Iteration #3

c. Large Gaps   d. Estimated Boundaries

FIG. 3.29.   All of the suggested boundaries are collected into a single "contour string" image. (b) These are then averaged by an iterative process. (c) Certain smoothing and cleaning algorithms are then applied (e.g., where lines filling long gaps are removed) to produce(d) the final spatially averaged output.

algorithms extracted only partial boundaries. Sometimes spurious identifications were made of boundaries that did not appear to be present visually. As shown in Figure 3.28, multiple and irregular boundaries suggest the variations in boundary estimates that can be generated by the different algorithms. This was the tangle of boundaries that had to be integrated by the combining algorithm's spatial statistics.

To quantify the capability of the entire texture segmenting algorithm, we compared the final images in Figure 3.30 with visual estimates of the boundaries between textured regions by graphically superimposing the two in the same

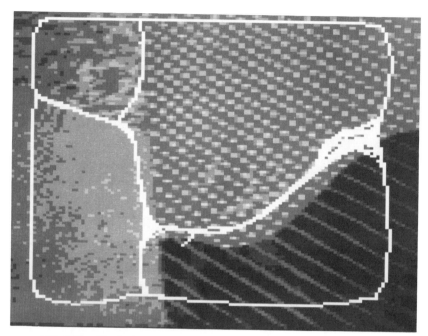

FIG. 3.30. The final output of the contour string combining algorithm described in the text has been superimposed on the original image Tex2.im to show the competency of the system.

FIG. 3.31. The final texture boundaries produced by the combination algorithm for input image Csub.im.

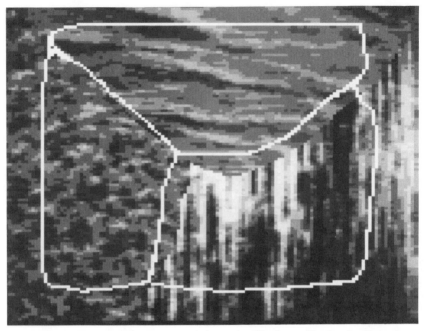

FIG. 3.32.   The final texture boundaries produced by the combination algorithm
for input image Wowapig.im.

space. An error factor (E) was calculated by evaluating the root mean square of
the error distances measured between each pixel on all boundaries in the final
image and the closest pixel on the nearest visually estimated boundary. The
distance between the computed boundary pixel and the nearest visually estimated
boundary pixel is calculated by searching progressively larger local regions
around every computed boundary pixel until any visually estimated boundary
pixel is found. Local region sizes for this search start at 1×1 and increase by
increments of two to 3×3, 5×5, up to a 75×75 pixel maximum limit. Half
the width of the largest local region that had to be used to locate a pixel in the
visually estimated boundary was used as the nominal error distance of the suggested boundary pixel.

E showed small differences between humans and computers, but E is at best
an approximate value since city-block distances instead of Pythagorean distances
were used in its calculation. However, its purpose is only to give a rough
estimate of the deviation of the computer texture boundaries from those produced
visually. We also compared the results of this calculation for several visual
estimates of the boundaries by different observers without generating significant
differences in E.

We can also evaluate the efficiency of the integrated texture segmenting algorithm in an informal way by examining the pictorial properties of the final

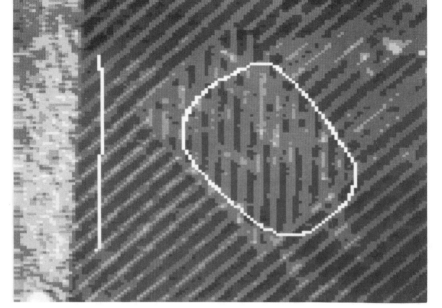

FIG. 3.33. The final texture boundaries produced by the combination algorithm for input image Stripes.im.

images shown in Figures 3.30 to 3.33. Sometimes, artifactual boundary estimates are produced by the spatial averaging process itself. Bifurcating intersections, as exemplified in Figure 3.30, were especially prone to this type of boundary distortion. Typically, pixels along one branch of the bifurcation mutually attract pixels from the other two branches. This type of distortion is clearly evident in the final output of all images, especially in Figures 3.30 and 3.31.

A second type of distortion occurs at boundary corners, as also exemplified in Figure 3.30. This distortion results in the rounding of angular corners and is most evident in the final outputs of the images Stripes.im (Figure 3.33) and Csub.im (Figure 3.32). A third type of distortion occurs at line terminations and when only one or two boundaries are suggested by the segmenting algorithms. In these cases, the terminations may be progressively eroded and large gaps may be introduced into the infrequently suggested boundaries.

An important issue concerns whether the six texture analyzers that we used are truly sensitive to texture and not just to intensity differences. The following test determined the relative sensitivity of the analyzers to the geometric aspects of texture as opposed to average intensity differences. Two test images were created in which two textured regions were joined at a common boundary. The first image (Figure 3.34) was constructed from two regions that differed only in

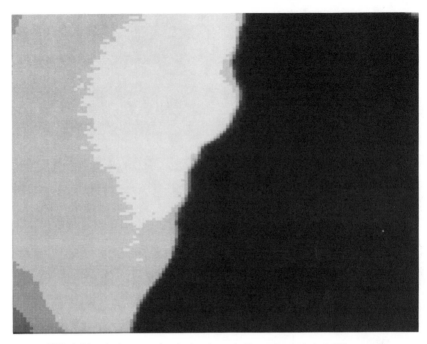

FIG. 3.34.   An input test image showing only first-order statistical differences in the texture.

intensity (i.e., in their first-order statistics). The second image (Figure 3.35) consists of two textured areas of the same average intensity but of different second-order statistics. All six texture segmenting algorithms were applied to these two images. This miniexperiment showed that all of the analyzers that were combined, with the exception of Laws's isomorphic Microtexture Mask and the vertical area differential operator, tracked the boundaries of the image shown in Figure 3.35. This indicates a generalized sensitivity to intensity differences along on the part of most of the analyzers, a property that could distort the analysis and in some situations pollute the discrimination of textures.

However undesirable sensitivity to intensity (i.e., first-order statistical differences) is an unavoidable property of most texture analyzers. The key question now arising is, do the texture analyzers discriminate boundaries between regions that differ in their second-order textural differences but not in their first-order differences? We now report the results of the application of the six algorithms to these test stimuli. With these sample images, the sample-and-match algorithm and the e5s5 and r5r5 Microtexture Masks did not produce good results. Nevertheless, the other segmenting algorithms all produced good estimates, suggesting a useful degree of effectiveness in discriminating textures with second-order statistical differences as shown in Figure 3.35 but with constant first-order statis-

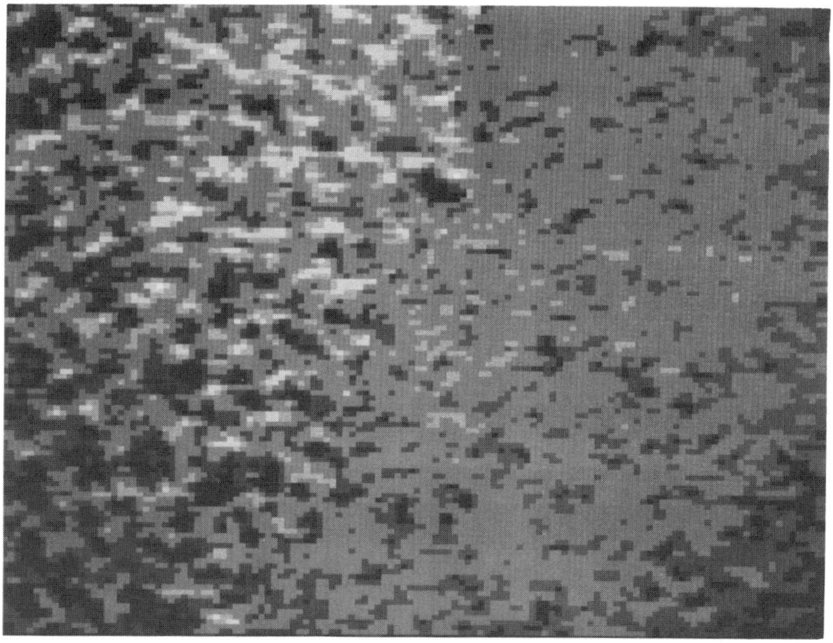

FIG. 3.35.   An input test image showing second-order statistical differences in the texture.

tics. The pattern of specific failures would be different with a different set of test stimuli.

One of the most important problems we currently face concerns the various parameters and threshold values that are variables in the execution of the many parts of the integrated texture segmenting procedure. Among the most important parameters passed from the script to the component algorithms of the procedure are the size of the local areas used in the various transformations, the definition of a weak boundary pixel, the ratio of the number of weak pixels to the total boundary length, and several critical intensity thresholds. We set these parameters empirically and did not adapt in any way to the properties of the image being processed. We intend to automate this part of the process and seek criteria for adjusting parameters to the specific attributes of the input image. We will address the problem of automatic correction of the known kinds of distortions that occur because of the spatial averaging process, by using the directional attributes of local areas along boundaries.

To summarize, we presented a method for integrating the outputs of six frail and idiosyncratic segmenters to produce estimates of the true boundaries of images that are superior to the estimates available from any one alone. An important advantage of this approach is that it works in a much more general way than any of the individual segmenters and will not fail catastrophically, as each of the individual segmenters must for one image type or another. As one segmenter fails, however, another one of the six succeeds. This is the foundation of the system's success.

The cost of this integrated approach is an increased computational load expressed as prolonged processing times on conventional computers and very large storage requirements. However, these are only technical problems. The forthcoming availability of parallel processors, faster arithmetic units, fast algorithms, streamlined code, and increased memory size promises to alleviate these difficulties.

We emphasize that a major theoretical advantage of the integrated procedure reported here is that it models one important aspect of human perception. Like the human visual system, the final output is the result of a combination of partial and incomplete information transmitted along parallel channels.

3.4. OBJECT RECONSTRUCTION

Another important and desirable attribute of both computer and human vision is the ability to reconstruct the full shape of an object when only partial information about its shape is available. The computer science aspects of this problem are dealt with in detail by Blake and Zisserman (1987) in their extremely timely book on visual reconstruction. They describe some general problems, of which the one discussed here is one special case, namely, the reconstruction of surface form from sparse dotted or pointlike samples that do no more than indicate a location on the surface of an otherwise invisible object in three-dimensional space.

The ability of the human to fill in or complete an object that has only been partially presented is often astounding. This ability to make a discontinuous image appear continuous is a foundation of Perceptual Theory. The long tradition of Gestalt Theory grew from early observations of ubiquitous phenomena. Unfortunately, and in spite of the fact that the Gestalt orientation was probably more correct than not in describing perceptual phenomenology, Gestalt psychology has been in a state of decline and disinterest for many years. The main reason for the decline was that the explanatory theories produced by this classical holistic tradition did not stand the test of time. Nevertheless, as a descriptive approach, *Gestaltism* or, more generically, holism, seems a more valid model of human visual performance than the local feature ideas so popular today. Gestaltism stands at the other end of the theoretical spectrum from an associative elementalism, the main distinction being that Gestalt theory stresses the influence of global rather than local properties of visual form on perception.

There are many examples and demonstrations of global processing and figural completion or reconstruction in human vision. The well-known two-dimensional subjective contour phenomenon shown in Figure 3.36 is one example of the

FIG. 3.36. The Kaniza triangle, a subjective contour phenomenon. (Courtesy of Dr. Gaetano Kaniza.)

power of this visual process. Another example is shown in Figure 3.37. Here a stereogram of a dotted surface is presented. If the pair of stimuli is fused, the perception of a complete surface, darker and slightly different in texture than the surround, is generated. The impression of a black feltlike surface is generated by processes in the human visual system that are presumably comparable in outcome to the interpolation processes used in reconstructing images in computer vision laboratories, although almost certainly different in exact mechanism. Psychophysical studies (Uttal, 1985, 1987; Uttal, Davis, Welke, and Kakarala, 1988) show how powerful this human perceptual reconstruction is even when there is no motion. When motion is added as a cue, the results are even more astounding. The work of Ullman (1979) and others has effectively proven that point.

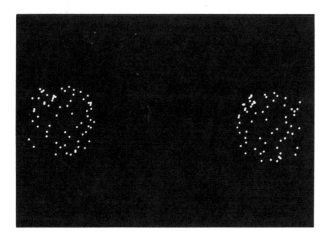

FIG. 3.37. A stereoscopic image that, when fused, produces the subjective impression of a continuous surface (a paraboloid of rotation) even though it is only sparsely sampled. *Note:* From *A Taxonomy of Visual Processes* (p. 131) by W. R. Uttal, 1981, Hillsdale, NJ: Lawrence Erlbaum Associates.

While some progress was made in imitating these human skills with computer algorithms, it cannot be overemphasized that computer vision programs probably do not even remotely resemble the internal algorithms that the organic vision system uses to accomplish the task.

The following sections consider our progress in reconstructing three types of surfaces that have been defined by only a few points:

1. Single-valued ("functional") surfaces drawn from the constrained list of standard quadrics and cubics (e.g., a hemisphere).
2. Single-valued ("functional") surfaces unconstrained in any way.
3. Unconstrained two or more valued ("nonfunctional") surfaces such as a sphere, an ellipsoid, a cube with all six surfaces present, a torus, any irregularly closed or folded shape.

In each case there are two steps to be carried out to reconstruct the surface from a few sample points. First, the surface must be tessellated or divided into bounded empty region between the sample points. The boundaries of this tessellation most often and most naturally form triangles. The boundaries, therefore, will generally be the straight lines connecting pairs of sample points.

Second, an interpolation expression must be found that represents the surface patches of the tessellated regions so that values for any point on the patch between the given points can be determined. The interpolating expression must be derived from information about the spatial relationships among the sample points. To determine the shape of the interpolating patch, one must know where the sample points are and some other characteristic of the surface, such as a polynomial expression that fits it, the partial derivatives, or the normals to the surface. There are examples of classic problems encountered in Interpolation and Approximation Theory.

A Simple Method for Reconstructing Single-Valued, Constrained Surfaces from a Few Sampled Points

In our SWIMMER simulation we initially modeled the perceptual process of surface reconstruction observed in our earlier psychophysical studies (Uttal et al., 1988). In a more or less straightforward manner the problem was formalized in the following way: Given a set of sparse samples taken from a single-valued, three-dimensional surface generated by an appropriate quadric or cubic polynomial, reconstruct the shape of the surface and the polynomial that generated it. Figure 3.38 shows the eight sample surfaces from which the dotted samples were generated. While these surfaces are shown here in the form of projective two-dimensional drawings, the stimuli were actually presented to the computer simulation in the form of a table of the three-dimensional coordinates of the sampled

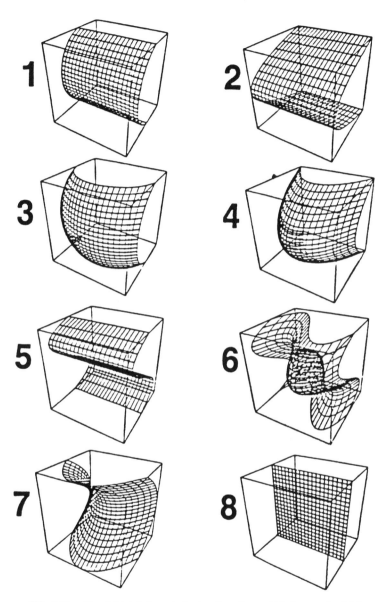

FIG. 3.38. The eight dotted constrained surfaces from which the sample of dots discussed in the text were drawn. The grid lines and surrounding cubes are merely aids to visualization and were not present on the surfaces when displayed. *Note:* from The Perception of Dotted Forms (p. 39) by W. R. Uttal, 1987, Hillsdale, N.J.: Lawrence Erlbaum Associates.

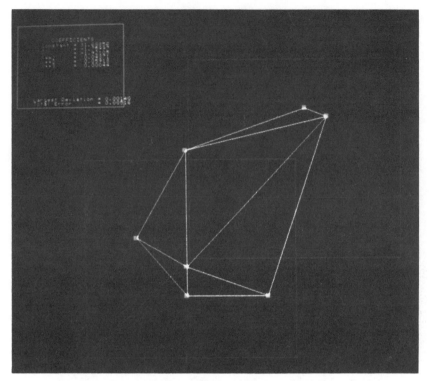

FIG. 3.39.   A wire-frame representation of a surface reconstructed from the few sample points. The table of numbers in the upper left corner contains the coefficients of the polynomial used for the interpolation process.

dots. The reconstruction simulation program required steps were carried out in order and displayed in various stages of completeness.

First, the display in Figure 3.39 shows the sampled dots connected by straight-line segments to create a polygonal wire-frame representation. In general, the polygons are triangular, but on occasion four-sided polygons might be generated. This wire-frame network is then filled in with appropriately lighted tiles to produce an approximation to the original surface from which the dots are sampled. While these graphical interpretations are being presented, a polynomial surface-fitting program is also running in the background. The results of this calculation are shown in the table in the upper left corner of these figures. The numbers in the table represent the coefficients of the best-fitting polynomial, an equation of the form

$$z = G(Cx^3 + Dx^2 + Ex + Ty^3 + Uy^2 + Uy + W)^F + H. \quad (3.22)$$

When the computation of the polynomial converges so that a sufficiently good fit is obtained, the iterative polynomial surface-fitting program is terminated.

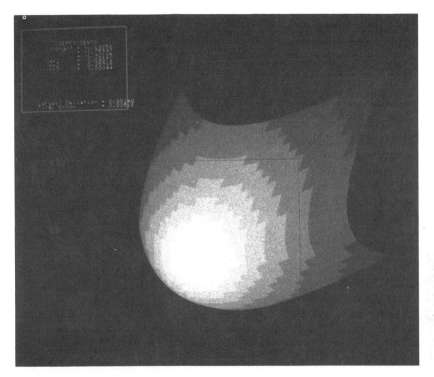

FIG. 3.40.   The continuous surface reconstructed from a few sample dots by the interpolation polynomial. The surface is a parabola of rotation, and the sample dots were originally constrained to this surface.

The next step of the graphical display—a continuous representation of the surface from which the original set of sampled dots—had presumably been drawn. This is shown in Figure 3.40.

Interesting tasks, subtasks, and results made this preliminary single-valued surface-fitting exercise worthwhile. One concerned the superficially simple task of connecting the points into a wire-frame representation—that is, triangulating or tessellating the surface.

A tessellation of a finite planar domain is a partitioning of the plane into a finite number of closed and nonoverlapping polygons. The tessellation can be constrained by the area of the generated polygons, by enforcing convexity and other geometric properties on them, and by other methods.

On curved surfaces with randomly distributed dots, tessellation cannot be accomplished without creating a chaotic jumble of lines unless certain exclusion rules are applied. To accomplish this task, therefore, we performed the following steps. First, the three-dimensional coordinates of the array of dots are reduced to their two-dimensional equivalents by simply ignoring the z coordinate. This projects the dot array onto a two-dimensional, planar surface at $z = 0$. The dots are then interconnected into a lattice subject to the following two exclusion rules. First, all possible line segments (generated by all possible pairwise combinations of the sampled dots) are examined to determine if they crossed any other line. This is accomplished by comparing the coordinates of each point on each line against those on all other lines. (Since the number of points in our simulations is relatively modest, this does not place too much of a demand on the computer.) If two points are determined to be coincident, then the three-dimensional coordinates of the respective lines are checked and the one in back deleted. The second exclusion rule determines whether two or more lines in the wire frame are actually collinear. The equations of all of the generated lines are compared to determine if any two (or more) are the same line. If so, the shorter one is deleted.

Following the application of these two exclusion rules, the z coordinates are restored and a two-dimensional projection of the three-dimensional wire-frame object is displayed on the screen. The viewpoint could be selected by the observer from among a slightly offset front, side, or top perspective.

Another interesting issue concerns the minimum number of dots required to uniquely define the surface from which the dots are sampled. While this is a question often asked and answered for lines (two dots) and planar surfaces (three dots), it is not usually discussed for the single-valued quadric and cubic surfaces examined here. Grappeling with this issue suggests a first approximation to an ideal model of the process of surface reconstruction by humans. The model is then compared to human performance in the similar task described by Uttal et al. (1988).

A mathematical answer to the question of how many dots are necessary for reconstruction can be obtained in a straightforward manner. Observe that the quadric surfaces are represented in our stimulus set by the general equation

$$z = G(Dx^2 + Ex + Uy^2 + Vy + W)^F + H \qquad (3.23)$$

and that we ask only about the general class of surface (i.e., *is it a hemisphere?* and not *which specific hemisphere is it?*). Then we assume that there are only five unknowns (D, E, U, V, and F) in this equation; G, W, and H may remain undefined. A minimum of five dots (i.e., five solutions to the equation, each of which is represented by a triplet, the x, y, and z coordinates of a point) are, therefore, required to designate a quadric surface.

Similarly, assuming that the cubics are represented by the equation

$$z = G(Cx^3 + Dx^2 + Ex + Ty^3 + Uy^2 + Vy + W)^F + H, \qquad (3.24)$$

a minimum of seven dots (i.e., solutions to the equation) are needed to reconstruct the form given only that the class of the surface (and not the specific surface) is to be determined; G, W, and H also remain undefined in this case. In both cases, the generation of a precise polynomial expression for a surface requires 8 and 10 dots, respectively.

In the three experiments of the Uttal et al. (1988) study, the human observer actually outperformed the criterion minimum number of dots defined by Equations 3.23 and 3.24; performance was nonrandom with fewer dots required for perceptual reconstruction (i.e., four dots allowed a 50% correct recognition) than even the relatively small number (five and seven) required for the reconstruction of quadrics and cubic. Furthermore, the scores did not seem to systematically differ for the quadric and cubic stimulus forms. Obviously, the human observer is operating under some additional constraints that provide him or her information not available to the simple polynomial curve-fitting model.

An Improved Reconstruction Method for Single-Valued, Unconstrained Surfaces from a Few Sample Points

Polynomial interpolation of the kind just described for surfaces constrained to the standard surfaces defined in solid analytic geometry cannot easily be generalized to unconstrained or irregular surfaces. The increasing order of the polynomials required for more complicated surfaces and the possibility of producing expressions that oscillate, rather than smoothly fitting the sampled surface lead to an inevitable breakdown in the polynomial approach. In addition, the computational complexity of polynomial interpolation increases with the number of sampled points. (For a general discussion of Interpolation Theory, see Davis, 1975.)

Furthermore, polynomial surface fitting and interpolation of numerous surface points usually involve a computationally expensive solution to a linear system of equations and could result in a system of equations with no solution. In other words, numerical stability and practical computability can become bottlenecks for any scheme based on polynomial interpolation when the number of points becomes large or when they are sampled from a generalized, as opposed to constrained, set of surfaces.

The implementation of the polynomial interpolation programs described in the previous section performed well on "well-behaved" and constrained surfaces. However, for the reasons just mentioned, we have not pursued that approach but have used an improved and more powerful technique. This new method is not based on the generation of an interpolating polynomial for the entire surface but on interpolating functions that operate only over local regions, specifically the triangles generated by a tessellation algorithm between the vertices defined by the sampled points.

These local interpolations are smoothed and made continuous at the seams between adjacent triangles in a way that produces a globally continuous surface. One advantage of a scheme based on local interpolation is that any surface, no matter how irregular or how unconstrained, can be reconstructed. Another is that gross discontinuities in the surface such as the edge of a cube can be handled without necessarily distorting (rounding) the entire object. The major disadvantage is that it is not possible to provide a formal expression for most surfaces.

The improved, generalized reconstruction procedure we report here is based on a two-stage process. First, the sampled points are connected in a grid of polygons (as in the polynomial method described earlier, but by an improved method.) Second, the surface of each of those polygons is interpolated in a manner that provides for smooth continuity between adjacent polygons. The influence of polygons on each other, however, is relatively local compared to the extended influence of distant polygons in the polynomial method.

The first step requires that the surface to be reconstructed be approximated by a set of planar tiling polygons (which as noted optimally turn out to be triangles). The second step requires that the individual tiling polygons be warped into the best-fitting curved and smoothed surface for a subset of nearby points. These curved tiles must be continuous with their neighbors at their common edges. This second step is accomplished by means of a specially designed interpolant or interpolating function tailored for each surface.

The First Step—Triangulation of the Domain.   One of the first problems faced is the choice of an appropriate polygon for the tessellation of the domain. (The domain is defined as the two-dimensional *xy* planar image of the surface onto which the sampled *xyz* surface is collapsed by removal of the *z* coordinate, the third dimension.) We believe that triangles provide the most elegant and simple scheme compared to higher order polygons. The preliminary stage of our improved reconstruction process, therefore, involves the subdivision of the domain into triangular subdomains. This task is not as easy as may initially seem, because of some simple geometrical facts of life.

First, there is no unique triangulation of any set of sample points, even when they are all lying on a plane. Unless the triangulation process is constrained in some way, numerous triangulations of any sample point set are equally possible. Second, the nature of the sample can result in an "uneven" triangulation; that is, even and "good-looking" triangles may obtain in some parts of the domain, and thin, long, and "ugly" triangles in others. Unfortunately, thin and long triangles can pose a problem regardless of which scheme will be used later to interpolate to their interior points. Notwithstanding these difficulties, since the quality of the surface generated depends on the nature of the triangulation, this step is critical. At best, the interpolation process does not produce an exact reproduction of the underlying surface; bad triangulations will distort the process from the outset. The goal is to keep these distortions to a minimum.

The Delaunay algorithm (Lee and Schachter, 1980) is probably the most widely used and efficient triangulation scheme. It was adopted as a reliable and fast method in such diverse fields as Finite Element Analysis, Network and Graph Theory, and many scientific areas where analysis is performed with lattice-based or topological criteria.

The Delaunay Algorithm uses a technique based on a max-min criterion to obtain locally optimal triangles. The max-min criterion maximizes the minimum angle of triangles in a local triangulation. The final triangulation emerging across the entire domain is also globally optimal with respect to the max-min criterion. The Delaunay triangulation is the only one of the known triangulation schemes that uses a local optimization process to converge to a globally optimal one. Also, it possesses important geometrical and topological properties that make it a robust and useful tool. One such property is that the same triangulation will always be obtained regardless of the order in which the sample points are processed.

One advantage of this approach is that the points on a single-valued surface in the *xyz* space can be collapsed onto a plane (the domain) in the same manner as in the polynomial algorithm described in the previous section. The triangulation is then performed over the domain where each point is defined only by its (x, y) coordinates. When the z values of the vertices are reintroduced, the resulting mesh of triangles in three-dimensional space is somewhat distorted, depending on the curvature of the original surface, but it is still useful for the subsequent interpolation process.

Another powerful property of the Delaunay triangulation method applied to the two-dimensional domain is that the mesh can be obtained by a trivial construction from the Voronoi (also called Dirichlet, Weiner-Seitz, or Thiessen) Tessellation (Shamos, 1977) of the sampled points. The Voronoi Tessellation of a set of points lying on a plane partitions or splits the plane into convex non-overlapping regions or "cells" such that each cell contains only one point. More importantly, the cells are constructed in such a way that any point in a cell is closer to the sample point around which that cell is built than to any other sample point in any other cell. The dotted lines in Figure 3.41 shows the Voronoi Tessellation of a set of points sampled from a single-valued surface.

In Figure 3.41 any edge of the tessellation common to more than one polygon is situated along the perpendicular bisector of the line joining the points enclosed in those polygons. The points sharing such edges need only be joined by straight lines to yield a triangulated tessellation. Conveniently, this turns out to be the Delaunay triangulation. Because of this close relationship, the Voronoi Tessellation and the Delaunay triangulation are referred to as *geometric duals*. Figure 3.41 also shows the Delaunay triangulation (in solid lines) of a set of sampled points collapsed to the domain.

The Second Step: Interpolation Across the Triangulated Tessellations.   The goal in the second step is to specify an interpolating function, or *interpolant*, that estimates the location of points on a curved patch. This interpolation must produce a better approximation to the original surface than the small planar triangles produced by the Delaunay technique even when those tiles are reconstructed from the domain to their three-dimensional form by the reintroduction of their z coordinates.

The sampled points by means of which we are trying to fit a surface are

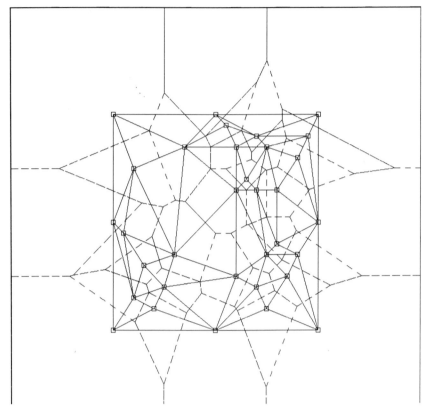

FIG. 3.41.   The Voroni Tessellation (dotted lines) and the Delaunay triangulation
(solid lines) of a set of 0-dimensional points collapsed onto the planar domain. The
two are geometric duals of each other.

nothing more than locations in space. By themselves, the information they represent is not sufficient to design an interpolation function that will not only successfully fill in the values of unsampled points across the tessellation tiles but
will also produce continuity at the seams between triangles.

To develop a successful interpolant we must know, in addition to the (x, y, z)
coordinates of each sampled point, something about the shape of the surface. In
the usual situation, some measure of surface shape is given. But this is not true in
the present case. Here, only the coordinates of the sample points are available. It
is necessary to estimate the surface shape from this information.

One way to estimate the surface is to use a polynomial as a surface-fitting
algorithm. We already considered that idea and rejected it as a feasible option for
reasons of numerical stability and practical computability. An alternative is to use
the point coordinates to determine the partial derivatives of the underlying func-

tion at those points. (Another method, based on surface normals, will be discussed in the next section.) This step is critical because the quality of the reconstructed surface depends on the accuracy of these estimated partial derivatives. However, the problem is, in a sense, circular. To precisely and rigorously determine the partial derivatives, we must know the shape of the surface. However, in the present situation, the partial derivatives are necessary to know the whole surface. Fortunately, the necessary information to approximate the surface is available in a computationally tractable form by looking at the spatial relationship coordinates among the sampled points.

The partial derivatives at a sampled point can be approximated by examining only a limited patch of the whole surface. This approximation can be done in a number of ways. If we fix a finite-sized neighborhood around each point, we can fit a first approximation surface (using any simple interpolation technique) to all the points that fall in this neighborhood. That rough surface is then used to obtain an approximate estimate of the partial derivatives in that local region.

This divide-and-conquer technique depends on its accuracy for several factors. The first factor is the quality of the local interpolant. In extreme cases, a poor local interpolant gives totally misleading partial derivative values. Second, the spatial distribution of the sampled points on the surface will undoubtedly influence the local interpolant. Uneven and skewed points will produce inaccurate estimates regardless of the method used.

The method chosen to estimate gradient values at the sampled points is based on a concept called the "Minimum Norm Network over a Triangulated Domain" (Nielson, 1983). It involves a preprocessing step in which the surface is also collapsed to the xy domain by ignoring the z coordinate values. This collapsed planar representation is then triangulated by the Delaunay triangulation method. The next stage creates a network of curves over the edges of each triangle when it is reconstructed into the third dimension by the reintroduction of the z value to each of the (x, y) coordinate pairs.

For an edge e_{ij} between vertices v_i and v_j, if $F(v_i)$ represents the function value, i.e., z value at v_i (and similarly for v_j) and if $\partial F/\partial e_{ij}$ is the derivative of the function in the direction of the edge between v_i and v_j, then a unique cubic curve can be defined between the two vertices as

$$c(t) = H_0(t)F(v_i) + H_1(t)F(v_j)$$

$$+ H_0(t) \frac{\partial F}{\partial e_{ij}} (v_i) + \bar{H}_1(t) \frac{\partial F}{\partial e_{ij}} (v_j), \tag{3.25}$$

where t is a real value that varies between 0 and 1 as we move from vertex v_i to v_j, and $H_0, H_1, \bar{H}_0,$ and $\bar{H}_1$ are the cubic Hermite basis functions.

From this process, each edge acquires a cubic curve defined over it. In accord with the Theory of Cubic Splines, the minimum norm technique then performs a minimization process over all the edges of the triangulation. That is, given data

(t_i, s_i), where $i = 1, \ldots, n$ and $t_1 < t_2 \cdots < t_n$, the cubic spline in one dimension can be characterized as the unique solution to the minimization problem

$$\text{Min} \int_{t_1}^{t_n} [f''(t)]^2 \, dt \qquad (3.26)$$

subject to

$$f(t_i) = s_i. \qquad (3.27)$$

The minimum norm network criterion yields a system of equations that involve the coordinates of the sample points and the partial derivatives in the x and y directions. This procedure is guaranteed to have a unique solution and thus can be solved for the unknowns, the partial derivatives.

The solution to this system of equations is obtained in an iterative manner until all of the values converge to a constant value. The method performs very well for single-valued surfaces, and we have tested it over a wide variety of test functions. With the partial derivatives in hand, we can develop a specific, more precise interpolant.

A large class of interpolation strategies for this type of surface fitting exists that requires only the partial derivatives and the sampled point locations. To achieve the additional goal of extending the interpolational procedure to reconstructing multiple-valued surfaces, we selected the side vertex technique (Nielson, 1979).

The goal of this interpolation is to obtain the z value of the surface at any point (x, y) in the interior of the triangle. The side vertex interpolation method for triangles is based on the concept of univariate interpolation along a line segment joining a triangle vertex and the side opposite it. The line must pass through the point (x, y) whose z coordinate is being determined. Consider one of the triangles in the Delaunay triangulation of the sample points shown in Figure 3.41. At each vertex its coordinates and the partial derivatives of the function in the x and y directions are available for the interpolation.

The side vertex method thus fits a cubic curve from each vertex of a triangle to a point on the side of the triangle opposite the vertex. As shown in Figure 3.42, the z value of any interpolated point within the triangle is then obtained as a weighted sum of the three cubic functions, as represented in the expression

$$F(x, y) = \frac{w_1 I_1(x, y) + w_2 I_2(x, y) + w_3 I_3(x, y)}{w}, \qquad (3.28)$$

where I_1, I_2, and I_3 are the three cubic functions each corresponding to one of the vertices of the triangle; w_1, w_2, w_3, and w are the weights, which are functions of the position of the evaluation point (x, y) within the triangle; and $F(x, y)$ is the interpolated function value or the z value corresponding to the (x, y) location. The weights are obtained as a function of the position of the evaluation point with

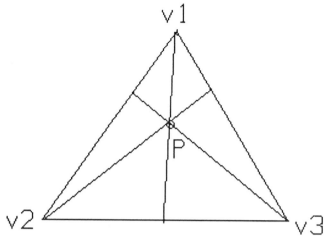

FIG. 3.42.   Means by which the three cubic curves are fit from the three vertices
of the triangle through an interpolated point. The actual z value of the point is then
estimated from the weighted sum of the values of the three cubics.

respect to the vertices of the triangle. Thus, as each point is evaluated, a check is
made to determine the triangle in which the point falls.

This method produces an interpolated surface that is continuous over the
domain and has a continuous first derivative everywhere, thus achieving our goal
of reconstructing a single-valued, unconstrained surface. Figure 3.43 shows the
reconstruction obtained from 33 points sampled from such a surface. The triangulation of the surface is also shown in the figure. An additional attribute of
this approach is that this method of reconstruction produces visually pleasing
images when they are displayed. Since these reconstructions are ultimately to be
viewed in our model, this property is useful.

Some Steps Toward the Reconstruction
of Multiple-Valued, Unconstrained Surfaces

This section considers the problem of reconstructing surfaces that may have
two or more z values for any (x, y) points; i.e., it deals with nonfunctional data.
Such surfaces are either closed (e.g., a sphere, an ellipsoid, or a torus) or wrap
around themselves one or more times (e.g., the catastrophic cusp).

The interpolation techniques described in the previous two sections to process
single-valued surfaces must necessarily fail in the case of multiple-valued surfaces. Therefore, other strategies were invented for this part of the problem. One
of the first solutions proposed was to convert it into the single-valued problem by
halving the set of sampled points and performing the interpolation separately on
the two halves. Although this expedient takes care of the problem of some two-
valued surfaces, the results are not generally satisfactory for four main reasons.

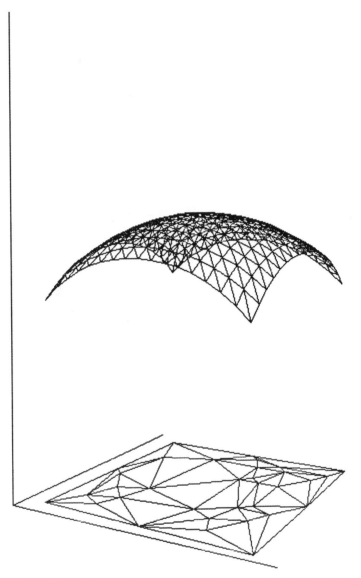

FIG. 3.43.   The interpolated reconstruction of a two-dimensional, single-valued, unconstrained surface as described in the text.

1. The semisurfaces produced on the halves of such a surface typically will not blend smoothly at the seams. The combined surface is nearly always distorted at the plane of the slice. Therefore, some type of mathematical "seam" clamping would be needed to ensure that the two halves blend in a smooth and geometrically continuous manner. This, we concluded, would be a formidable task.

2. The distribution of the initial set of sample points in Euclidean space might be skewed to one side with samples unevenly distributed on the surface. Such a skewing makes it very difficult to specify a good plane with which to slice the surface into two parts.

3. One slicing of the sample of points may not disambiguate the multiple-valued nature of the surface. For surfaces that wrap around themselves several times, it may be necessary to slice the surface more than once to carry out the interpolation process. Specifying several successive optimal slices is a difficult task even when performed interactively by the human operator. Automating the process would also be extremely difficult.

4. The simple version of the side vertex method of interpolation also fails for multiple-valued surfaces. The simple algorithm is based on the concept of an underlying single-valued surface and it needs modification for multiple-valued surfaces

The First Step—Triangulation of the Surface in Space. By analogy with the strategy used for single-valued surfaces, the first step in a reconstruction algorithm suitable for multivalued surfaces was the triangulation of the sample-point-defined surface. At this point the sample points can no longer be uniquely collapsed into the *xy* domain as they could for a single-valued surface. The sampled points must be considered in the form in which they were originally provided—points located in space. But the principle remains the same; a triangulation of the sample points must be generated. In this case it must be a connectivity network of the points in three-dimensional space rather than in the plane.

The technique of obtaining a Delaunay triangulation described earlier cannot be directly extended to the three-dimensional setting. Therefore, we chose an alternative method of triangulation. The new method restricts the algorithm to process purely convex two-valued surfaces. That is, there can be no depressions or dimples on the surface that we reconstruct, and all interior points will be ignored.

The task is to compute the triangulated *convex hull* of a set of points sampled from a two-valued surface. The convex hull is defined as the smallest, outermost wrapper that can be placed around a collection of sampled points in three-dimensional space with the restriction that there can be no concavities on that wrapper.

The computation of the convex hull of a set of points is accomplished by means of a technique called Giftwrapping (Shamos, 1977). The algorithm works (figuratively) in the manner in which one would wrap a cover or "skin" around an object until it is covered. The initial step of the algorithm examines one valid triangle of the convex hull that may be generated by three nearby points. Then, taking each edge of the first triangle into consideration, it forms another triangle by selecting a nearby point in such a way that the convexity requirement is not violated. This process is continued until there are no more unprocessed edges.

Note that an unprocessed edge is one that is present in only one triangle. When the algorithm terminates, all the points will be connected by triangles, with every edge in the structure shared by exactly two triangles.

The Second Step—Interpolation of the Triangles.   Following the completion of the triangulation of the sample points the next step is to define an appropriate interpolating function. Estimation of the partial derivatives cannot be applied here because of the possibility of multiple z values of the surface at single points in the xy domain. Instead, the new method obtains estimates for the surface normal vectors at the sample points based on the results of the application of the initial triangulation algorithm. Estimates of the normal vectors totally depend on the outcome of the triangulation. Because there is no unique triangulation of a set of points in three-dimensional space any more than in two-dimensional space, every distinct triangulation will yield a different surface normal and, hence, a different surface. The positive side of this difficulty is that the variations in the surface normals resulting from different triangulations are relatively small and will, in most cases, not make a visual difference when the interpolated surfaces are displayed.

For these multiple valued surfaces we used a modification of the side vertex method (Nielson, 1987) of interpolation over triangles for single-valued surfaces. Instead of the coordinates of the sampled points and estimates of the partial derivatives at those points on a triangulated domain, the information now available includes a three-dimensional structure made up of triangles and a surface normal defined at each vertex.

The modified and extended side vertex interpolating function generates a curved, tentlike patch over each of the triangles. This patch is constrained by the surface normals located at the sample points. The surface normals are themselves determined by all of the triangles that meet at that point. Just as the reconstructed single-valued surface had continuous first derivatives at the triangle boundaries, this double-valued interpolated surface is characterized by a continuously varying surface normal. In other words, it will be displayed as a "visually continuous" surface. This is not a complete mathematical representation of the surface. However, our objective is to reproduce the surface of the object so that the object recognition and classification phases can operate on it. This is sufficient for our needs.

Figure 3.44 shows the triangulated convex hull of a set of five points sampled from a two-valued surface. Figure 3.45 shows the wire-frame rendering of the interpolated surface. (These small triangles help us see the surface computed from the interpolation function, but note that they are not the same as the original tessellation triangles.)

We have described a method for solving the problem of reconstructing a surface from point samples—in other words, scattered data interpolation. We considered three cases: (1) single-valued surfaces constrained to the standard

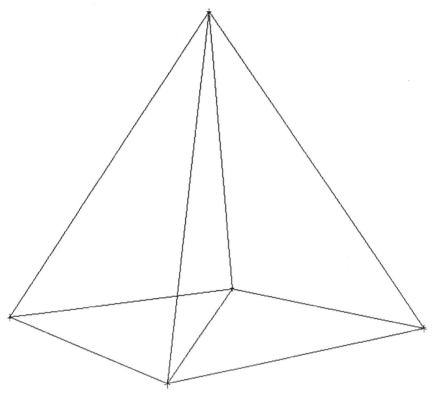

FIG. 3.44.   The triangulated convex hull of a set of five points sampled from a
two-valued surface.

solid geometric forms; (2) single-valued surfaces unconstrained to any form; and
(3) multivalued surfaces unconstrained to any form. The techniques used here are
not totally general. The problem of defining two-valued, nonconvex surfaces
remains.

Furthermore, there are other limits of our work that should be noted. One is
that the computational algorithms are approximations and not mathematically
rigorous. This may distress pure mathematicians, but our discomfort is greatly
assuaged because these algorithms reconstruct some surfaces that would be
mathematically intractable when approached in a more formal manner.

Another of the most profound principles is that there is no universal procedure
that will work for all reconstruction problems (or for that matter for all image
processing problems). Different situations require different mathematical and
computational techniques. This conclusion may extend to the human perceptual
system. There may be no single solution to all of the reconstruction problems
faced in a complex visual environment. The SWIMMER has developed by

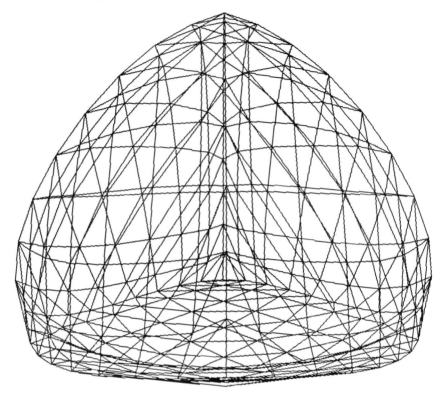

FIG. 3.45.   The interpolated reconstruction of the surface in Figure 3.44. Depending on the value selected for the tension at the vertices, this may be a softly
rounded or a sharply cornered form.

evolutionary, as well as accretionary, steps. This is not unlike human vision that
also has evolved a complex of visual image processing "tricks" that allow us to
function adaptively in our environment.

3.5.   OBJECT RECOGNITION

The simulated organism described here is supposedly searching for salient, regular objects (i.e., simulated food) and avoiding irregular (and, therefore, irrelevant) objects. At this stage of development of our model the SWIMMER only
has available visual information concerning the two-dimensional geometric form
of the objects to make the discrimination between salient and irrelevant objects.
For this reason, and the general importance of the process, the simulation of
visual form recognition became a major programming activity. This section deals
with our progress in developing form recognition algorithms.

There are several important considerations in developing a form recognition system so that it can be applied generally and not limited to excessively narrowly defined classes of forms. To the maximum extent possible, the algorithms should deal with forms in a very general way analogous to the human visual system. Thus, generalizability and adaptability were important criteria in the design of the simulated form recognition system.

A very desirable attribute of the model's visual recognition system, therefore, is a high degree of competence in recognizing an object independent of its position, orientation, or apparent size. For an organism, simulated or real, to perform with this degree of flexibility, it must identify and use information that is invariant as the object moves, rotates, or changes in distance and apparent size. Ideally, position-, size-, and orientation-invariant information should be extracted from an analysis of the relationships between the features that make up the image rather than from an analysis of the features themselves. This attribute suggested that some degree of sensitivity to the global organization of a form should be incorporated into the model.

Another important attribute of a powerful visual recognition system should be a relatively low sensitivity to noise. To the degree that the model can simulate human perception, it must be able to tolerate subtle (and sometimes not so slight) perturbations in the global shape of the objects or of the components of which it is constructed. Spatial perturbations of the type that might incapacitate a form recognition algorithm may arise if an object is blurred, distorted by viewing conditions, or partially occluded by another object. Interfering distortions may also occur because of sampling errors in the original recording of the image or from idiosyncrasies of the algorithms used at an earlier stage of processing. This attribute suggested use of a more relaxed and discrepancy-tolerant kind of form matching process than the usually rigid template image correlation.

Beyond simply discriminating between regular (food) and irregular (nonfood) objects, the simulated organism should be able to describe the objects in terms that may be far divorced from geometrical or mathematical simplicity to provide a more subtle, and sometimes more ambiguous, kind of recognition category. For example, the program in some instances is directed to recognize an object and to name it "circle" as well as provide the formal analytical geometric expression for a symmetrical form with a radius (r) located with its origin at (x, y). Both forms of categorization are useful to humans and both would be useful in our simulation.

Finally, the recognition system should be adaptive in the most powerful way; it must learn from its environment and its experiences. To simulate this important aspect of human visual information processing, we designed the recognition algorithm to add newly encountered forms to its memory when they did not match closely enough previously encountered forms.

As a result of these considerations, the SWIMMER's recognition system consists of two stages. In the first stage, a purely geometric analysis is made. In the second, the object is associated with a symbolic name and descriptors that characterize the intangible properties and attributes of the recognized form.

The first stage, which provides a geometric analysis of the object, requires a more or less conventional, deterministic algorithmic strategy. The global form matching portion of this part of the program is, however, quite unconventional in terms of its tolerance to noise and size, position, and orientation variations.

The second stage associates symbolic names with objects in a way that depends on the program's previous experience. Therefore, built into the system is an adaptive and experiential learning environment. In other words, the program constantly reorganizes itself so that the output depends not only on the immediate input and its own transformations but also on all of its previously recorded experiences. If the organism encounters a familiar object, it is able to retrieve specific information about similar objects belonging to the same class, to use in guiding its behavior. Even if the object is unfamiliar the simulated organism is designed to be able to often designate its properties and features when the object shares some attributes with other objects that were previously encountered by the simulation algorithm. Thus, the SWIMMER has the ability to classify objects it encountered before while maintaining its ability to describe objects it has not encountered.

In the computer simulation of the recognition process, familiar and unfamiliar objects were analyzed somewhat differently. The program is only able to describe an unfamiliar object, identify its features, and make general classifications based on those features. However, when dealing with more familiar objects or objects that share some properties with known ones it can identify similarities among different objects or variations of the same object by using classes of objects that are defined less rigidly than is often the case.

It was for these reasons that we used the two-stage recognition analysis in our model. As noted, the first stage decomposes a two-dimensional object into its constituent local features and identifies those features along with the object's more general, global properties. The second stage compares this representation of an object with the larger set of representations of previously encountered forms stored in the recognition system's memory. This second stage, at first glance, seems to incorporate a template matching process, but as we will see it is a much less rigid system than that; it depends on the attributes of the object in a much more subtle manner than simple geometrical cross-correlation.

Other methods for feature-based form recognition include those proposed by Wu and Stark (1985), Henderson and Anderson (1984), and Wojcik (1987). Alternative methods for extracting features from an image include those proposed by Nagy (1969), Gupta and Wintz (1975), Rosenfeld and Thurston (1971), Rosenfeld, Thurston, and Lee (1972), and Nevatia and Binford (1977). A general review of feature detection methods is presented by O'Gorman (1988).

The First Stage

The first stage of processing is a straightforward analysis of an object into its constituent local features. Our approach to feature analysis in this first stage of processing requires that the program identify and segregate linear from nonlinear features of the outline of a segmented object.[7] Feature analysis of this kind can be considered as a context-independent approach to object recognition, in the sense that each feature is independent of all others. This process is, therefore, comparable to the *hard-wired* analytic mechanisms of early processing in organic visual systems. While this approach does transform the input, substantial amounts of subsequent processing are required to characterize an object and make decisions about the category to which it belongs. This distinction, from our point of view, is analogous to the preattentive-attentive dichotomy in human visual perception.

To reduce the effects of noise and aliasing in the binary edge image, the coordinates of points in the image are averaged locally. Let $F(x, y)$ represent the binary edge image. Each point, (x_i, y_i) in the edge image is connected to at most two other points. To smooth the edge image a new set of points (x_{ai} and y_{ai}) is calculated as

$$x_{ai} = \frac{x_i + x_j}{2}, \tag{3.29}$$

$$y_{ai} = \frac{y_i + y_j}{2} \tag{3.30}$$

The new coordinates (x_{ai}, y_{ai}) replace the original points (x_i, y_i) and (x_j, y_j) in the smoothed image. The number of cycles determines the amount of smoothing. As this number gets larger, the contours in the image become smoother and more rounded. It also reduces small gaps in the edge image.

The new binary edge image defined by $F(x_{ai}, y_{ai})$ contains much smoother contours than the original does. Smoothing of this sort is not always required, but it is sometimes useful for dealing with noisy and degraded images. The smoothing process can be applied to the incoming edge image or to the extracted features. Some approaches to image smoothing may be found in Pratt (1978) and Klaus and Horn (1986).

Following smoothing, we tabulate sequential sets of points, taken from an object's outline, and examine them for linearity or curvature. The angular relationships characterizing sequences of points organized in straight or curved lines are determined by measuring the angles formed by the lines connecting adjacent pairs of points. For example, assume that points 1 and 2 define one such line, points 2 and 3 a second line, and points 3 and 4 a third line. If the slopes of these lines do not differ (within the constraint of some small and arbitrary threshold

---

[7]The outline of the objects with which this part of the simulation deals had previously been generated by the image segmentation algorithms. Objects were edge enhanced as described earlier, and a serial tabulation was made of the x and y coordinates of each point on this enhanced perimeter. It was this set of points—those constituting the edge of the object—upon which the algorithms we are now discussing operate.

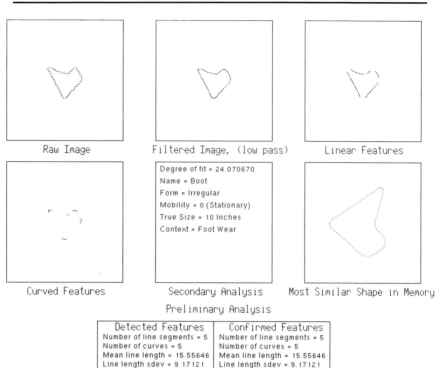

Raw Image   Filtered Image, (low pass)   Linear Features

Degree of fit = 24.070670
Name = Boot
Form = Irregular
Mobility = 0 (Stationary)
True Size = 10 Inches
Context = Foot Wear

Curved Features   Secondary Analysis   Most Similar Shape in Memory

Preliminary Analysis

Detected Features	Confirmed Features
Number of line segments = 5	Number of line segments = 5
Number of curves = 5	Number of curves = 5
Mean line length = 15.55646	Mean line length = 15.55646
Line length sdev = 9.17121	Line length sdev = 9.17121
Mean angle size = 1.46625	Mean angle size = 1.46625
Sdev of angle size = 0.47645	Sdev of angle size = 0.47645
Shape name =	Shape name =
irregular	irregular
Pentagon	Pentagon

FIG. 3.46.   The display presented on the computer screen during the computation of the recognition algorithms. The upper left picture is the boundary of an
object segmented from the original input image. The next picture shows the
smoothed version (low-pass-filtered) of this object. Next are the extracted linear
features and then the extracted curved features. The two tables show the properties
of the features that have been extracted in raw form and after confirming that each
exceeded a threshold size value. The last picture shows the best-matching item
from the computer's memory of previously encountered forms. The center panel
conveys information about the meaning and nature of the object that, once at-
tached to this object by the experimenter, can be automatically passed to matching
objects. Note that a good match occurs even though there are large differences in
the size, orientation, and position of the object and the stored reference.

amount), then the lines connecting these points are considered to be samples
from a straight portion of an object's outline. If, on the other hand, there is a
continuous and above-threshold change in the slopes, then this portion of the
object's outline is considered to be a curve with a curvature defined by the rate of
change of the slopes. If there is an abrupt discontinuity in slope between two
otherwise straight segments, then an appropriate angle is defined. Adjusting the

criteria for comparing the slopes of the interpoint lines, and the sensitivity of the program to minor irregularities such as missing or displaced points, allows us to make this analysis relatively insensitive to slight perturbations in the position of individual dots.

After the individual linear and curved portions of the outline are properly segregated, a purely geometrical description of the object is produced by tabulating the properties of the component line segments. The properties of the linear segments analyzed by the programs are length, orientation, and position. The properties of curved segments that are tabulated included, in part, the length of the arc, the location of the center of gravity (defined by the averages of the x and y coordinates of all of the constituent points along the curved segment), and a set of values r_n, θ_n (the length and orientation of the straight lines connecting each pair of points in the object's outline.) Some of this information is presented during the simulation as shown in the lower middle panel of Figure 3.46, a reproduction of the display appearing on the computer screen as the recognition portion of the program is processed. Other measures for defining curved line segments will be defined later.

This table of information is sufficient to reconstruct any of the linear and nonlinear segments of the original image even if the original coordinates of the constituent points of the object's outline are lost. Indeed, such a compilation of data, even though larger in volume than that of the original image, has some advantages over the raw data. A line reconstructed from these tables is idealized in the sense that it is conceptually continuous and complete. It may also lack some of the imperfections present in the original image. For example, a series of unaligned points may be aligned. Thus, this procedure is an implicit noise reduction and smoothing operation. This is an important step in enhancing the capability of the second stage of processing, because it helps to reduce the number of new categories that would otherwise be automatically generated by the second stage's adaptive learning capability and makes the recognition process more robust.

In addition to its length and orientation, a line segment's position must also be known before sufficient information is available to reconstruct it. The reference used by the program for this part of the recognition procedure is the point of bisection of the line. It is defined as the average of the x and y coordinates of the line's end points.

Describing curves requires more than a simple tabulation of the length, orientation, and position of straight-line segments. Curves have more degrees of freedom than do line segments because they must be represented by second (or higher order) equations rather than linear ones. Our goal was to represent all of the attributes of a curve with the fewest possible measurements. Measurements were chosen to reflect the curve's arc length, curvature, position, orientation, concavity, and form. This information is enough to allow an idealized reconstruction of the curves while providing a relatively simple basis for classifying and comparing them.

To compute a discretely sampled curve's arc length, we sum the distances between pairs of adjacent points on the curve. This sum serves as a reasonable approximation of the curve's true arc length, provided that the points are not too widely separated.

The curvature of a segment can be measured in such a way that it is position, orientation, and size invariant and still allows complete reconstruction of the outline of the object of which it is a part. Curvature is approximated in our system by taking the first derivative of the orientations between pairs of adjacent points on the curve. That is, we compute the differences between orientations of successive imaginary line segments connecting sequential pairs of points on the curve. This table of differences is a position-, orientation-, and size-invariant representation of the curve that can be combined with position, orientation, and size measurements to permit an exact reconstruction of the curve.

Determining concavity (i.e., whether the curve is concave or convex with respect to the object's center of gravity) follows directly from the measurement of curvature. If the points on a curved segment are processed in clockwise order, curves that are concave with respect to the object's center of gravity have a negative average curvature. Similarly, curves that are convex with respect to the object's center of gravity have a positive average curvature. Alternation of signs between the minimum, maximum, and average curvature reflects a reversal in curvature as exemplified by a sine wave or S-shaped curve.

To specify a curve's position, we decided to use the curve's center of gravity itself. A curve's center of gravity is defined as the point at which the weighted moments of all points on the curve sum to zero. Since the curves, in this case, are made up of discrete points, the center of gravity can easily be calculated by simply averaging the curves' x and y coordinates. The resulting values are a good approximation of the center of gravity's x and y coordinates. This point is invariant with respect to the curve's size and orientation and thus provides a stable and reliable measure of the curve's position.

A simple and fairly reliable method for specifying a curve's orientation is to use the curve's end points as indicators. The program accomplished this by simply dividing the difference between the y coordinates of the end points by the distance between them and taking the arc cosine of the result. This measure of orientation is independent of the curve's size and position. As with the orientation of line segments, the orientation of curves calculated in this manner is defined from $-90°$ to $+90°$.

Once the form of the curve is represented in the manner just described, it is possible to reconstruct the original curve (or an idealized representation of it) in any position, orientation, or size. This is possible because the curve's representation is based on the lengths and orientations of imaginary line segments between pairs of adjacent points on the curve. By normalizing the orientation and distance values representing the curve's form relative to the new size and orientation and calculating a starting point relative to the new position, the curve can be regenerated point by point.

To accomplish a smooth, idealized, or interpolated reconstruction of a curve (without using an formal expression), we compute a set of descriptive values by dividing the differences between the orientation values of two successive inter-point lines by the length of the first line. Given this set of values, the number of points to be computed, the curve's approximate arc length, and its orientation, a new representation of the curve that is as smooth and continuous as the discrete image allows over the curve's entire length can be generated.

To accomplish this position-, size-, and orientation-invariant interpolation, we must convert the data to a form based exclusively on the orientations of the tangents to the curve at any point. This is accomplished by computing a polynomial function θ_t from the invariant polar representation of a feature: (r_n, θ_n), where r_n is the distance and θ_n is the direction between each pair of points. Given this representation, the interpolated function θ_t can be approximated by

$$\theta_t \approx \left[\frac{r_n\theta_n + r_{n+1}\theta_{n+1}}{r_n + r_{n+1}} - \left(\frac{\theta_{n+1} - \theta_n}{r_n} \right) \left(\sum_{i=0}^{n} r_i - t \right) \right.$$

$$\left. - \frac{1}{2} \left(\frac{\theta_{n+2} - 2\theta_{n+1} + \theta_n}{r_n + r_{n+1}} \right) \left(\sum_{i=0}^{n} r_i - t \right) \right], \tag{3.31}$$

where

$$\sum_{i=0}^{n-1} r_i \leq t \leq \sum_{i=0}^{n} r_i.$$

This interpolation is based on the partial Taylor series:

$$\theta_t \approx \theta_0 + \theta_0' t + \tfrac{1}{2}\theta_0'' t^2. \tag{3.32}$$

Because our goal in this part of the project is to recognize and reconstruct complete objects rather than just straight lines and curves, additional global organizational information (beyond the specification of the attributes of the components) is needed about the *arrangement* of the features making up a form. This information must also be invariant with respect to the object's position, size, and orientation if it is to be used in a biologically realistic manner.

One of the more convenient ways to derive this information is to calculate the position of each linear or curved feature relative to the object's center of gravity. The Cartesian coordinates representing each feature's position are thus converted into polar coordinates with the object's center of gravity serving as the origin. Given these polar coordinates and a measure of the object's size, position, and orientation, it is possible to recalculate each feature's descriptors in a way that preserves the relationships among the features while maintaining position, size, and orientation invariance for the entire object. This information also allows two

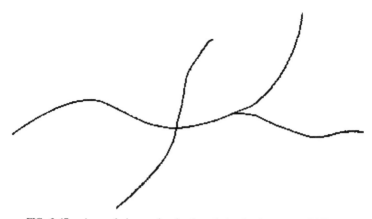

FIG. 3.47.   A sample image showing boundaries that intersect and bifurcate.

entire shapes, even if they differ in these dimensions, to be compared on the basis of files of information describing their respective features. This type of comparison is the basis of the second stage of processing in our recognition algorithms.

Finally, another important aspect of our recognition algorithm is that it should be able to resolve the problem of overlapping objects and the resulting bifurcating contours. When lines overlap or intersect, as shown in Figure 3.47, there is uncertainty about which lines exiting the bifurcation are continuations of each other and which represent separate contours. We used the criterion of mathematical continuity to resolve this uncertainty in the same way suggested years ago by Ratoosh (1949) to explain the psychological phenomenon. Details of this algorithm will be presented later.

The Second Stage

The comparison of two two-dimensional objects in terms of their features, in a way that is less rigid than a conventional template matching procedure, involves two essential steps. The first step identifies the best-matching pairs of corresponding features from each object. The second step makes a detailed comparison of those pairs of features. This two-step comparison process is based on the concept that geometrically similar objects will tend to have similar features in similar relative positions even if they are in different positions and orientations and are of different sizes.

To pair the corresponding features of two objects, the program first identifies the best-matching feature positions' shapes. Because feature positions are represented in a system of polar coordinates distributed about the object's center of gravity or the centers of gravity of all of the other features, the set of polar coordinates of all of the identified features on one object is compared with the set of polar coordinates on the other. Instead of looking for a perfect or least-squares match between the sets of polar coordinates, the program computed a set of differences with a minimum average score. In this manner we are able to maintain orientation and size invariance. The transformation to polar coordinates has already provided the objects being examined with position invariance.

Once the two sets of features from the two objects are appropriately matched for position, the individual features are then compared. Again, the criterion for a best match is that the distribution of differences over all features has a minimum standard deviation. Visual similarity between two objects is then defined as the degree to which the two feature sets meet these criteria. That is, the corresponding features must be similar to each other, and each object's features must be similarly arranged. This balance between featural similarity and compositional similarity plays a very important role in increasing the tolerance of the comparison to possible distortions of one of the objects.

Distorting an object's features will alter its visual appearance, as will rearranging them. But, these two kinds of distortion have different effects. If an object's features are rearranged, it may still be possible to recognize the object by its individual features. By the same token, if the object's features are distorted, it may still be possible to recognize the object by the arrangement of those features.

By taking into account this balance between the global integrity of an object and the integrity of its local features, we have made it possible for the simulated SWIMMER to cope better with degradations of the images, such as occlusion, noise, and distortions. Now it is possible to identify objects as being "similar," even when they may not be exactly alike.

One major problem arises when using this type of comparison process in the recognition algorithm. Before features can be compared, they must first be segregated and identified. To identify an object's features, we must break it down according to some rules of geometrical syntax. However, there are no generally accepted criteria or rules for dividing an image into its constituent features other than in an ad hoc manner. For example, consider the way in which a simple figure such as a triangle can be constructed from a wide variety of different features (as well as from an even larger variety of formulae and algorithms). Triangles may be constructed from angles or line segments only, they may be drawn using solid lines, dotted lines, dashed lines, or any variety of smaller shapes, and they may even be formed subjectively from the features of other objects as shown in Figure 3.36.

In each case, the category of triangularity remains constant even though every exemplar triangle may be composed of a wide variety of different features. Indeed, many different triangles are easily recognized as such even though they have no features in common.[8] Therefore, how an object should be divided into its constituent features is arbitrary and often depends on what the object is. Such an

---

[8]From a purely theoretical point of view, this line of thought is a strong argument that the human recognition process operates more on the basis of image components' organization than on the nature of the components or features. There is a gross discrepancy between the holistic phenomenology of visual perception and contemporary feature-oriented recognition theory that has yet to be resolved.

arbitrariness introduces a paradoxical circularity into the rules for identifying and segregating an object's features. If the object's features are not properly identified and segregated, it cannot be identified by using a feature analysis, yet if the object is not already known its features cannot be properly identified and segregated.

One way to overcome this difficulty is to treat the object as a single unitary whole and not attempt to break it down into its constituent features. This worked for closed nonbifurcating shapes or shapes that had the bifurcations resolved and the overlapping forms separated. It is also possible to define a set of relational values that represents the objects in a way that is position, size, and orientation invariant by treating an object's contours as a single, though very large, trace or vector. In the same way as the form of a curve was represented earlier, an object's contours can be represented as a list containing the orientations and lengths of imaginary line segments connecting adjacent points in the object's image. Using such a list, the object can be reconstructed at any arbitrary size, position, and orientation in its original form or an idealized (i.e., interpolated) form simply by varying a few parameters. The generation of the interpolated representation of an object requires, in addition, that the first derivatives of the interpoint line segments be determined and placed in a list. This list describes the course of the contour of the object.

Once two objects are processed in this way, they can be directly compared even though of different position, orientation, and size. Invariances are maintained in the comparison by reconstructing both objects with the same position, size, and orientation values or by factoring out the differences in these values. Not only are the objects compared without analyzing them into their constituent features, it is also often possible to fill in missing features in each object. As with a feature comparison process, this process can be made tolerant with regard to image degradation and occlusion by limiting the lengths of the lists representing each object.

Although this sort of global shape analysis has some advantages over feature analysis, it also has some disadvantages. The principal disadvantage is that global analysis lacks the ability (as do humans) to identify an object whose features are rearranged. Another disadvantage is its inability to abstract specific details for describing the object. This becomes a serious constraint if the program is trying to describe an unfamiliar object, a task that is much easier to do in terms of its parts. Features often lend themselves to simplified generic descriptions, while more holistic descriptions of complex objects may not.

To extract as much useful information from an object as possible, it is important to consider both the constituent parts and the relationships of those parts. It is particularly useful to be able to associate some parts with a behavioral function. Because the simulated organism is supposedly aquatic and seeks food on the basis of visual form recognition processes, ideally it should be designed with the ability to recognize objects on either basis, that is, their overall form or their meaningful parts. For example, if the prey is a fish, the organism would be well served by the ability to recognize fins and eyes as well as the ability to recognize a complete fish. Under extremely poor viewing conditions, only a few parts of an object may be visible. Because both global and feature analyses provide unique and useful information, we have sought to strike a balance between the local features and holistic shape analyses in order to produce a better simulation of organic visual processes. Ideally, they should be integrated into a combined process.

Global and feature analyses may be integrated several interesting ways. A global analysis may serve to identify objects and guide the segregation of their features. A feature analysis can then provide a more detailed description of the object and confirm or disconfirm the results of the global analysis by identifying subtle differences between visually similar objects, thus allowing more detailed classifications. Information about function and behavior can also be stored along with the results of global and feature analyses. This is particularly useful for dealing with new and unfamiliar objects. An unfamiliar object, while not recognized using the global process, might have features or groups of features in common with other objects with related behavioral repertoires. Conceivably an aquatic organism could identify the behavioral properties of an unfamiliar fish by the shape of its fins, eyes, and mouth.

Details of the Recognition Algorithms

Let us now consider some of these functions in detail. As described earlier, the process of comparing two objects in terms of their respective feature sets is accomplished by first pairing features in one object with the best-matching features in the other. Corresponding features in the two sets are matched in such a way that the average deviation between all comparable features in the two sets is minimized. The principle that guided our work is that these data comparisons must be relational rather than absolute. Initially, each feature in one object is compared with all of the features in the other in a way that is position, size, and orientation invariant. To accomplish this invariant, relational comparison, we generated a data set of feature characteristics for each object being compared and transformed the characteristics to relative values. The length of each feature in each object is first divided by the lengths of every other feature in the object's feature set. The transformed result is another, larger data set that represents the length of each feature in a relative, rather than absolute, manner.

Next, the orientation of each feature in an object is compared with the orientation of every other feature in the object. This is done by computing the difference in orientation between each feature and every other feature arbitrarily limiting orientation values to a range of $-90°$ to $+90°$. These values, also a large data set, represent the orientation of each feature relative to all of the other features in the object.

The last set of relative values needed to perform the feature comparison expresses the position of each feature as a function of the positions of the other features in the object. This is accomplished by calculating the distance and direction between the center of gravity of each feature and the center of gravity of every other feature. The transformed or invariant distance values are then computed by dividing these Euclidean distances by the average distance between the compared features to normalize it for size. The resulting data constitute a redundant set of relative position-, orientation-, and size-invariant values that describe the relationships between features making up an object rather than simply listing their absolute values. Redundancy in these data makes the comparison process less sensitive to subtle changes in the form and arrangement of the object's features and, therefore, tolerant of image degradations and even, to a certain degree, occluded objects.

Once the three invariant, relational data sets for position, orientation, and size are computed for each object, it can be compared with any other. To compare two objects with different size data sets, each data item in the smaller of the two sets is compared (differenced) with each item in the larger set; the average deviation between each item in the smaller set and all of the data items in the larger set is calculated. The data items in the smaller set are then sorted from largest to smallest in terms of these average deviation values. Next, in order from largest to smallest average deviation, each item in the smaller set is compared with all of the items in the larger set until the best match is found. These two items are then paired for the final comparison, and the process is continued until each data item in the smaller set is uniquely paired with a data item in the larger set. When the sets are equal in size, either one may be treated as the smaller set. This process is relatively fast, requires little computation, and is very effective at identifying the optimal pairing of data items that minimizes the average deviation between the two sets.

Once the data sets are paired in this way, each data item in the smaller set is compared with its corresponding data item in the larger set. The deviations between the data items are averaged to give an estimate of the overall fit between the two sets. This estimate represents the degree to which one shape matches another, independent of size, position, and orientation.

Let us now describe more formally the comparison procedure we used. The features making up two data sets are compared in terms of their invariant representations. Let

$$[L_{r_1}, \theta_{r_1}, (r_{p_1}, \theta_{p_1}), (r_1, \theta_1)] \qquad (3.33)$$

and

$$[L_{r_2}, \theta_{r_2}, (r_{p_2}, \theta_{p_2}), (r_2, \theta_2)] \qquad (3.34)$$

be the invariant representations of two features. The total disparity, $D_{1,2}$, between the two features is

$$D_{1,2} = \sum_{i=0}^{n} \min_{j=1,\ldots,m} \left[a[L_{r_{1,i}} - L_{r_{2,j}}] + b[\theta_{r_{1,i}} - \theta_{r_{2,j}}] \right.$$
$$\left. + c[r_{p_{1,i}} - r_{p_{2,j}}] + d[\theta_{p_{1,i}} - \theta_{p_{2,j}}] \right] \qquad (3.35)$$
$$+ e\left[\sum_{k=0}^{n} [r_{1,k}^2 + r_{2,k}^2 - 2r_{1,k}\,r_{2,k}\,\cos(\theta_{1,k} - \theta_{2,k})]^{0.5} \right],$$

such that each value of i, j, and k occurs only once, $n \le m$, and a, b, c, d, and e are weighting constants expressing the relative importance of each component in the total sum. For the continuous case the last term of Equation 3.35 becomes

$$e\left[\int_0^{L_{a_1}} F_1(t) - F_2\left(\frac{tL_{a_2}}{L_{a_1}} \right) dt \right], \qquad (3.36)$$

where L_{a_1} and L_{a_2} are the arc lengths of the two features L_{a_1} and L_{a_2}.

The value of $D_{1,2}$ is the minimum disparity for the two features. To achieve this minimization, values in the data sets representing the two features must be optimally paired. This is done by competition between features or by pairing in order of greatest to least average deviation. The method of average deviation was used first because it was faster. Competition for pairing was used in later versions because it was more accurate, even though slower because more comparisons had to be made. This competition ensures that the components of the two representations are optimally paired.

In the event that the data sets

$$[(r_{1,0}, \theta_{1,0}), \ldots, (r_{1,L_1}, \theta_{1,L_1})] \qquad (3.37)$$

and

$$[(r_{2,0}, \theta_{2,0}), \ldots, (r_{2,L_2}, \theta_{2,L_2})] \qquad (3.38)$$

representing the encoded shapes of the features contain different numbers of elements, a hashing function is applied to the sets. The results of the hashing function are the new sets

$$[(r_{1,0}, \theta_{1,0}), \ldots, (r_{1,L'}, \theta_{1,L'})] \qquad (3.39)$$

and

$$[(r_{2,0}, \theta_{2,0}), \ldots, (r_{2,L'}, \theta_{2,L'})] \qquad (3.40)$$

having equal numbers of elements. For continuous features, this hashing function is unnecessary. A general discussion of disparity calculation is provided by Barnard and Thompson (1980).

Special consideration must also be made to handle closed contours. For example, in a circle, there is no clear definition of where the feature begins and where it ends. To handle this problem, multiple feature matches are performed, where each point in the closed contour is used as the starting point. It is therefore possible to handle both properly closed contours and contours that are broken because of errors in processing. For example, if two images each contain a circle and the circle is closed in only one of the images, both circles may be identified as the same feature if this iterative approach is used.

This same procedure can be applied if the object is represented as a single continuous contour rather than a set of individual features. The method of representation used for an entire contour is the same as the method used to describe the shapes of individual curves in the feature-based analysis described earlier. In this case, however, the lengths and orientations of the whole set of line segments approximating the contour are stored as one large vector as opposed to the smaller vectors that make up, for example, the individual sides or features of a triangle. The resulting data set is therefore inherently position invariant, but still varies with size and orientation.

To obtain size invariance, we compress or expand the single continuous vector by computing the percentage of the contour's total arc length accounted for by each element of the data set, thus converting segment length into relative scores. Orientation invariance is achieved by computing the average deviation between the corresponding values in the two arrays representing the two shapes being compared. Any rotation of one shape produces the same change in all of the orientation values in its respective array. When two shapes are the same or highly similar, this average orientation deviation reflects the total orientation difference between the two shapes. Once this value is determined, it can simply be added to all of the orientation values in either array to maintain orientation invariance for the final comparison.

The two vectors are then compared again by using the adjusted values. The newly calculated average orientation deviation value now reflects the degree to which the two original contours differ in form independent of their respective sizes, positions, and orientations, the former two parameters having already been normalized. The same results can be obtained by computing the variance or standard deviation of orientation values in the unadjusted arrays; however, this would entail additional and superfluous computations.

Two forms are compared by pairing their best-matching features and summing the disparity values produced by the individual feature comparisons. If

$$[[L_{1r_1}, \ldots, L_{1r_n}],[\theta_{1r_1}, \ldots, \theta_{1r_n}],[(r_{1p_1},\theta_{1p_1}), \ldots,$$
$$(r_{1p_n}, \theta_{1p_n})],[(r_{1,1}, \theta_{1,1}), \ldots, (r_{1,n}, \theta_{1,n})]] \quad (3.41)$$

and

$$[[L_{2r_1}, \ldots, L_{2r_n}],[\theta_{2r_1}, \ldots, \theta_{2r_n}],[(r_{2p_1},\theta_{2p_1}), \ldots,$$
$$(r_{2p_n}, \theta_{2p_n})],[(r_{2,1}, \theta_{2,1}), \ldots, (r_{2,n}, \theta_{2,n})]] \quad (3.42)$$

are the invariant representations of two forms, the total disparity $D_{p_{1,2}}$ between these forms is computed as

$$D_{p_{1,2}} = \sum_{i=1}^{n} \min_{j=1,\ldots,m} (D_{i,j}),\qquad(3.43)$$

such that each value of i and j occurs only once and $n \leq m$.

The value of $D_{i,j}$ is the total disparity between the i-th feature of the first form and the j-th feature of the second. To calculate the value of $D_{p_{1,2}}$, we must optimally pair the features making up forms 1 and 2. Competition is again used to ensure that each feature in one form is paired with the best-matching feature in the other.

The number of features in one form may differ from the number of features in the other. To correct this problem, the form with the fewest features must be matched against the other, so that $n \leq m$, where n and m are the numbers of features in the two forms. This ensures that the total number of optimally paired features cannot exceed the number of features in either form.

Unpaired features are taken into account when making the comparison. This is done by calculating the percentage of unmatched features:

$$Pu = \frac{m - n}{m + n}.\qquad(3.44)$$

The values of $D_{p_{i,j}}$ and $P_{u_{i,j}}$ are then combined into a composite disparity value:

$$D_{comp} = \left[\frac{D_{p_{1,2}}}{P_{u_{1,2}}} \right],\qquad(3.45)$$

which takes into account both degree of fit and completeness.

In addition to identifying familiar objects and describing unfamiliar objects, our simulated organism must be able to add new objects into its memory—that is, to make the unfamiliar familiar. This involves storing either an exact representation of the object or a simplified description of it. The ideal representation for an object in the present context is the normalized (i.e., position, size, and orientation invariant) data set or vector just described. These vectors describe objects in a way that simplifies the recognition process, because only the incoming object needs to be transformed and normalized.

Whenever a new object is viewed by the SWIMMER simulation program, an automatic decision must be made by the algorithm as to whether the object is similar enough to one in memory to be familiar or if it is a new object. This decision is instantiated by imposing a threshold for the average deviation measure between an object being identified and its most similar object in memory. If the deviation score exceeds the threshold, the object is considered to be unfamiliar, and its vector is added to the list of familiar objects. If the deviation score is less than the threshold, the test object's vector is discarded, and it is considered to be an exemplar of a known object. If an object is determined to be the same as a familiar object, it is tagged with the name and any other attributes of the familiar object, thus fully implementing the recognition process. This information is also displayed in Figure 3.46.

In addition to adding the vectors representing the forms of unfamiliar objects to memory, the SWIMMER must store functional, behavioral, and contextual information relating to an object. In some ideal future model, this information should be obtained by observing a recognized object and determining how it behaves and interacts with other objects. In the present simulation, however, this information is provided by the programmer to the SWIMMER simulation directly. The form, function, behavior, and context of an object may all be correlated to different degrees. For this reason, any such background information should be stored along with a weighting value that reflects the degree to which it is correlated with the object's visual form.

This background information and its associated weighting values are used to make inferences about the function, behavior, and context of the object being identified. Each weighting value represents the probability that a piece of background information is directly applicable to the object. The average deviation measure between a newly encountered object and its best-matching counterpart in memory is used to adjust these probabilities for the new object. Any background information whose weighting value is greater than a threshold (some value of the average deviation measure) is then reported as a likely property of the object being identified. When the new object is unfamiliar, this information is added to the stored vector of the new object instead.

The weighting values of background information that are added to the memory for a new object are thus adjusted to reflect the similarity between the new object and its best-matching counterpart in memory. The more dissimilar the two objects are, the lower the weighting values for the new object's inferred background information will be. This adjustment is made by dividing each weighting value by unity plus the average deviation measure between the object being identified and the best-matching object in memory, from which the background information is inferred. Adjusting the weighting values in this manner produces a generalization gradient such that the more visually similar two objects are, the more functional, behavioral, and contextual properties the two objects are assumed to share. Ideally, this information would be verified in every case, but because of constraints on computation time, it was not possible to do so in the present simulation.

The current form recognition algorithms now operate on two-dimensional objects oriented anywhere in three-dimensional space, while maintaining many of the features of size, orientation, and translation invariance that characterized the two-dimensional version. In addition, the system is still relatively insensitive to occlusion and degradation. The modified system is able to identify certain classes of three-dimensional shapes from their two-dimensional projections on the frontoparallel viewing plane virtually independent of their three-dimensional orientations. Size- and position-invariant information is extracted from a two-dimensional projection, and the series of rotational transformations is applied to normalize the orientation information. Recognition is then accomplished by comparisons that are identical in concept to those for the two-dimensional case.

While this general approach may seem at first to be a brute-force solution to a subtle and complex problem, it shares a major advantage with human form recognition, namely, that because the recognition system does not operate on the basis of an exact match (as does a conventional template matching process) or even on an approximate match (as does a fuzzy template matching process) the number of rotational transformations required to achieve full orientation invariance is relatively small. In this case, only 20 rotational transformations per plane are required.

Debifurcation

A modified recognition program compares and identifies arbitrary binary spatial dot patterns. Earlier versions of the system are designed to work only with nonbifurcating closed contours or simple outlines of shapes. As a result of this improvement, the recognition subsystem can now identify objects that contain interior details, such as writing or texture patterns. It is also able to recognize stimuli with bifurcating contours that more closely resemble complex line drawings rather than just simple outlines.

The first step in the resolution of the bifurcation uncertainties requires that the edge image be broken down into a set of nonbifurcating contours. A nonbifurcating contour is one which does not branch or divide. A search process is used to find all points of bifurcation in the edge image. A point (x_j, y_j) is considered to be connected to another point (x_i, y_i) if

$$[(x_j - x_i)^2 + (y_j - y_i)^2]^{0.5} \le C \tag{3.46}$$

and no other point (x_k, y_k) exists such that

$$[(x_k - x_i)^2 + (y_k - y_i)^2]^{0.5} < [(x_j - x_i)^2 + (y_j - y_i)^2]^{0.5} \tag{3.47}$$

and

$$tan^{-1}\left[\frac{x_k - x_i}{y_k - y_i}\right] - tan^{-1}\left[\frac{x_j - x_i}{y_j - y_i}\right] \le \theta, \tag{3.48}$$

where C is a constant describing the average separation of adjacent points in the image and θ is a constant describing the maximum angle formed by three successive points in a straight line.

Any point in the edge image which is connected to more than two other points is regarded as a bifurcation point. Breaking the edge contours at each bifurcation point results in a set of nonbifurcating contours which are then traced from end point to end point.

After tracing, all contours which meet at a bifurcation point are tested for mathematical continuity at the end where they meet. This is done by computing the weighted sum of their first and higher derivatives near the bifurcation point. The results of these tests determine which contours may be joined to form larger contours. Let

$$[(x_i, y_i), \ldots, (x_j, y_j)] \tag{3.49}$$

and

$$[(x_k, y_k), \ldots, (x_l, y_l)] \tag{3.50}$$

be discrete samples of points from the ends of two such contours which meet at a bifurcation point.

These points may be represented in parametric form as $G_1(t)$ and $G_2(t)$. Let $G_1(0) = G_2(n) = (x_b, y_b)$, where (x_b, y_b) is the bifurcation point at which the two contours meet. Next, let

$$D(i, j) = \frac{1}{n + 1} \sum_{t=0}^{n} \left[\sum_{d=1}^{n} a_d [|G_i^{(d)}(t) - G_j^{(d)}(t)|] \right], \tag{3.51}$$

where $G_i(0) = G_j(n)$. Then contours 1 and 2 are joined at (x_b, y_b) if and only if

$$D(1,2) \le M_{con}, \tag{3.52}$$

$$D(1,2) < D(1,m), \tag{3.53}$$

$$D(1,2) < D(m,2) \tag{3.54}$$

for all m such that $G_m(n) = G_1(0)$, or $G_m(0) = G_2(n)$. Here, $G^{(d)}(t)$ is the d-th derivative of $G(t)$, a_d describes the relative weight of the d-th derivative in the total sum, and M_{con} is the maximum value of this sum for which the two contours may be joined. REA (1978) and Zwillinger (1989) provide additional background information.

Derivatives described here are approximated for discrete data by calculating differences on x and y between adjacent points and their subsequent derivatives. While it is possible to fit polynomials to the sampled points, taking the derivatives of such polynomials tends to produce unstable and unreliable results. When the weighted sum of derivatives calculated in this manner meets the criteria stated above, the two contours are joined at the point of bifurcation. The result is a new nonbifurcating contour which is more complete and meaningful than its individual parts. All such nonbifurcating contours extracted from the edge image serve as features in later analyses.

As before, the system maintains position, size, and orientation invariance, is still relatively insensitive to degradation of the stimulus by occlusion, but is more sensitive to changes in form than previous versions.

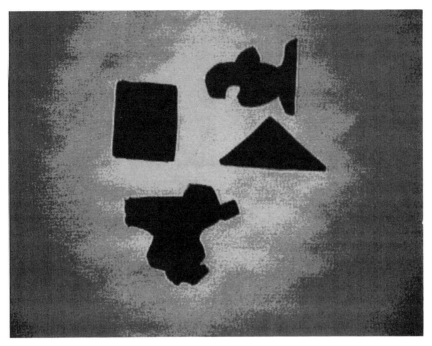

FIG. 3.48.   An array of nonoverlapping shapes shown in a sample input image.

Experimental Results

Two kinds of experiments were carried out. The first dealt with nonoverlapping objects, the second with overlapping objects with bifurcating contours. Let us now consider the nonoverlapping objects. An array of incoming shapes segmented from a scene is shown in Figure 3.48, and a sample output of the recognition process is shown in Figure 3.49. Figure 3.49 demonstrates the shift-, rotation-, and scale-invariant recognition of a single shape segmented from the image. In all, the memory set for this experiment consisted of 41 different shapes. Each shape in Figure 3.48 was compared with the memory set 10 times under random shifts of ± 100 pixels, random rotations of $\pm \pi$ radians, random scalings of $2^{\pm 1}$ times, and no distortion. Under these conditions, recognition accuracy was 100% for all seven shapes.

Another test was then performed with the same shifts, rotations, and scalings as before plus 50% random distortions. These distortions were performed by randomly modifying all values (r, θ) in the invariant representations of the features by $\pm 50\%$ of their original values. For this test case, accuracy was 88.57% on average, with four shapes achieving 100% accuracy. With 100% distortion, overall accuracy dropped to 64.29%, with three shapes producing peak accuracies of 80%. These results demonstrate the distortion tolerance of the feature

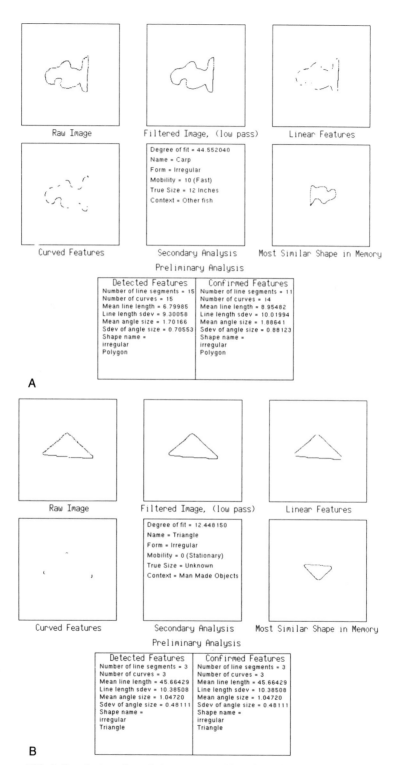

A

Raw Image   Filtered Image, (low pass)   Linear Features

Curved Features   Secondary Analysis   Most Similar Shape in Memory

Degree of fit = 44.552040
Name = Carp
Form = Irregular
Mobility = 10 (Fast)
True Size = 12 Inches
Context = Other fish

Preliminary Analysis

Detected Features	Confirmed Features
Number of line segments = 15	Number of line segments = 11
Number of curves = 15	Number of curves = 14
Mean line length = 6.79985	Mean line length = 8.95482
Line length sdev = 9.30058	Line length sdev = 10.01994
Mean angle size = 1.70166	Mean angle size = 1.88641
Sdev of angle size = 0.70553	Sdev of angle size = 0.88123
Shape name = irregular Polygon	Shape name = irregular Polygon

B

Raw Image   Filtered Image, (low pass)   Linear Features

Curved Features   Secondary Analysis   Most Similar Shape in Memory

Degree of fit = 12.448150
Name = Triangle
Form = Irregular
Mobility = 0 (Stationary)
True Size = Unknown
Context = Man Made Objects

Preliminary Analysis

Detected Features	Confirmed Features
Number of line segments = 3	Number of line segments = 3
Number of curves = 3	Number of curves = 3
Mean line length = 45.66429	Mean line length = 45.66429
Line length sdev = 10.38508	Line length sdev = 10.38508
Mean angle size = 1.04720	Mean angle size = 1.04720
Sdev of angle size = 0.48111	Sdev of angle size = 0.48111
Shape name = irregular Triangle	Shape name = irregular Triangle

FIG. 3.49. Analyses for each shape segmented from the original image in Figure 3.48. See Figure 3.46 caption for details.

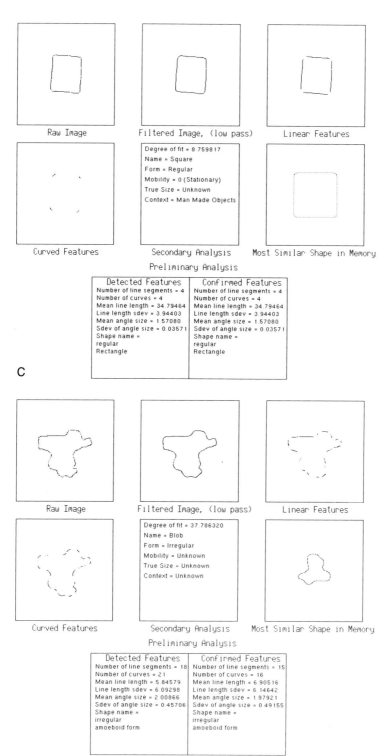

Raw Image

Filtered Image, (low pass)

Linear Features

Curved Features

Degree of fit = 8.759817
Name = Square
Form = Regular
Mobility = 0 (Stationary)
True Size = Unknown
Context = Man Made Objects

Most Similar Shape in Memory

Secondary Analysis

Preliminary Analysis

Detected Features	Confirmed Features
Number of line segments = 4	Number of line segments = 4
Number of curves = 4	Number of curves = 4
Mean line length = 34.79464	Mean line length = 34.79464
Line length sdev = 3.94403	Line length sdev = 3.94403
Mean angle size = 1.57080	Mean angle size = 1.57080
Sdev of angle size = 0.03571	Sdev of angle size = 0.03571
Shape name =	Shape name =
regular	regular
Rectangle	Rectangle

C

Raw Image

Filtered Image, (low pass)

Linear Features

Curved Features

Degree of fit = 37.786320
Name = Blob
Form = Irregular
Mobility = Unknown
True Size = Unknown
Context = Unknown

Most Similar Shape in Memory

Secondary Analysis

Preliminary Analysis

Detected Features	Confirmed Features
Number of line segments = 18	Number of line segments = 15
Number of curves = 21	Number of curves = 16
Mean line length = 5.84579	Mean line length = 6.90516
Line length sdev = 6.09298	Line length sdev = 6.14642
Mean angle size = 2.00866	Mean angle size = 1.97921
Sdev of angle size = 0.45706	Sdev of angle size = 0.49155
Shape name =	Shape name =
irregular	irregular
amoeboid form	amoeboid form

D

FIG. 3.50.   Complex form with hand-drawn overlapping and bifurcating lines.

comparison process. Feature smoothing prior to encoding and recognition greatly increases the accuracy of such comparisons under random distortion or noise.

The recognition process was also applied to complex forms. For this test, the incoming images were hand-drawn contours and shapes which were digitized but processed at the full resolution of 512 × 512. These contours and shapes were allowed to intersect and overlap. In this case, each form contained several features, all of which were used in the recognition process. Thus, the debifurcation and feature extraction processes were applied and the entire form was recognized as a whole. Individual features extracted by using this process may also be recognized independently. This allows overlapping forms to be recognized separately when necessary. Figure 3.50 shows an example of a complex form made up of hand-drawn shapes and contours. Figure 3.51 shows the components into which it was separated. Figure 3.52 shows the match, and Figure 3.53 shows the set of forms in memory with which it was compared.

In this experiment, 15 forms stored in memory were recognized 10 times each under the same random shifts, scalings, and rotations as in the previous experiment. For the first test, the forms were undistorted. Under these conditions recognition accuracy was 100% for all 15 forms. For the second test, 50% random distortions were introduced as before. Recognition accuracy in this case was 94.67%, with 11 of the forms achieving accuracies of 100%.

A third test with 100% random distortions produced a recognition accuracy of

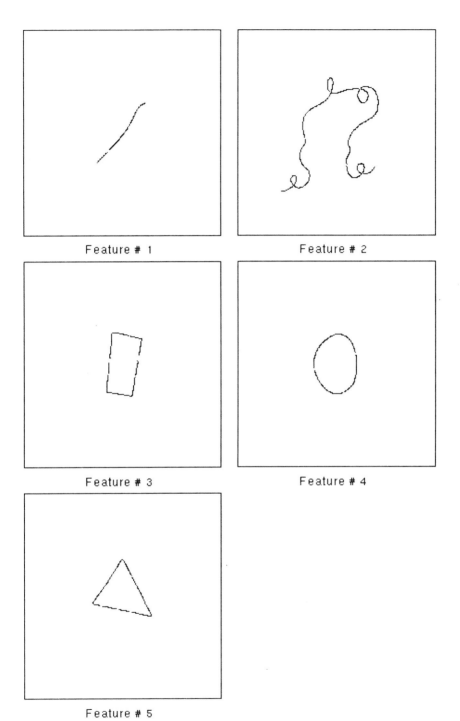

Feature # 1

Feature # 2

Feature # 3

Feature # 4

Feature # 5

FIG. 3.51. The components into which Figure 3.50 is analyzed by the recognition algorithm.

Incoming Pattern   Best Match

FIG. 3.52.   The recognition process for the complex form, showing the best-matching object from among those stored in the computer's memory and shown in Figure 3.53. Note the invariance of the process as exhibited by the size, orientation, and translation differences between the input image and the matched object. Matches can also be carried out on the components of the complex object.

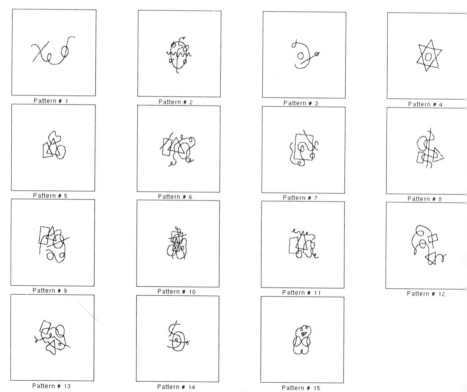

Pattern # 1   Pattern # 2   Pattern # 3   Pattern # 4
Pattern # 5   Pattern # 6   Pattern # 7   Pattern # 8
Pattern # 9   Pattern # 10   Pattern # 11   Pattern # 12
Pattern # 13   Pattern # 14   Pattern # 15

FIG. 3.53.   The set of objects stored in the computer's memory from which the discrimination shown in Figure 3.52 was made.

144

74%, with four forms achieving 100% accuracy and three more achieving 80% accuracy. These tests were performed after debifurcation and feature extraction to improve processing time and compensate for extraneous variables affecting the feature extraction process.

Separate tests were also performed on the debifurcation and feature extraction processes. Results of these tests indicated conditions under which these processes fail. Bifurcation points were generally detected correctly; however, in addition to the correct detections, some false alarms also occurred, generally where a series of points in a contour were very closely grouped and staggered. This was due primarily to errors in the thinning process which resulted in staircasing of diagonal lines.

Under these conditions the angular constraint θ of Equation 3.48 was violated by the staggered points forming the diagonals. Setting the value of θ at $\pi/2$ generally corrected the problem in these cases, but it also decreased the number of correct detections. This problem was subsequently eliminated by improving the thinning algorithm. As a result, a value of $\pi/4$ for θ in Equation 3.48 produced correct detection rates near 100% and under most conditions completely eliminated false alarms.

In general, such errors do not greatly affect the output of subsequent processing stages, because the recombination of subcontours in the next stage of processing compensates for false alarms in the detection process by rejoining improperly divided contours. False alarms did affect subsequent stages of processing by producing large gaps in contours where a string of false alarms occurred.

Through additional program modifications, recognition can even be achieved for a uniform random sampling of points from a surface. Simple orientation invariance was implemented with this new matching algorithm as well, but the complexity of the problem made it computationally demanding; about 20 min were needed to identify a complex shape from among only 10 possible matches. The process of matching random dot patterns requires that the algorithm find the best match in one shape for every point in the comparison in a manner comparable to the solution of the correspondence problem in stereopsis. This was done after normalizing the two dot distributions for size, translation, and orientation as described earlier. Once so normalized, rather than comparing fuzzy boundaries or contours, the best pairwise matching of all of the points in the two shapes is made. The Euclidean distances between each pair of points are then summed to provide a measure of the total shape disparity between the two sampled forms. When the two randomly dotted forms being compared are identical, then the calculated form disparity is zero. When the two spatial distributions of dots differ, then the summed form disparity indicates the degree to which the two distributions are dissimilar or how much they have to be transformed to become identical. This then serves as a good quantitative measure of visual similarity for this kind of stimulus—a distribution of dots.

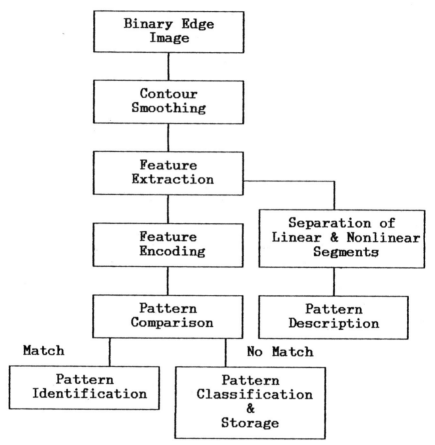

FIG. 3.54.   A flowchart of the recognition process.

These algorithms were generalized from binary dot patterns and the two-dimensional projection of three-dimensional objects to the solid objects themselves. The modified algorithm remains completely invariant to size and position and relatively insensitive to degradation.

Because the transforms required to maintain rotational invariance of solids must now be applied on each of the three dimensions, the computational load is substantially increased (by a factor of 20^2), making it very difficult to actually carry out the salient experiments on our Apollo system. A few preliminary tests, however, show that it is possible to recognize complete, arbitrary three-dimensional forms with full position, size, and orientation invariance in a way that is still relatively insensitive to degradation and minor occlusions. Our procedures work for solids defined by continuous surfaces and random assemblages of points scattered about in three-dimensional space.

Further training of and experimentation with the algorithms in the object recognition system demonstrates their ability to generalize to similar, but not identical, stimuli. We now know the system can handle distortions of an object, such as those that occur underwater, in a way that allows successful recognition.

It should be evident from the examples given here that an accurate model of visual recognition must involve much more than a simple feature-based image comparison. Ideally, it must be driven and guided in terms of what has meaning for the organism as well as by similarities in function and context. It is in these directions that the development of our recognition algorithms will proceed in the future.

The present version is flowcharted in Figure 3.54 to sum up the discussion in this section.

4 Response Processes

4.1. THE WORLD VIEW

Because a real-world environment to test the image processing and decision-making aspects of our model was not available, we had to simulate the SWIM-MER's localization, planning, and navigation actions in an artificial world. This chapter describes the procedures and algorithms used to imitate a three-dimensional, dynamic reality and to model how the SWIMMER responds to the information being passed from the visual information processing algorithms described in Chapter 3.

It must be noted at the outset of this discussion, that the work described so far (with the exception of some of the more recent and advanced image reconstruction and recognition algorithms) concentrated mainly on two-dimensional surfaces that are themselves oriented frontoparallel to the line of sight of the SWIM-MER. To make the simulation of the response processes interesting and meaningful, we simply assigned each of the successfully segmented two-dimensional objects to a random position in the simulated three-dimensional world space and allowed the SWIMMER to go about its navigation and response duties as if they were genuinely located in a real three-dimensional world.

The task assigned to the SWIMMER was to search for the planar objects that were segmented, recognized, and randomly positioned in its environment and then to approach each object in order of propinquity to its current location. At a given distance from each object, the SWIMMER had to decide if the detected object was food (i.e., a regular object) or nonfood (i.e., an irregular object). If food, the SWIMMER was instructed to pass through the center of the object; if nonfood, it was instructed to swim around and avoid the object. The main

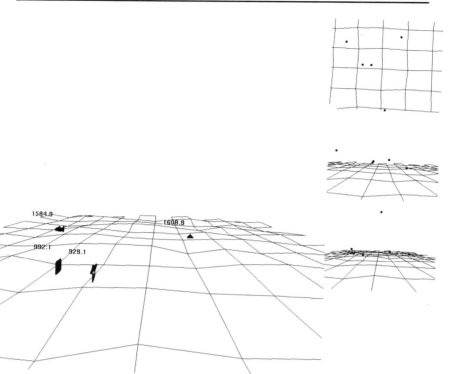

FIG. 4.1.   A sample of the display presented during the navigation phase of the model. The large picture is the SWIMMER's-eye view of the scene, while the other three pictures present the "God's-eye" view from the top and side views and the view of another observer looking over the shoulder of the SWIMMER, respectively.

visualization of the environment is presented as through the eyes of the SWIM-MER, an egocentric display. In addition, smaller "God's eye" or external observer views from the top and side were also displayed. Occasionally, we also added an over-the-shoulder (of the SWIMMER) view. Figure 4.1 is a sample of one stage of the view presented on the Apollo workstation screen.[1]

As the simulation begins, the set of objects acquired from the video camera and segmented, recognized, and randomly placed in the scene are displayed from the viewpoint of the SWIMMER as if at a great distance. Successive images following the initial scene are seen at discrete time intervals to give an impression of the motion of the SWIMMER. The current field of view of the SWIM-MER is stored in what we call a *local composite scene* file. As the SWIMMER

---

[1]As noted, we also had the option of displaying the scene on a Tektronix truly stereoscopic, three-dimensional display as well as the projective drawings on the Apollo two-dimensional display. All of the figures in this book are from the Apollo display.

moves past objects or as objects leave the field of view, they are placed into a more comprehensive *global composite scene* that represents the entire space in which the simulation is occurring. The global composite scene also includes the segmentation and recognition information that has been transmitted to the scene from preceding stages of processing.

The graphics space simulating the SWIMMER's world is defined as follows: The z axis[2] represents the depth of the water where the surface is at zero and the ocean floor is below at simulated depths that can range down to $-65,535$ (i.e., $[-(2^{16} - 1)]$) units. We arbitrarily chose 1 unit to represent 1 m of distance. Currently, the floor of the simulated environment is located at a depth of 300 m. The volume of the environment was arbitrarily limited among the four vertical planes defined by

$$x_{min} = -65,535, \tag{4.1}$$

$$y_{min} = -65,535, \tag{4.2}$$

$$x_{max} = 65,535, \tag{4.3}$$

$$y_{max} = 65,535, \tag{4.4}$$

and the surface and ocean floor as just defined. The SWIMMER can operate anywhere within this volume.

At the beginning of each test, the SWIMMER is aimed along the positive x axis and positioned on the surface. This position defines the origin of the coordinates of the system [i.e., world location $= (0, 0, 0)$]. The displayed objects, which have been segmented and recognized from the original captured image, are planar surfaces oriented parallel to the yz plane perpendicularly to the SWIMMER's initial line of sight. As the SWIMMER moves and changes its orientation, the appropriate perspective corrections are made in the depictions of the objects and the scene, but the objects remain in the same orientation to the scene.

The floor of the simulated world is represented by a relatively coarse grid of lines drawn at intervals of 200 m and is programmed to appear with some irregularities in depth to add to the realism of the visualized scene.

The action of the SWIMMER is displayed as a sequence of the kind of views in Figures 4.2 through 4.12. Because of the large amount of computing involved in simulating the SWIMMER's scene interpretations and actions and the relatively low operating speeds of our current computer system, this series of views does not appear rapidly enough to produce a sense of movement on the part of the

---

[2]Although the coordinate system we use is arbitrary, we have followed the convention usually used in computer graphics. The depth of the water in our simulated world is measured along the z axis (i.e., up [+] and down [−]); the x axis stretches in front of what is the initial orientation of the SWIMMER (i.e., ahead [+] and behind [−]); and the y axis is perpendicular to and in the plane of the x axis (i.e., stretching off to the left [+] and right [−]). Once established by the initial orientation of the SWIMMER, the origin and axes remain constant regardless of the SWIMMER's subsequent motions.

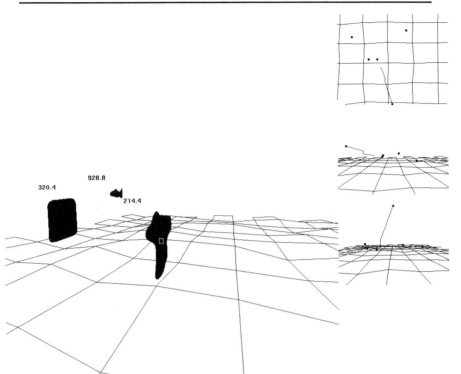

FIG. 4.2.–4.12   The continuation of the action of the navigation phase of the model as the action progresses. The SWIMMER, in turn, approaches the object, avoids two irregular objects, and swims through two regular objects following the simple rules described in the text.

observer; only a sequence of still images appear at intervals of several seconds. However, by storing each of the computed scene images in a separate file and then dumping them sequentially as rapidly as possible onto the screen of the cathode ray tube (CRT) display, a sense of motion is created.

As the SWIMMER moves, the display changes in appropriate ways. At great distances, objects appear simply as red dots along with an associated numerical distance reading. As the SWIMMER approaches an object, it is displayed with all of the available details of its shape and the appropriate projective distortions due to its orientation (fixed with regard to the scene) with respect to the SWIM-MER (whose orientation with regard to the scene varies).

Currently, the simulation system computes the behavior of the vehicle by assuming an ideal hydrodynamic response. If the SWIMMER rotates to a new heading and orientation, the model carries out this action precisely without accounting for any lag, drag, or overshoot. The model assumes that the movement from one point to another and one orientation to another can be decom-

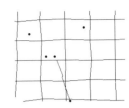

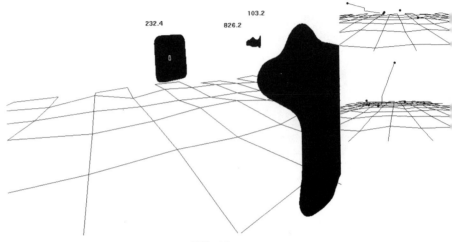

232.4   826.2   103.2

FIG. 4.3

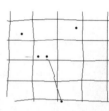

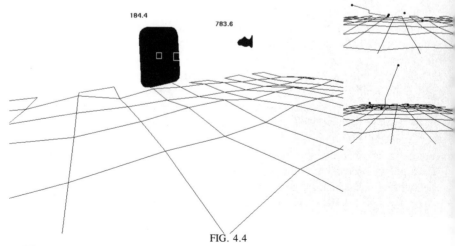

184.4   783.6

FIG. 4.4

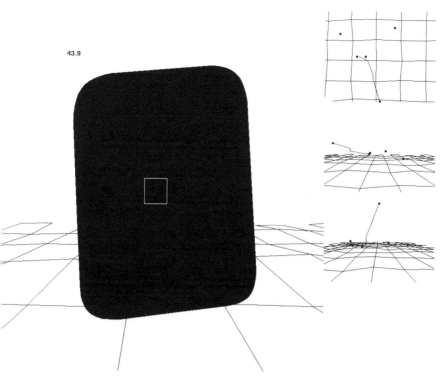

FIG. 4.5

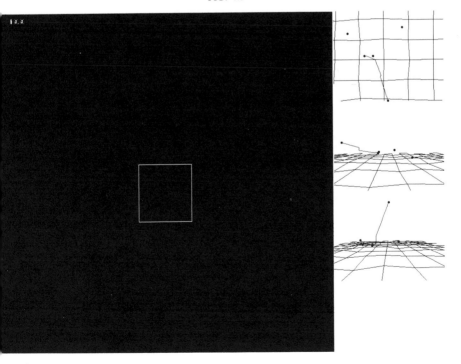

FIG. 4.6

153

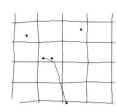

626.1

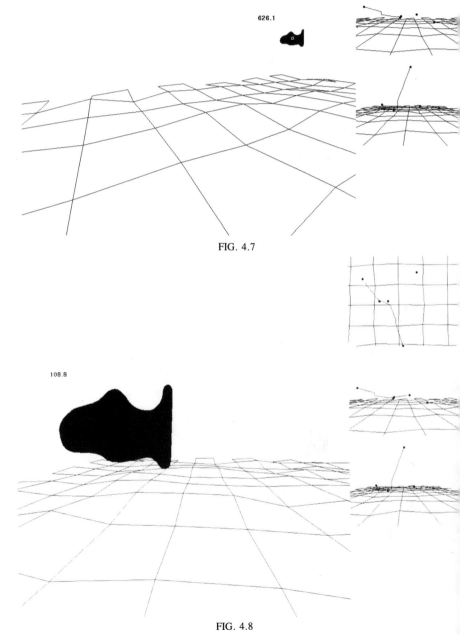

FIG. 4.7

108.8

FIG. 4.8

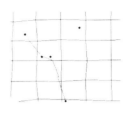

108.8

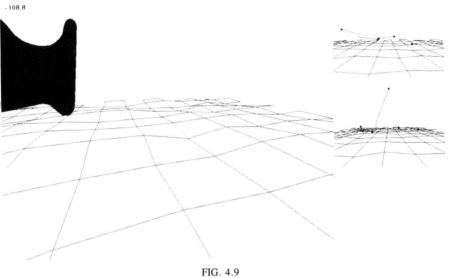

FIG. 4.9

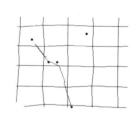

1025.4

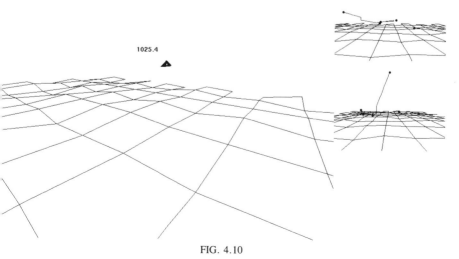

FIG. 4.10

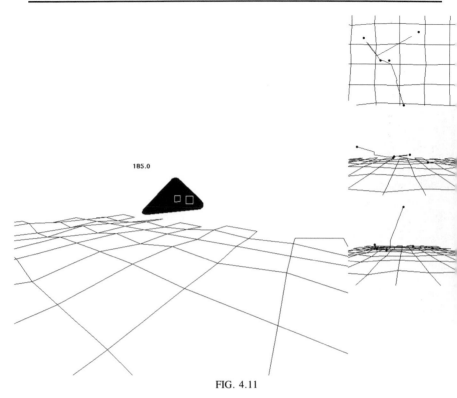

FIG. 4.11

posed into a rotation and a translation. In the future, to make the simulation more realistic, we plan to introduce the complete Newtonian hydrodynamics of the SWIMMER in an underwater environment.

We define the local composite scene as the data base of all of the objects and environmental features in the simulated undersea world that are in the field of view of the SWIMMER. These objects influence path planning for the next sequential display. The global composite scene, on the other hand, is the complete world map and includes all objects and environmental features whether or not they are in the field of view of the SWIMMER. The global composite scene is constantly updated from information fed to it from the local composite scene, but it may also contain objects that are currently unseen. The properties of each object in the global composite scene are stored in a computer file that consists of a record of its last known location as well as its geometrical properties. When we extend the scene to include moving objects, the global composite scene will also include information concerning a moving object's velocity and present course and even make extrapolations to where it may be at some future time.

A major challenge for this type of model is the matching of objects in the composite local scene with those in the composite global scene. The problem arises because of discrepancies in the shape or position of the representation of

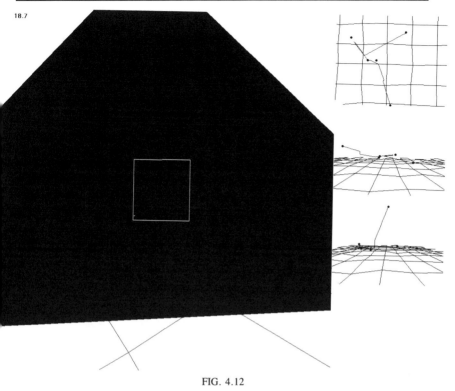

FIG. 4.12

objects in the two scenes. The difficulty is minimal for stationary objects; similar location and shape enable the match to easily be made. But as we extend our model to incorporate moving objects, the matching process becomes much more difficult. Matches made on shape alone benefit from the assistance of our form recognition algorithms, because the object may have changed orientation and position relative to the SWIMMER. Course extrapolation for moving objects in which the position and velocity of the object must be used to estimate a new position will always be problematic because of the possibility of unseen course corrections.

4.2.   PATH PLANNING AND NAVIGATION

Once objects in the SWIMMER's simulated world are recognized and located, decisions can be made concerning the movements required of the SWIMMER to approach them. Decisions like these in an underwater environment are less constrained than in an overland situation and, in a certain sense, are easier to implement than, for example, those required for an autonomous road-following vehicle. This is so even though the transition from two to three dimensions would, at first glance, seem to complicate the matter. But because underwater navigation can occur by going over or under an obstacle as well as around it and because our SWIMMER need not follow a constrained two-dimensional road, navigation often becomes straightforward in this kind of three-dimensional environment.

In our simulation of the behavior of the SWIMMER, many practical problems are associated with the visualization of the scene. The general task assigned to the SWIMMER is to approach and swim through food (i.e., regular) objects and to approach but swim around nonfood (i.e., irregular) objects. For the scene to be increasingly realistic, all objects and obstacles in the field of view must be *bloomed* or enlarged to fill an appropriately larger visual angle as they are approached. These features are also part of our simulation.

Another modeling problem to be resolved was how to define the location of an object that had spatial extent. We chose to use the center of gravity of each object as the point at which the object was considered to be located.

In a stable environment, planning the SWIMMER's path becomes one of connecting the current location of the SWIMMER and that of the nearest object. Planning occurs recursively for each time frame. The straight-line path connecting the SWIMMER's current location and the destination is computed and then recomputed at each step of the path. If obstacles lie along this path, their locations and extent are taken into account. Hypothetical lines are drawn from the SWIMMER's current location to the object. After arriving at each new destination and appropriately responding, a new straight-line path to the next nearest destination is computed. Complexities arise when a nonfood object or some other obstacle must be avoided. We cannot simply connect the centers of gravity of the series of food objects, however. The environment and the objects it contains are real to the SWIMMER, and it must constantly adapt to new navigational challenges such as large obstacles.

The situation is further complicated when there are disturbances or perturbations in the medium through which the SWIMMER is supposed to move. These disturbances may be constant (currents) or random impulsive events (surges) that alter the position, orientation, and course of the SWIMMER. The model includes forces that would lead to deviations from straight-line path planning to illustrate the necessary calculations and transforms required to adapt to such a dynamic environment. A formal presentation of the mathematics of path planning in this complex, hydrodynamic environment is presented in the Appendix.

Each path must also be considered in terms of its desirability and cost. A cost is associated with a path based on its length, danger, and computational load. Currently only the shortest path is chosen; in the future we plan to use other heuristics to determine the feasibility of a path based on the meaning of any object encountered. For example, if one of the objects encountered along a path is determined to be a shark, this portion of the path should be avoided.

Other algorithms will evaluate navigational costs. It would be desirable to estimate how many maneuvers must be executed and what type of navigation must be used to navigate around an object. The introduction of such factors as behavioral significance, adaptive responses, meaning, and navigational costs to the model add complexly—a cost—but also realistic richness—a benefit—to a model that would otherwise be little more than an exercise in a pure, but unrealistic, physics. While not all of these criteria are yet added to our model, we developed capabilities within the recognition algorithms in particular that go beyond simple geometrical analyses to characterize an object in terms of its meaning (see page 136).

Because the segmented and recognized objects are randomly located at the beginning of each run, each run is unique. Because the SWIMMER is guided mainly by spatial location of the objects, it is unpredictable what course it will actually follow. In addition to object location, the SWIMMER must obey a few simple rules:

1. Always approach the nearest object first.
2. The distance to any object is always defined by the three-dimensional Pythagorean distance.
3. Avoid irregular "nonfood" objects by detouring around them.
4. Swim directly through the center of any regular "food" object.
5. Always swim through a "food" object on a course that is perpendicular to its surface.

The result of the random placement of the objects and these simple rules is an astonishingly complex behavior pattern closely mimicking organic predatorial behavior.

Figures 4.2 through 4.12 present a sequence of the views of the SWIMMER as it executes one sample plan. As noted, these displays also include top and side views of the cumulative path to help the reader understand the path planned and taken by the SWIMMER. The small squares shown help one to visualize path planning. They show the current goal, where the SWIMMER must be at some future time. A mathematical treatment of the navigation and path planning aspects of our model is presented in the appendix.

5 System Processes

5.1. THE MENU-DRIVEN EXECUTIVE SYSTEM

The integrated model of a perceptual-motor system described here is designed with a high priority given to the ability to combine a library of individual process algorithms into a simulation of a smoothly functioning complex behavior. There are, in addition, several fundamental psychological assumptions guiding our work that directly impact the organization and nature of the computer programs we are producing. For example, we explicitly assume that perceptual processes can be partitioned into a series of sequential steps, some of which may have some intrinsic parallel organization. We also assume that global organization (rather than local features) should be the basis of the most realistic model of perception.

Another psychological principle that has influenced us is that perceptual processes, in general, are the outcome of the integration of multiple attributes of the stimulus and multiple serial and parallel channels of neural encoding and processing. These assumptions not only influence the design of specific algorithms but the nature of the executive system described in this chapter. In no place is this better illustrated than in the design of the Macro Processing Facility (MPF) discussed later.

The individual algorithms that simulate the steps of a perceptual and behavioral process must be able to interact smoothly and efficiently with preceding and succeeding program units. The design of the menu system was guided by this requirement and the MPF facilitates experimental tests of new computer simulations.

The primary input to the system is a visual (i.e., geometric) image. This image is processed and transformed into a sequence of representations, with each stage of processing operating on the information provided by the previous stage or, if a parallel operation, stages. Maintaining the smooth flow of information between stages is the essence of the automation process and the responsibility of the menu-based executive.

To briefly recapitulate, our simulation of the SWIMMER consists of four main stages:

1. Image segmentation
2. Object reconstruction
3. Form recognition
4. Navigation

Each stage is distinguished by the nature of the information on which the individual steps in the process operate. For example, the image processing operations operate primarily on image data in the form of a spatial array of pixels wherein numbers represent the raw value of the pixel at each image location. The recognition stage, which is concerned with providing qualitative and quantitative information about the nature of the objects in a scene, must operate on what are, in some instances, abstractions of the pixel-based information, sometimes counting features or comparing forms in a way that goes far beyond the properties of the raw image space. The navigation processes that characterize the third stage require information about the nature of the objects and their locations in space and thus represent an even higher level of abstraction than that required by the recognition stage. The navigator operates on the descriptions of the objects in the scene and their locations in a totally nonexistent domain—the SWIMMER's world.

These four stages of processing are ordered in a straightforward, if not necessarily unique, manner. The preliminary image processing, object segmentation, and reconstruction processes are performed before the recognition stage. The recognition stage uses the outputs of the segmentation stage and passes its outputs to the navigation stage.[1] The different modules in the computer model are invoked sequentially, ensuring that the previous processing stage generated the appropriate input for the next processing stage. Problems can arise when there is interaction between two successive processes, e.g., when the two processes have an interlaced mode of execution with, say, process A carried out in the breaks in the execution of process B or in the execution of what are intrinsically parallel processes. In such cases a reliable method of communication has to be established between the processes to maintain integrity of the model as a whole.

---

[1]In the future, the recognition algorithms will be embedded in the navigator so that will be executed in real time (i.e., as encountered in the path of the swimmer) rather than prior to the navigational stage.

Appropriate sequencing of an adequate communication between algorithms is also an important goal that helped define the nature of the menu-based operating system.

To handle the housekeeping tasks associated with a system of the nature, size, and complexity described in this book and to provide a convenient means for carrying out computer experiments, we developed a master program known as the Executive (or the Procedure Manager). The Executive serves as a supervisory process that executes all operations that can be performed by invoking them as a sequence of program calls. It also provides many useful utilities to the operator, including the communication algorithms linking individual algorithms, interfaces with various peripheral devices such as the ITI image-capturing subsystem, the monochrome and color printers, and the file storage and recovery protocols.

The Executive is also an interactive aid to the user running a version of the model on an experimental basis. It provides a graphical menu system that helps the user to select and execute program sequences in arbitrary configurations. Most significantly, the Executive controls the operation of the MPF.

The Executive provides a convenient means of access to and linkage of the algorithms available in the extensive library we created for the present simulation. Any library algorithm can be executed by simply typing in its program call code, a specific sequence of function keys. Progressively more detailed menus are called in sequence as the function keys are depressed. The Executive provides a convenient and easy means of stringing algorithms together by simply selecting items from the treelike menu to allow a simulation to be constructed.

Depending on their location in the menu hierarchy, one or more function keys (e.g., F1, F2, . . . , Fn) must be pressed to select an algorithm. After the Executive is invoked, the top-level menu (shown in Figure 5.1) is activated. For each menu level, as many as 14 function keys may be available (F1–F6 and shifted F1–F8). Each key can be assigned to represent any operation in the menu system. Unshifted F7 and F8, however, are committed to system functions and are not available to the user: F7 is the HELP code and accesses programs that provide help in using the SYSTEM executive; F8 is the RETURN/EXIT function that returns the screen to the previous menu level (for menus other than the top menu) and that exits the Executive when invoked from the top menu level.

Each user-defined key can call a processing algorithm, an ITI program (an image acquisition program), or another menu, or it can be assigned to some other capability at a later time. Within a menu level each defined function can be selected for immediate execution or *accented,* thus delaying its execution until the next keystroke. To accent a function key, move the cursor to the box marked for that function in the menu display, using either the mouse or the arrow keys. After the menu function is accented, it can be executed by pressing the space bar or the left button of the mouse.

Help is provided for all defined menu functions. Help for a given function can be accessed by accenting the function Fn and pressing H, h, or ? or the center or

Arizona Perceptual System – Top Menu:

F1 M	F2 M	F3 M	F4 M	F5 M	F7	F8
Image Process-ing	Navig-ation	Macros	System Utilities	Demos	Help me use MENU	EXIT APS PROGRAM

FLAGS

A   B   I

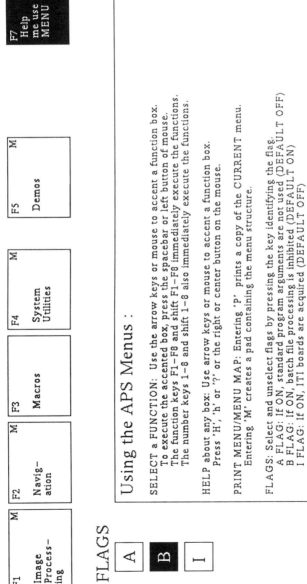

Using the APS Menus :

SELECT a FUNCTION: Use the arrow keys or mouse to accent a function box.
    To execute the accented box, press the spacebar or left button of mouse.
    The function keys F1–F8 and shift F1–F8 immediately execute the functions.
    The number keys 1–8 and shift 1–8 also immediately execute the functions.

HELP about any box: Use arrow keys or mouse to accent a function box.
    Press 'H', 'h' or '?' or the right or center button on the mouse.

PRINT MENU/MENU MAP: Entering 'P' prints a copy of the CURRENT menu.
    Entering 'M' creates a pad containing the menu structure.

FLAGS: Select and unselect flags by pressing the key identifying the flag.
    A FLAG: If ON, standard program arguments are not used (DEFAULT OFF)
    B FLAG: If ON, batch file processing is inhibited (DEFAULT ON)
    I FLAG: If ON, ITI boards are acquired (DEFAULT OFF)

FIG. 5.1. The top level of the menu-based Executive system.

163

right buttons on the mouse. Help always appears in the large lower box, where the initial HELP instructions were originally presented.

Special flags define various program standards and modes of operation. Each flag is identified by a single character in one of the small display boxes to the left of the HELP box. No flag is originally selected when the Executive is initially invoked. Each flag is selected or deselected by pressing the character that identifies it. The flags are defined as follows.

A Flag   When the A (Argument) flag is in the default (unaccented) mode, program calls are made with a standard set of arguments, as defined for each function in an associated menu text file. If the flag is activated (accented), arguments are entered interactively, after the program call and before program execution. The A flag value is ignored for those programs that do not pass arguments.

B Flag   If the B (Batch) flag is in the default (unaccented) mode, then standard input for program calls is redirected to the function's default batch file (if any). If the B flag is activated (accented), standard input is not redirected and remains the keyboard. If no batch file is available for a function, the B flag is ignored.

I Flag   If the I (ITI) flag is in the default (unaccented) mode, then the ITI image acquisition algorithms do not have control of the ITI boards. If the I flag is activated, then the ITI process has acquired the ITI image acquisitor boards. It is not necessary to manually acquire the ITI boards before attempting to run an ITI program, since the system will make the linkage to the boards when necessary. If an attempt to acquire the ITI boards is unsuccessful, an error message to this effect is printed in the HELP/ERROR box. Only one process in the network can have control of the ITI boards at any time.

As mentioned, there are four types of function calls for user-defined functions in each menu level display. They are executed as follows.

Menu   If a function key is designated to call a subsidiary level menu, then the menu level for the selected function is activated. Menu functions that call other menus are designated with an M in the upper right corner of the respective function box.

Program   If the function calls a program, the program call is executed, as defined in the menu text file and according to the flag settings.

ITI   If the function calls an ITI program, then the icon for the ITI process is turned into a window (one of the multiprogrammed operations being carried on in the Apollo system environment) and the program is executed in that window. Before running the program, the system attempts to acquire the ITI image acquisition boards if it does not already control them. If it cannot acquire the ITI boards, an error message is printed in the HELP/ERROR function box and the program is not executed. If the function call is undefined, an audible beep is sounded.

Undefined   If the function call is undefined, an audible beep sounds when the function is accessed.

Menu functions are defined by parameters and arguments stored in an associated menu text file. The function definition consists of the function name, the help text, the type of function call (MENU, PROGRAM, ITI, or NONE), and the program call with arguments, if any. If there is no menu text file assigned to a function key, a new program can be allotted to that function number by creating an appropriately formatted menu text file for it. The next time the Executive is invoked, the new function will be available for use.

Two additional utility operations are built into the menu-driven Executive system to aid the user. Pressing P or p prints a copy of the currently active menu. The file will take a couple of minutes to print, since it is a display screen plot (bitmap) file. However, executing a p command will not interfere with program execution, since the printing is executed in the background of the ongoing program.

Pressing M or m creates a window and a file with the current overall structure of the model, i.e., an updated version of the listing of all individual programs available in the menu system. This has been provided to aid users to find and locate specific programs in the hierarchy of the system and to help manage the inclusion and exclusion of programs. The required key-press sequences to activate an algorithm are listed in this printout of the menu's total structure. A sample of such a listing is shown in Figure 5.2.

Establishing a standardized format for the data upon which each process operates is also necessary. For example, most image files in the image processing phase consist of an array of pixel values with a matrix size of either 128×128 pixels or 320×320 pixels. As another example, the data produced by the recognition processes consist of a list of the attributes of objects such as size, degree of curvature, and orientation as well as the coordinates of the points defining an object's boundaries. Exceptions to the standard format of data in each stage involve processes that are located at points of transition between stages of processing. A program at the transition from the image processing stage to the recognition stage must have its input data in the pixel image format, but its output to the recognition stage must include, among other data, a tabular listing of all of the x, y, and z pixel location coordinates that make up the objects in the scene. Within the limits of a few exceptions such as this, all programs in the three stages have been implemented to adhere to standard input and output data formats.

5.2. THE MACRO PROCESSING FACILITY

To enable users of the system to easily carry out a predetermined sequence of processing steps on a captured image, we have incorporated a Macro Processing Facility into the menu-driven Executive system. The MPF allows the user to create and execute macros either interactively or as a totally automatic sequence of processes previously chosen from the menu.

PTD System Menu Structure Map :

F1   Image Processing

   F1.F1   Image Acquisition Functions

      F1.F1.F1   Image Acquisition
      F1.F1.F2   Freeze   Image

   F1.F2   Image Smoothing and Noise Reduction

      F1.F2.F1   *Image Averager
      F1.F2.F2   *Image Autocorrelator
      F1.F2.F3   Image Smoothing

   F1.F3   *Contrast Enhancement
   F1.F4   Object Detection From Spatial Form

      F1.F4.F1   Line Detection
      F1.F4.F2   Edge Detection

         F1.F4.F2.F1   Roberts Cross Edge Detector
         F1.F4.F2.F2   Sobel Edge Detector
         F1.F4.F2.F3   Vertical Line Detector
         F1.F4.F2.F4   Canny Edge Enhancement

      F1.F4.F3   Determine Threshold
      F1.F4.F4   Threshold
      F1.F4.F5   Region Extraction
      F1.F4.F6   Dilation/ Erosion
      F1.F4.SF1   Medial Axis Transform (skeleton)
      F1.F4.SF2   Remove "Twigs"
      F1.F4.SF3   Image Subtraction
      F1.F4.SF4   Detect Closed Regions
      F1.F4.SF5   Contour Closure
      F1.F4.SF6   RGB SEGMENTING

         F1.F4.SF6.F1   Shrink-RGB
         F1.F4.SF6.F2   Sobel edge   detector on R,G & B
         F1.F4.SF6.F3   Auto threshold   R,G & B
         F1.F4.SF6.F4   Merge   R, G & B
         F1.F4.SF6.F5   Extract   regions
         F1.F4.SF6.F6   Medial   axis transform
         F1.F4.SF6.SF1 Remove   twigs
         F1.F4.SF6.SF2 Extract   contour   co-ords
         F1.F4.SF6.SF3 Reorder   contour   co-ords

   F1.F5   Object Detection From Motion
   F1.F6   Image Sampling
   F1.SF1   Image Reconstruction

      F1.SF1.F1   Stereo Reconstruction

         F1.SF1.F1.F1   Image Filtering
         F1.SF1.F1.F2   Stereo Matching
         F1.SF1.F1.F3   *Surface Interpolation & Equation Fitting
         F1.SF1.F1.F4   Perspective Cross Section Display
         F1.SF1.F1.F5   *Create Random Dot Stereograms

      F1.SF1.F2   *Contouring
      F1.SF1.F3   *Side Scan Shadows
      F1.SF1.F4   *Spot Ranging

FIG. 5.2.   A sample listing of a few of the levels of the menu system showing the hierarchy of key presses (e.g., F1.SF1. F1.F2) necessary to call up a sequence of program modules. This is part of a four-page listing of the various programs that make up our computational model.

The concept behind the MPF system is quite similar to the automatic image processing system *apE* developed by The Ohio Supercomputer Center in Columbus, the *AVS* system marketed by the Stardent Computer Corporation, as well as others now emerging as commercial products. The idea behind all of these systems is to use a library of very high level computational modules and link them with simple text or graphic commands. The text command approach used in this project is obviously obsolete in light of the development of the more modern graphic programming and visualization systems. We plan to use one of the graphic options on the new generation of computers being introduced into our laboratory in the next stage of our work.

In the MPF system, macros are created and stored as standard text files. The content of a macro file is nothing more than a linear list of program invocations in the order in which the programmer desires to execute them. A period (.) is used to indicate the end of a processing sequence in a macro. A typical macro file has the form

Threshold_image
Sobel_edge_detection
Extract_regions
Trace_contours

.

A graphical interface was built into the MPF along with the necessary HELP instructions to lead a novice through the steps required to create and execute a customized macro. Figure 5.3 displays the initial MPF menu used by the programmer to indicate how a macro is created or used. Other displays associated with the MPF will be discussed shortly.

Two distinct modes of operation are provided for the execution of user-defined macros—the interactive and the automatic. In the interactive mode, the user is prompted for all the input parameters the program requires at each step. Data such as the names of input or output files are inserted manually. As each subprogram in the macro is invoked, a brief description of the function it is performing is displayed for the user's benefit along with any relevant graphics. In this manner, the user is led through the steps in the macro, interactively specifying the parameters required at each step.

In the automatic mode, an entire macro is executed without user intervention. The output file of each stage of processing is directed automatically to the input of the next stage. The user is only required to provide the name of the original input image file (or to tell the ITI system to capture the current scene from the camera) prior to the first stage of processing. In this mode the MPF is capable of integrating any logically valid sequence of processing steps and executing them in order. Each step of the sequence is presented in as much graphic detail as the algorithm allows on the CRT display.

APS

| THE APS MACRO PROCESSOR MENU |

F1

Create a macro file and save it.

F2

Execute a macro interactively.

F3

Execute a macro in auto mode.

F4

Quit the APS macro facility.

Select option using function keys.

USING THE APS MACRO FACILITY

The Macro facility has been provided to aid the users of the system to customize a set of program calls and then execute them.

This can help the user in storing sequences of frequently called programs in a macro and using the macro facility to execute the same.

The user has the option of creating a new macro or executing a macro which has been created and stored previously.

Two modes of execution are provided:

1. Interactive mode : in which the user is prompted for input and output file names and other parameters the programs may require.
2. Auto mode : in which at each stage of the macro, the program being executed uses the output of the previous stage as the input and so on.
   NOTE: It is the responsibility of the user to ensure that each program in the macro being run in auto mode provides the right number of input files to the next stage.

FIG. 5.3. The initial Macro Processing Facility (MPF) menu used to create or use a sequence of program modules.

```
Acquire an Image

Split Image into R, G and B Components

PAR_BEGIN

     Sobel Edge Detection

     Automatic Thresholding

PAR_END

Merge R, G and B Components

Extract Regions

Thin Boundaries
```

FIG. 5.4. A listing demonstrating the construction of a pseudoparallel operation within the context of the Macro Processing Facility.

The individual graphic displays can also be used to generate a total history of the macro, since an automatic flowchart generating facility has been included within the MPF. After executing a macro, the flowchart generator displays a graphical flowchart of the output of each processing stage. A sample MPF sequence is shown in Figure 3.13. This enables the user to verify the performance of each stage and to observe how the performance of one stage of processing affects succeeding stages. This information can be used to fine-tune the entire macro by modifying, adding, or eliminating stages of processing, and to identify difficulties within the macro being executed.

Another important property of the MPF is its ability to simulate parallel processing within a macro. Recent physiological and psychological studies (see page 58) show that many human perceptual and behavioral processes exhibit inherent parallelism. Current theories about the human brain's ability to process visual information along parallel channels and to combine these channels at a later stage to provide a unitary visual perception provides an incentive to incorporate a similar kind of parallelism into the model. It is also clear, from a computer science point of view, that far better processing will occur if the outputs of several algorithms, each with its own limitations, are combined into a joint estimate of some image attribute. The success with the texture and color algorithms is one clear example of how successful this approach can be.

Because the Apollo workstations used in the present level of simulation on this project are not true parallel machines, we produced a *pseudoparallel* mode of program execution within the MPF. Figure 5.4 shows how a parallel operation is programmed. The code PAR_BEGIN tells the program that the following algorithms (in this case, edge enhancements of the images stored in the three color planes of the ITI image acquisition system) are to be executed in parallel. The algorithms are then listed along with the name of the image each is to transform, and the code PAR_END is entered to indicate that the parallel subprogram is now complete. The outputs of all programs that occur between the PAR_BEGIN and PAR_END are processed by the next listed algorithm. This programming mode is a general-purpose procedure that can be used for any set of algorithms as long as their outputs are compatible with the algorithm following the PAR_END code.

6

An Integrated Model—
Conclusions

6.1. SOME CONCLUSIONS

We have reported the details of the accomplishments of a project to develop an integrated model of a fairly complete perceptual-motor system. The progress made has stimulated several kinds of results. Some of them are purely technical and factual and were reported in detail. However, some general conclusions can be made. First, we believe we have demonstrated that it is possible to develop a system that is adept and robust at carrying out the detection, discrimination, recognition, planning, and navigation goals of our original plan. Second, we also created some novel algorithms and procedures that accomplish these tasks in new and interesting ways. Second, there are conceptual, if not philosophical, conclusions emerging from this project that go far beyond the details of the specific algorithms and procedures. This chapter concentrates on presenting those broader conclusions and inferences.

This programming system instantiates one particular theoretical model of a perceptual-motor system. The very presentation of a flowchart of the steps that are executed in the model is, itself, tantamount to the promulgation of a new theory of a simple mind. Our presentation so far is exactly that. Now we consider some concepts that evolved during our work that altered or confirmed some of our preconceptions about the nature of visually guided behavior.

Several consequences of the raw details of our work bought to our attention some less tangible lessons with regard to computers, brains, and minds. Some lessons we learned are the direct outgrowth of the project. Nevertheless, whether through confirmation or discovery, we are becoming increasingly confident about the general organization that a perceiving-behaving system of the kind we model here must have. We now propose some of these less tangible conclusions.

6.2. SOME CONCEPTUAL CONCLUSIONS

6.2.1. The Need for a Network of Processes

We are convinced that no complex system, computer or organic, can accomplish its functions by a single processing stage or algorithm. The mass of contemporary empirical psychological and neurophysiological evidence, as well as the experiences that we and other workers in the computational modeling field have had, testify that not only does a serial sequence of processes characterize the overall processing of perceptual information, but there is a need for parallel processing within the many intermediate stages of the serial sequence.

This same idea is also expressed by Ramachandran (1990) in an expanded discussion of his "bag of tricks" hypothesis. His conjecture is that vision is mediated by a collection of utilitarian, but inelegant, "short-cuts, rules-of-thumb, and heuristics" (p. 24), none of which is sufficiently powerful to account for any aspect of vision, but each of which contributes something to a cumulative perceptual experience. Ramachandran's conjecture is based on the fact that no one has yet proposed an efficient and competent single, general-purpose algorithm to accomplish even as straightforward a task as texture segmentation. Most computer texture algorithms fail when extended to images other than the types for which they were originally developed. Which algorithms will work on which type of images is usually unpredictable. Progress in the development of a robust texture segmenting algorithm occurred simply because we chose not to seek a single all-powerful algorithm but to combine or integrate the outputs of several weak ones. It is this concept—the concatenation, integration, or combination, of weak processes into a strong outcome—that we model and champion here.

This demonstrated necessity for the integration of several weak algorithms also reminds us of another emerging basic axiom of visual processing. If many processes can be combined to produce an output, it is also likely that no one of them is necessary. The concept of redundancy is an immediate corollary of the concept of integration. Probably no single attribute of a cognitive processing mechanism is necessary for a given visual perception to be consummated, but a combination of different processes may be sufficient to produce the appropriate perceptual response. Even more important, the combination of processes involved may vary from instant to instant and from task to task.

A psychophysical implication (and one that is supported by a rich variety of failed experiments) is that there may be many ways for a human observer to solve the problem posed in a psychophysical experiment. The search for single, omnipotent answers to questions such as, Is a particular perceptual process carried out in serial or parallel? or Is perception guided by local features or global organization? may always be a search for a chimera. It seems more likely that such terms as multiple mechanisms and processes, alternative strategies, adaptive responses, and variable psychoneural structure may be much more realistic descriptors of the human's perceptual psychology.

Closely related to the idea that many processes can possibly be invoked to solve a problem is the observation that no single cue or attribute of the stimulus is probably *necessary* in generating the perceptual outcome. Many attributes of the stimulus may carry the critical information, and although none is necessary, any one of these cues may be *sufficient* to account for the perceptual outcome. A corollary of this idea is that if multiple attributes conveying redundant information are available, then the use of several of them may improve the perceptual performance over that obtainable with one alone. Specific empirical evidence for this conclusion in a psychophysical experiment can be found in Uttal et al. (1988).

The theoretical implication of this line of thought is that the search for a best-fitting or unitary process, for a single best stimulus attribute, or for a universally explanatory algorithm (the approach taken in most earlier research) is probably ill conceived. Processes of combination, integration, and aggregation of often totally inadequate approximations should be stressed in future research and development efforts.

6.2.2. The Evolution of a Computational Rather than an Analytic Model

A second major outcome of our work is evidenced by the *computational* rather than the *mathematical* nature of many of the algorithms we have produced. Many of our algorithms are formulated in terms of simple interactions, which may include such trivial logical processes as ORing, comparisons between individual pixels or local areas of the image, or the simplest kind of differencing operators. These algorithms are often represented in the form of local arithmetic, logical, or statistical transformations, but that is not really necessary. Transforming them to the elaborate analytic mathematics of integral and differential equations that characterize so much of recent work in the field of image processing may be more an illusion of progress than a real contribution.

The reasons for this apparent simplicity are manifold. First, some of the functions carried out by these simulations (as opposed to analyses) may be so complicated that the mathematics necessary to describe them simply does not yet exist and possibly may never exist. Some of the processes we implemented are intrinsically nonlinear transformations and are clearly beyond formulation, or, if formulizable, beyond solution in either a rigorous or practical sense. (See Stockmeyer & Chandra, 1979 for a discussion of the latter possibility.) The point is that the system of programs that make up our model is more of a computational simulation that a formal mathematical model.

Second, there is strong possibility, from our point of view, that differential or integral analysis, developed primarily to describe the continuous world of physical forces, is simply is not the right kind of mathematics to model the functionally discrete action of processes that are biologically instantiated in a network of anatomically discrete neurons or pixels. The simple discrete interactions may represent a more correct and more natural language for simulation studies than integrals or differentials. Formal mathematics may allow us to summarize many simple interactions, but this is more of a convenience than a necessity. In any event, a program loop accomplishes the same thing in a way that may be more useful operationally, if not notationally.

Third, it is even possible that conventional mathematical analysis may be misleading in this kind of endeavor. The search for neural mechanisms or logical processes that are formulizable with available kinds of mathematics may be misdirecting our attention and malforming our theoretical perspectives. The descriptive power of mathematics is so great that we tend to forget that it is neutral with respect to internal mechanisms and that powerful mathematical tools can carry extraneous conceptual baggage as well as being incomplete as models of some process.

Perhaps, no clearer example of such extraneous baggage can be found than in the application of Fourier Analysis to the visual system. While superbly suited to the description of stimuli and the presentation of qualitative results in a quantitative form, Fourier Analysis has often been misunderstood to demand or necessitate that spatial-frequency-sensitive *mechanisms* are real anatomical entities. The point is often forgotten that Fourier Analysis allows the representation of any linearly superimpositionable function with a finite number of discontinuities and maxima and minima to be represented by spatial sinusoids even if the spatial sinusoid mathematical entities do not physically exist.

In summary, many of the algorithms embedded in our model were designed on the basis of computational possibility rather than on the basis of mathematical rigor or solvability. Local interactions analogous to the mutual influence of neurons on each other were programmed without recourse to formal expressions that might have been enormously complicated. While some of our algorithms may be representable in the formal language of contemporary mathematics, we are increasingly suspicious that many of them are not so representable at present. It is possible that they merely await the invention of novel mathematical systems. On the other hand, it is also possible, that many of them are beyond conventional mathematical analysis and await the invention of novel mathematics suitable for modeling large numbers of simple interactions by building process analogs of the kind that have come to characterize the present stage of computational modeling.

After the presentation of these arguments about why conventional mathematics may not be a cure-all for the problems encountered when one simulates cognitive processes, one disclaimer is required. Please note that we do not eschew mathematical formalisms entirely. Please also understand that we do not reject mathematics as a method of power and elegance in many situations both within the domain of this project and more broadly. Our argument is only that conventional mathematics and a demand for mathematical rigor might actually inhibit some of the progress that we made on some of the tasks in our model some of the time.

All of the authors have been trained as mathematicians to a greater or lesser level. It is fair to say that we all love the "queen of the sciences" and appreciate that there are some questions that will require a more formal mathematical approach, if not now, then soon enough as our project continues. For example, we finesse the question of the computability and solvability of some of the tasks we have attacked. It is well known that some image processing questions are ill posed. (See Aloimonos & Shulman, 1989, for a discussion of these issues.) Mathematics can often provide answers to the question of computability or suggest additional constraints that may be needed to solve a problem. (It should be noted that none of the tasks that we have incorporated into our model proved to be completely intractable.) Mathematics of a more formal kind might also answer questions of efficiency and rank order the likelihood of success of alternative approaches a priori. Or, it might have made for a more elegant solution in some instances.

Furthermore, please note that we have liberally used mathematical notation and ideas throughout this project. Sometimes, this was done a priori (e.g., when we applied the Gabor filter technique) and sometimes they were used to summarize, in a concise way, the process of some algorithm. The comments just made should be remembered in the context of our championing of other computational approach than formal mathematics.

6.2.3. The Evolution of a Statistical Geometry

A further interesting outcome of work of the genre reported here is the concept that statistical ideas can be applied to geometry to combine or integrate the usually incomplete outcomes of a family of weak, ineffectual algorithms. The kind of spatial averaging to target the "best estimate" of the position of a texture boundary is but an early example of novel kinds of interactive processes that we believe is to be found in at least some of the intermediate stages of visual processing.

This kind of spatial statistics is important in its own right, but it may be even more important as a harbinger of the kind of unusual, unexpected, and unformulizable kind of transformational mechanisms that someday will be found to be ubiquitous in the visual system. In the long run, we are convinced that these interactive, integrative, network-like, spatial-temporal synergisms are more likely to describe the visual process than the mathematical tools we have so glibly adopted from engineering and physics.

6.2.4. The Need for Softer and Gentler Matching Criteria

In a similar vein, the idea that we can use an approximation to a successful match (a thresholded correlation) rather than exact congruence adds to the statistical-geometrical flavor of our work. We strove in the development of the recognition algorithms, to allow for a relaxed criterion for a match between two images. That is, objects that match to a certain degree (designated by a threshold) are assumed to be acceptable, if not perfect, matches. This allows objects that are slightly deformed, that are of poor contrast, or even those that are partially occluded to be recognized as exemplars of previously encountered prototypes.

6.2.5. The Need for Invariant Representation

A related conclusion emerges from the effort that we made to make our recognition algorithms invariant with regard to position, size, and orientation while maintaining the sensitivity of the algorithm to the shape of an object in an image. The goal in this case was to avoid having too strict a criterion for recognition (i.e., an acceptance that an input image was an exemplar of one that already been encountered). Indeed, as is characteristic of the human visual system, we were seeking to make the model of the SWIMMER capable of recognizing objects on the basis of their global or holistic attributes rather than on the specific metrics of size, position, or orientation. This effort was rewarded by the development of a system that modeled the well-known properties of stimulus generalization to a sometimes an astonishing degree. To the extent that the model is tolerant of deformations, it can also be thought of as having sensitivity to certain of the topological properties of the image.

Invariant representation of images is not only a convenient way of matching objects but also an essential for any model that purports to model vision. It is the direct analog of stimulus generalization. Our efforts at size-, orientation-, and shape-invariant coding are early stages of development of what must be a much more extensive set of invariances up to and including those geometrical ones that allow shapes that are distorted by perspective or incompleteness to be recognized as exemplars as a previously encountered and stored image.

6.2.6. The Need for Completing and Closing Processing

Closely related in principle to invariant representation is the need for pro-grammed processes capable of completing a figure. In contemporary psychology, closure and completion processes play what is virtually a vestigial role, only reminiscent of the attention paid to them by the great Gestalt tradition of the 1920s and 1930s. But when one is driven by the demanding detail of a computational model, it quickly becomes apparent that closure and completion are fundamental processes of far greater importance than ascribed to them by contemporary thinking. Matches, comparisons, segmentation, recognition, and discrimination all depend on an object being seen as a whole rather than as a disjointed collection of isolated parts. In one way or another, the concept of an organized and unified whole, either in the actual image or in the way in which a given algorithm processed the data, was essential to virtually all stages of the model. We feel that attention to these classic Gestalt ideas is also essential for any valid analysis of vision whether it be in the mathematical, computational, neurophysiological, or psychophysical domains.

6.2.7. The Need for Pyramidal Processing

The concept of a pyramid of processes emerges from our work and that of others (e.g., Marr, 1982; Rosenfeld, 1980; Uhr, 1974). The idea inherent in this statement is that it seems likely that the visual system initially operates at a rather gross level sensitive only to the most global attributes of a stimulus. Then, as in the most typical multilevel schema for solving the correspondence problem in stereoscopic perception, it moves on to a more detailed (i.e., higher spatial frequency, greater density of pixels, or more local feature oriented) process. The point is that a full-blown image analysis at the finest level of resolution is terribly expensive in processing time in a computer model and that the initial analysis should be carried out at the grossest possible level of analysis. Then as interest features are coarsely defined, the analysis should be carried out in progressively finer detail.

There is a question about whether the necessity for resolution pyramiding in computer modeling is generalizable to the neural networks of the visual system. It is entirely possible that the brain is organized in such a way that fine details are encoded and processed as promptly as the coarse details and that considerations of economy are actually unnecessary in this context. Either global or local attributes can take precedence as current attention is directed to either the whole figure or its components. For example, the perception of color depends from the start on the coded differences in the finest grain possible in the retina—the relationship between the activity in the three types of cones. We can fairly ask the question: although we perceive a global, unified outcome, is not the initial processing carried on at the finest possible level in this case? This possibility is anecdotally supported by the contradictory evidence that the details of an image can sometimes obscure the overall structure, while at other times we can lose the details because of the global organization of the parts (e.g., the famous paintings by Guiseppe Arcimboldo (1527–1593) of faces made from fruits or fish bodies, none of which are initially seen until locally scrutinized).

The role of pyramiding, driven by the need for computational economy in the computer, thus remains problematic in biological systems where an abundance of parallel processing computational elements exist and economy is not an essential criterion.

6.2.8. The Critical Role of Apparently Trivial Processes

Another important general conclusion to which our work leads is that some of the seemingly most uninteresting and trivial processes turn out to be at once some of the most critical and some of the most difficult to implement. Many of these are associated with key decision-making points in the operation of the model. For example, the automation of contrast thresholding procedures proved to be an immense challenge that we have not yet completely solved. Potential trade-offs between the introduction of noise and the loss of critical image information make implementation of threshold processes extremely difficult because there is no simple criterion, convergence rule, or even a benchmark that can be unambiguously used to specify what the threshold should be in a variety of conditions. Thus, thresholding in the computer model and decision criteria in the analogous psychological process play an important role in any analysis of vision.

6.2.9. The Inevitability of Compensatory Processes

The difficulty that emerges in the case of thresholds is a special case of a general property of many of the decisions made in the construction of this model as well as in many other levels of psychological processing. There are costs and benefits to be paid and enjoyed from virtually any criterion applied in the model; compensatory interaction is a universal concomitant of organic evolution and computational modeling.

For example, when coarse-grained, low-resolution images reduce the computational load, the result is a loss of detailed pictorial information that might have been useful or even critical to some later computation. But to increase the pixel density to preserve that information can often lead to a computational explosion that makes the program unexecutable in any practical sense.

Another instance occurred in the development of the algorithms for contour closure. The parameters of the algorithm could be manipulated so that virtually every gap would be closed. To do so, however, incurred the cost of closing false gaps (i.e., gaps that should not have been closed since they did not represent a true interruption in a single contour). A third example, has already been discussed in detail—the compensatory interaction between the obtainable depth resolution in a stereoscopic analysis program and the load imposed upon the computer.

In the organic eye, the compensatory balance is between spatial acuity and intensity thresholds. Thresholds are lowered by combining the outputs of several adjacent receptors. However, such a convergent combination increases the uncertainty of the location of part of an image and thus reduces acuity. To go in the opposite direction produces the reverse difficulties.

The important point is that these compensatory interactions are inherent in both organic vision and computer image processing. They cannot be completely resolved. The best we can hope for is that we can understand the nature of the interaction and the costs and benefits incurred as one shifts criteria.

Is this situation unique in our models? Of course not. An elaborate technology, called Signal Detection Theory, has been developed to handle situations like this in which the choice of the criterion can have significant effects on the outcome of a psychological decision. It is obvious that processes such as the Signal Detection Theory approach, in which the compensatory trade-off between errors of omission (misses) and errors of commission (false alarms) is at least understood and quantified, will have to play a role in future developments of any computer image processing system.

6.2.10. The Adaptive Nature of our Model

One of the most important outcomes of this research is that we were guided and directed to a model that is adaptive. Many programs we have written accommodate themselves to the vagaries of form and location defined by the input image. The behavior of the navigational phase of the system is responsive to the locations and forms of the image as they are analyzed by the image segmenters and classified by the recognition modules. No two experimental runs are ever identical, since there are random positioning algorithms built into the routines that locate objects in the SWIMMER's microworld.

Similarly, our recognition algorithms are explicitly designed to respond adaptively to the current image inputs and to learn from previous encounters with similar interests. Our model is an adaptive system in the fullest sense of the term as it may be used to describe a living system. Of course, its complexity is less, and its behavior is constrained by the simplicity of its repertoire of simulated logical skills. Nevertheless, we believe that adaptive systems programming of the type exemplified by our work is a sine qua non of any future programming effort in related fields.

6.2.11. Real-Time Operation Was Neither
Planned nor Obtained

For the simplest of reasons, the system of programs that we report in this book does not yet run at a speed that could be termed even approximately a real-time operation. The primary reason for this was nothing more complicated than the nature of the computers on which the project was developed. The Apollo workstations are simply not fast enough to allow rapid program execution, and many of our programs were actually elaborate systems of algorithms that often had to be run in parallel conceptually, if not in fact.

While this non-real-time operation is essentially a temporary technological constraint, there are some other aspects to the slow execution problem that have broader implications. Most of our image processing work is carried out in a world that is intrinsically parallel. An image is a two-dimensional array over which the various transforms and algorithms should best be considered to be operating simultaneously at every point. Unfortunately, conventional computers have to execute these transformations in serial order unlike the biological mechanisms that evolved to operate in parallel order. While there is no intrinsic conceptual difference between a parallel and a serial transformation in a model such as ours, there is a practical difference that often makes computer experimentation and program refinement discouragingly slow. Some of our macro algorithms, particularly those that integrated the outputs of several preceding stages of processing, take many minutes to run.

The solution to this problem lies partially in technology. Faster computers are available, and parallel processing systems, should they come into general use, will greatly alleviate this difficulty. Nevertheless, there are some structural problems suggest that it is not simply a matter of waiting for faster computer technology but, at least in part, a matter of certain inevitable constraints should continued efforts be made to simulate the kind of cognitive processes dealt with in this project. In this context, one has to consider the number of calculations that are carried out with two-dimensional images, ignoring for the moment the even greater demands of a three-dimensional calculation. There is strong need for clever new designs in fast algorithms or for transporting our programs to specially designed hardware that will actually carry out the critical program steps in parallel.

A practical consideration is that performance measures for our programs couched in terms of speed are meaningless. It was the conceptual organization of the processes that was important to us, not the relative computational efficiency of program execution. That "performance measure" is more a characteristic of the computers we used than the algorithms themselves. (Our new facility, installed at the time this book was completed, offers us a 100-fold increase in speed with no required change in conceptual organization.) In this context, it should be emphasized that the criterion of temporal "economy" (i.e., speed), an important factor driving the engineering design of computers, is vastly different than any of the criteria driving the evolution of the brain.

Memory capacity is another problem that interacts directly with the computational speed problem. Most of the calculations produced by our algorithms generated either a new image of the same pixel density or multiple new images. *In some cases the number of new images was as great as the number of pixels in the original image.* There is, therefore, an extraordinary amount of image storage space required. Even with an aggregate system storage capacity of almost

600 Mbytes, we were always "disk poor." We now believe that successful execution of a project such as this requires computer storage capabilities in gigabytes, a number also typical of the brain.

The point is that image processing, so effortlessly carried out by the parallel networks of the retina and the higher regions of the nervous system, are extremely demanding activities in a computer simulation project. In terms of memory capacity and algorithmic execution time, even the best modern computers are severely challenged by these tasks. How does the human visual system do it? The contemporary conclusion is that it does so by virtue of sheer numbers of processing units operating in parallel. Perhaps even more important is that it depends on the execution of a kind of simplifying, heuristic-based processing of which we have virtually no knowledge. To repeat, our models are analog executing processes comparable to those performed in the organic brain but should not be interpreted as a reductive, homologous kind of explanation of those organic processes. They remain invisible to us, and despite some claims to the contrary, to psychobiologists of all persuasions.

6.2.12. Top-Down (Heuristic Rule) Processing is Probably Necessary in Any Successful Simulation of a Cognitive Process

Finally, we come to a conceptual conclusion that we can not completely justify nor prove, but which is becoming a compelling force in our thinking about computation models of the kind presented here. On the basis of the experience we have had with this project we believe that no simulation of any cognitive process of any depth can be successful if based on a purely bottom-up (algorithmic) approach. That is, no deterministic procedures can be invented that will not quickly explode combinatorially or simply fail. All efforts to simulate cognitive processes seem to require additional rules that exclude certain exceptional cases or handle uncertainties in a way that goes beyond the simple computational evaluation of a pixel mapped image or scene. Some such additional rules (e.g., the exclusion of uniques in the texture combination process) are relatively straightforward and simple. Others are likely to be more complex and mysterious. While these may be elusive they also may be essential for successful computational modeling.

We suspect that the great breakthroughs in computational modeling are going to come about when we understand how general heuristic rules, that look at the image in a way that transcends local interactions, can be combined with the algorithmic image manipulation processes we have mainly used in this project. This is not only a practical matter for computer science. It is also likely to be the key to understanding the way the human perceptual-motor system operates.

6.3. A SUMMARY

We conclude by professing one major point—that the system of programs developed, however incomplete, is a specific, detailed, quantitative theory of a perceptual-motor process. Collectively the flowcharts used to document the steps in the entire system constitute a statement of how the nervous system carries out this behavior. But it must be interpreted as a descriptive theory, not as a reductionistic one. It is the transforming processes themselves, and not the algorithms in which they are instantiated, that are critical. In this context, we point out once again that this model is at best an analog of the perceptual-motor system. We do not claim that the algorithms we generated are identical to the neural mechanisms underlying organic vision or decision making in either structure or logic. They only define what we believe are the transforming steps that are necessary to go from the original image to the predatory behavior of the SWIMMER. Any model that aspires to represent this form of behavior must account for these steps, but each can be constructed in virtually an infinite number of ways.

The computational details represent the current development of our model. In the future, we must take into account movement and other cues that help in the segmentation phase of the process. These additional cues will be added to the color, intensity, stereoscopic, and textural cues that now contribute to the segmentation process. We also have to attend further to the problem of automation. As we have indicated, the problem of sequencing between steps has turned out to be much more challenging than we initially expected.

Finally, we look forward to working on more realistic modeling of the SWIMMER's undersea world. We want to make both the hydrodynamics and the appearance of the environment more realistic. Most important to us is the continued development of an integrated model of the perceptual process using the latest information from the psychophysical or neurophysiological laboratory about the organization of the visual system.

We hope that our model will be useful to psychologists interested in a deeper understanding of cognitive process and to computer scientists, who may benefit from some of the algorithms and procedures stimulated by that increasing understanding.

Appendix: A Primer on Navigation and Path Planning

Gary Bradshaw

A.1. INTRODUCTION

This appendix is an introduction to navigation in underwater environments. It acts as a guide to some of the algorithms we used in the navigational portion of the simulation of the SWIMMER. The equations that were developed and specialized for underwater navigation, but are related to general navigation formulas used in water-surface, land, and air navigation. Beginning with simple problems in dead-reckoning navigation, successively more complex and more realistic treatments are discussed. Much of the information here can be derived by anyone familiar with basic trigonometry and vector algebra. Our intention is not to describe esoteric navigation principles but to outline the basics for those who have little familiarity with navigation problems.

A.2. STRAIGHT-LINE NAVIGATION

Navigation, as defined in this book, is the process of directing the movement of our simulated SWIMMER from one point to another in the simulated three-dimensional space in which it resides. *Dead-reckoning* navigation is the determination of a course from the initial and final locations without allowance for currents. Let the coordinate system be a simple two-dimensional xz plane. (The coordinate system used is slightly different than the one used in the rest of this book. The z and y axes have been interchanged.) Euclidean geometry is assumed; the formulas can be applied to spherical earth systems only at a local level. We can assume that the positive Z axis points North while the positive X axis points

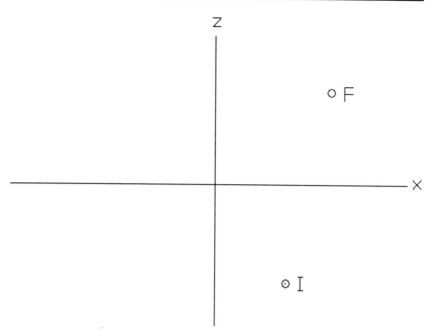

FIG. A.1.   The simple navigation problem faced when one wishes to move from an initial point (I) to a final point (F).

East. The simplest problem imaginable is represented in Figure A.1, where we intend to navigate from an initial location $I = (x_i, z_i)$ to a final location $F = (x_f, z_f)$.

A.2.1. Planar Navigation

Given that the initial position I and the final location F are known to a reasonable degree of precision, the navigation problem requires a determination of the compass heading Q_h and the length of the navigation course L. As shown in Figure A.2, Q_h is the compass angle for our course, and L is the length of the course. The value of Q_h may be determined from simple trigonometric relationships:

$$tan(Q_h) = \frac{x_f - x_i}{z_f - z_i} \tag{A.1}$$

or

$$Q_h = arctan\, \frac{x_f - x_i}{z_f - z_i} \tag{A.2}$$

Where L is determined as the length of the hypotenuse:

$$L = \sqrt{[x_f - x_i]^2 + [z_f - z_i]^2}. \tag{A.3}$$

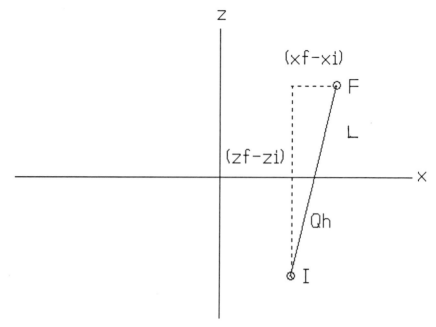

FIG. A.2.   The geometry of the solution to the simple navigation problem shown in Figure A.1. The solution requires that the compass heading (Q_h) and the course length (L) be specified.

The time required to traverse distance L depends on the speed (S) of the SWIMMER, since $L = ST$. At any time T_n, the location of the SWIMMER can be computed, since $x_n = ST \sin Q_h + x_i$ and $z_n = ST \cos Q_h + z_i$.

This solution is unrealistic in that it ignores environmental effects on the SWIMMER. Usually an object is moving through an active medium influenced by events such as flowing currents or winds. Only in vacuums or totally stable, and thus unrealistic, spaces can environmental forces be ignored. The next section derives a more complex model where a single constant force, corresponding to a current or wind, acts to displace the SWIMMER as it travels.

A.2.2. Compensating for Currents

Assume that a current force acts on the SWIMMER while it is maneuvering between I and F. The current is represented as a vector of a particular heading (clockwise from North) and specified length (i.e., a 2-knot current with a heading of 90° will push the SWIMMER to the right). Currents represent forces that act over time. Compensation for currents requires us to consider speeds as well as distances. One simplifying assumption is to treat the SWIMMER as inertia free. This implies that top speed can be achieved instantly, a conclusion that simplifies the computation of distances along the navigation course.

The current (Q_c, C) can be decomposed into its rectilinear components C_x and C_z by using the formulas $C_x = C \sin Q_c$ and $C_z = C \cos Q_c$. These values represent the x and z drifts per unit of time. A SWIMMER located at position (x_0, z_0) at time T_0 would drift to $(x_0 + [T_n - T_0] C_x, z_0 + [T_n - T_0] C_z)$ by time T_n. Current drift affects the navigation track and must be compensated for by shifting the heading of the SWIMMER. This section describes the computations necessary to derive the corrected heading and the true speed (referenced to land or the ocean floor instead of the speed through water) for the SWIMMER. A prerequisite for these computations is knowledge of the current vector. The next section will describe how a current model can be developed from experience.

Assume that our SWIMMER starts at point I and maneuvers along course Q_h for one unit of time. If no currents acted on the SWIMMER, the new location would be $(x_i + S \sin Q_h), z_i + S \cos Q_h$. A current displaces our true location to $(x_i + S \sin Q_h + C_x, z_i + S \cos Q_h + C_z)$. Vectors obey the commutative property of addition, so an abstraction of this situation is to consider the SWIMMER beginning at location $(x_i + C_x, y_i + C_z)$ and heading in direction Q_h. To correct the heading for our SWIMMER, note that in one unit of time the SWIMMER can maneuver a distance S in any direction away from the adjusted beginning point. The possible locations reachable from $(x_i + C_x, y_i + C_z)$ form a circle of radius S around that point. One of the points on the circle intersects the original course from I to L. This point of intersection can be used to compute the revised heading Q_h' and the effective ground speed S' as shown in Figure A.3.

Determining the points of intersection between a circle and a line is a tedious but straightforward procedure. A simplification may be realized by translating the coordinate axes so that $(x_i + C_x, z_i + C_z)$ is the origin of the new axes. The initial and final points are translated into this coordinate system by

$$I' = (x_i', z_i') = (-C_x, -C_z) \tag{A.4}$$

and

$$F' = (x_f', x_f') = (x_f - x_i - C_x, z_f - z_i - C_z). \tag{A.5}$$

The line from I' to F' is described with a simple slope-intercept equation of the form $Y = MX + B$, where M and B are determined from the translated initial and final points by the equations

$$M = \frac{z_f' - z_i'}{x_f' - x_i'} \tag{A.6}$$

and

$$B = z_i' - Mx_i'. \tag{A.7}$$

Our translation of the coordinate axes allows us to represent the set of points reachable from the origin at speed S by the simple equation

$$S^2 = X^2 + Z^2 \tag{A.8}$$

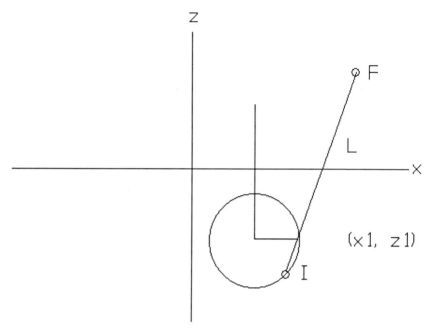

FIG. A.3.   When currents are present, the problem of navigation becomes more complicated. The heading must be corrected. To do this, we must construct a circle that represents the locations reachable from the initial point within a unit time.

or, equivalently,

$$Z^2 = S^2 - X^2 \qquad (A.9)$$

We wish to determine the point (x_1, z_1) that represents the intersection between the circle and the line. Substituting $z_1 = Mx_1 + B$ into the circle equation results in

$$(Mx_1 + B)^2 = S^2 - x_1^2. \qquad (A.10)$$

By expansion,

$$M^2x_1^2 + 2BMx_1 + B^2 = S^2 - x_1^2. \qquad (A.11)$$

Collecting terms gives

$$(M^2 + 1)x_1^2 + (2BM)x_1 + (B^2 - S^2) = 0. \qquad (A.12)$$

By the quadratic formula,

$$x_1 = \frac{-2BM \pm \sqrt{4B^2M^2 - 4(M^2 + 1)(B^2 - S^2)}}{2(M^2 + 1)} \qquad (A.13)$$

Simplifying, we get

$$x_1 = \frac{-BM \pm 2\sqrt{(M^2 + 1)S^2 - B^2}}{M^2 + 1} \tag{A.14}$$

The term z_1 may be determined by substituting the value of x_1 into the linear equation $Z = MX + B$. In most cases there will be two points of intersection. Selecting the point that is closest to the navigation course is left as an exercise for the reader.

Once the point (x_1, z_1) has been determined, the revised heading and true ground speed can be calculated by using a simplification of the planar equations from Section A.2.1:

$$Q_h' = arctan \left(\frac{z_1}{x_1} \right) \tag{A.15}$$

and

$$S' = \sqrt{x_1^2 + z_1^2}. \tag{A.16}$$

A.2.3. Computing a Current Model

Compensation for currents can only occur when the current force is known. Free-floating SWIMMERS cannot directly measure the current, and so must estimate current strength from indirect methods. All methods are based on the principle of measuring drift over time. Drift is computed from knowing the SWIMMER's location fairly precisely at two different times. The SWIMMER's location may be computed by transponder localization, landmark tracking, inertial navigation instruments, and so on. We will assume that the SWIMMER's location can be determined at any time without significant error.

Assume that the SWIMMER begins to navigate toward F without any estimate of current forces. As it approaches the destination point, the SWIMMER will be displaced away from the track IF by the current. The magnitude of the displacement will initially be small and will increase linearly over time. Figure A.4 shows the intended and actual SWIMMER tracks. When the discrepancy becomes sufficiently large with respect to the error of measurement of SWIMMER localization, the current vector (Q_c, C) can be estimated. Suppose at time T_n we observe a significant deviation from our intended track. At that point, we determine our location to be (x_n', z_n') (Figure A.4). The intended location (x_n, z_n) at T_n is $(x_i + T_n \times sin\ Q,\ z_i + T_n \times cos\ Q)$.

We can compute the rectilinear components of the current directly as

$$C_x = \frac{x_n' - x_1}{(T_n - T_0)S} \tag{A.17}$$

and

$$C_z \frac{z_n' - z_1}{(T_n - T_0)S} \tag{A.18}$$

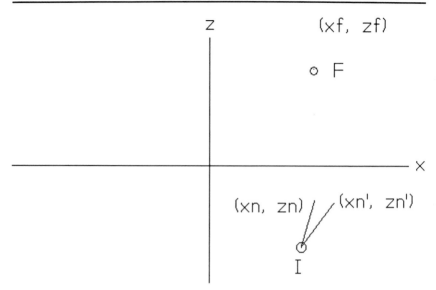

FIG. A.4. Actual and intended paths with and without current compensation.

If desired, the magnitude of the current C can be derived from the Pythagorean Theorem, and the direction Q_c from the arctangent of C_x and C_y.

Although the formulas we describe are general, in practice these equations should only be used in two conditions: when the SWIMMER is not actively trying to maneuver in the environment, and when it is maneuvering along a straight line. When the SWIMMER is maneuvering along an arc, computations of the intended direction and distance become problematic. Turning movements are often performed by applying differential force to two sides of the SWIMMER. Calculating the distance the SWIMMER will travel along the arc requires a knowledge of the dynamics of the SWIMMER thrusters in the underwater environment. These dynamics are usually nonlinear and require elaborate models for their computation (Yoerger & Slotine, 1985).

A.2.4. Extensions to a Three-Dimensional World

Ordinarily, the generalization of the navigation and current model equations developed in the past two sections to handle a three-dimensional world requires the use of spherical, instead of planar, trigonometry. This treatment results from the *spherical radius* limitation: The SWIMMER can only travel distance S in a single interval of time. If the SWIMMER is traveling downward, the forward distance will be shortened. If the SWIMMER has independent control over its depth and forward movement, it does not obey this restriction. Downward movement is (largely) independent of forward and lateral motion. In this case, the complexities of spherical geometry can be ignored for a simpler three-dimensional model.

Consider a navigation volume (x, y, z), where the x and z coordinates again represent compass headings of East-West and North-South, respectively, while the y coordinate represents depth above the bottom. (This model was chosen to be consistent with the Apollo 3D graphics package and is, as noted, inconsistent with the coordinate system used in this book.) The initial point I is described by (x_i, y_i, z_i), and the final point F is described by (x_f, y_f, z_f). Disregarding current effects, the compass heading can be determined from Equations A.1 and A.2. The dive angle D can be computed analogously:

$$tan\,(D) = \frac{y_f - y_i}{z_f - z_i} \qquad\qquad (A.19)$$

or

$$D = arctan\left(\frac{y_f - y_i}{z_f - z_i}\right), \qquad\qquad (A.20)$$

and L is the Euclidean distance of the hypotenuse. That is,

$$L = \sqrt{[x_f - x_i]^2 + [y_f - y_i]^2 + [z_f - z_i]^2}. \qquad (A.21)$$

The y component of the current C (C_x, C_y, and C_z) is computed by deriving the distance between the expected and observed locations divided by the time interval during which the deviation occurs:

$$C_y = \frac{y_1' - y_1}{(T_n - T_0)S}. \qquad\qquad (A.22)$$

Current corrections in three dimensions rely on the same analysis as that for the two-dimensional case, because corrections in the xz plane are largely independent of corrections in the yz plane. Using Equations A.6 through A.15, Y values may be substituted for X values to obtain the modified dive angle D'. Since SWIMMER speed in the xz plane is not affected by the action of the vertical thrusters, Equation A.16 can be used in its original form to compute true speed.

A.2.5. Summary and Limitations

These computations are based on a few simplifications and are only approximate. The first simplification we considered was to treat the effect of forces on the SWIMMER as instantaneous. We computed the distance traveled by the SWIMMER, using only maximum velocity and average current. These forces do not act instantaneously, but can only accelerate the SWIMMER; this acceleration is balanced by drag from the water. Only when the thruster and current forces are balanced by drag forces will the system reach its final velocity. A more sophisticated model of the intended location and exact current can be derived by using a full acceleration/drag model for the thruster and current forces.

The next simplification derives from the assumption that the SWIMMER's pitch, roll, and yaw will not be perturbed by outside forces. For an actively maneuvering SWIMMER, each of these forces alters the effect of an action. Consider what happens when a SWIMMER is pitched downward by a small angle N. The horizontal thrusters push the SWIMMER along *its* horizontal axis, not the world horizontal axis. Depending on the size of angle N, the SWIMMER descends more rapidly and moves forward more slowly than on the path specified by the control system.

If these factors are not measured, they will affect the computation of the current model. A downward pitch causing a course deviation can only be interpreted as a downward current if the model does not include any pitch computations. Roll and yaw variations can have a similar effect. The correction requires a more sophisticated model to compute the intended SWIMMER location given measured pitch, roll, and yaw deviations.

Whether these problems are serious enough to warrant correction depends on two factors: the stability of the SWIMMER and the reliance on dead-reckoning navigation. If the SWIMMER is quite resistant to changes in pitch and roll but now yaw, the correction can be limited to yaw deviations only. Whenever the SWIMMER is piloting (obtaining its location by active scanning instead of projection from courses and speeds), course computation is of little importance, and these factors can also be safely ignored. In search tasks, where there may be few cues to location, dead reckoning becomes more important, and it may prove necessary to include pitch, roll, and yaw sensors to allow a more complete model of currents and maneuvering to be derived.

A.3.   CURVED PATHS BETWEEN TWO POINTS

Straight-line navigation can be used if one wishes to go to a particular destination, but does not care about the final orientation upon arrival. If the SWIMMER can rotate about its axis, straight-line navigation followed by a reorientation upon arrival will suffice. An important case where straight-line navigation is insufficient is when a SWIMMER can only look forward. If the field of view is largely forward looking, the SWIMMER should probably approach its target from a nearly perpendicular orientation; in other words, when approaching the target location, the SWIMMER will have the target in full view. This navigation task requires us to move to a location and to have some specified orientation at the destination. Accomplishing this approach requires our path to assume an arc from the current location to the destination location. This section describes the computation of an arc connecting two points.

First, note that there are an infinite number of arcs that connect any two

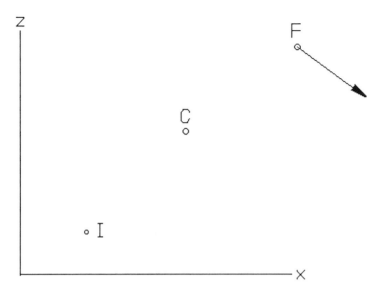

FIG. A.5.   Means of computing the midpoint between the initial and final positions in a navigation problem in which a curved path is being computed.

points. Specifying the arrival orientation uniquely determines the arc, because the SWIMMER must lie on the tangent to the arc connecting the points. Only in rare circumstances will the SWIMMER begin the arc in the proper orientation. Our arc navigation will require a rotation to begin the path, followed by a smooth curve to the point. (If the SWIMMER cannot rotate about its axis to begin the path, a two-arc solution is required. This case is not covered here.) As in previous discussions, we begin with simple cases and work toward more complete and realistic solutions. Our first analysis ignores the effect of currents on the SWIMMER. The goal is to compute a curved path between I and F. The orientation at the destination point (x_f, z_f) is Q, which is specified as the clockwise angle with respect to the z axis (an orientation of zero is parallel to the z axis looking toward infinity; positive angles are clockwise, while negative angles are counterclockwise). Figure A.5 shows the initial and final SWIMMER locations.

Determining the equations for the arc are tedious but are not complicated. We consider only circular arcs so that points I and F lie on a circle. This simple fact has an important implication: The center of the arc must lie on the perpendicular bisector between the two lines. A second constraint is that the SWIMMER orientation must be tangent to the circle at the destination location. The line segment connecting the circle center and the SWIMMER center at the destination point must be perpendicular to the destination orientation. The perpendicular bisector and the orientation radius will intersect at the center of the circle connecting the points. Once the circle center is determined, it is a simple matter to derive the radius of the circle and length of the arc.

To find the center point, we determine the parameters of these two lines and solve for their intersection. Each line is expressed by an equation of the form $Z = MX + B$. Before the equations are developed, it is helpful to define a few terms that can simplify our equations. The point midway between the two positions,

$$C = (x_m, z_m) \qquad (A.23)$$

shown in Figure A.5 can be computed as

$$x_m = \frac{x_f + x_i}{2} \qquad (A.24)$$

and

$$z_m = \frac{z_f + z_i}{2}. \qquad (A.25)$$

Next, we need to know the x and z displacements from the initial point to the target point. The term x_{disp} is defined as $x_f - x_i$, and z_{disp} is defined as $z_f - z_i$. These terms permit us to specify the slope and intercept values for the orientation radius line and the perpendicular bisector line. Considering the orientation radius line first, we observe that the slope M can be quickly determined from angle Q. Our radius line must be perpendicular to the SWIMMER orientation Q and will have an angle of $\pi/2 + Q$ with respect to the Z axis. The tangent of this angle is the x displacement over the z displacement. The slope of the radius line M is rise/run, that is, z displacement over x displacement. Thus, the slope of the radius line is

$$M_t = \frac{1}{tan\ (Q + \pi/2)}. \qquad (A.26)$$

The radius line must pass through (x_f, z_f), so $z_f = Mx_f + B_t$. Solving for B_t gives

$$B_t = z_f - \frac{xf}{tan\ (Q + \pi/2)}. \qquad (A.27)$$

The perpendicular bisector line has a slope that is the negative inverse of the slope connecting (x_i, z_i) and (x_f, z_f). The equation is

$$M_p = -\left(\frac{x_{disp}}{z_{disp}} \right). \qquad (A.28)$$

This line must pass through (x_m, z_m), so the intercept may be determined by

$$B_p = z_m + \left(\frac{x_{disp}}{z_{disp}} \right) x_m. \qquad (A.29)$$

To summarize, the equations for each line are

$$z_t = \frac{1}{tan\ (Q\ +\ \pi/2)}\ x_t + z_f - \frac{x_f}{tan\ (Q\ +\ \pi/2)} \tag{A.30}$$

and

$$z_p = -\left(\frac{x_{disp}}{z_{disp}}\right) x_p + z_m + \left(\frac{x_{disp}}{z_{disp}}\right) x_m. \tag{A.31}$$

Both lines are shown in Figure A.6.

The intersection of these lines is the center of the arc that connects the two points. We solve for this intersection by noting that (x_c, z_c) must be a point on both lines. Substituting x_c for x_t and x_p and z_c for z_t and z_p gives us two equations whose left sides are identical (z_c and z_c). The equations are therefore equal and can be solved for x_c:

$$\frac{1}{tan\ (Q\ +\ \pi)}\ x_c + z_f - \frac{x_f}{tan\ (Q\ +\ \pi)} = -\left(\frac{x_{disp}}{z_{disp}}\right) x_c + z_m + \left(\frac{x_{disp}}{z_{disp}}\right) x_m$$

$$\tag{A.32}$$

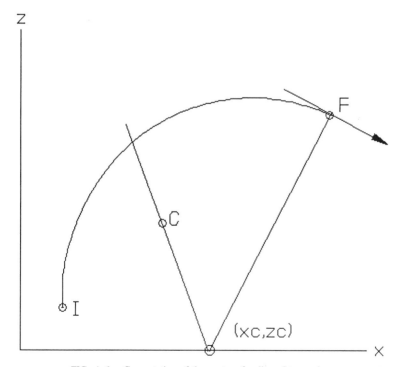

FIG. A.6.   Computation of the center of radius of two points.

Simplifying gives

$$x_c = \frac{z_m + \left(\dfrac{x_{disp}}{z_{disp}}\right)x_m - z_f + \dfrac{x_f}{tan(\pi + Q)}}{\dfrac{1}{tan(\pi + Q)} + \dfrac{x_{disp}}{z_{disp}}}.$$ (A.33)

The term z_c may be determined by substituting the value of x_i obtained from Equation A.33 into Equation A.30 or Equation A.31. The point (x_c, z_c), used in conjunction with either of the original points, determines the radius of the circle:

$$r_c = \sqrt{[x_c - x_i]^2 + [z_c - z_i]^2}.$$ (A.34)

The arc center (x_c, z_c) and the radius r_c can be used to determine the length of the arc around the circle. This can be derived by knowing the length of the angle A_f that subtends the arc from $(x_c + r_c, z_c)$ to (x_f, z_f) and the length of the angle A_i subtending the arc from $(x_c + r_c, z_c)$ to (x_i, z_i). We begin this analysis by determining the arc from the point $(x_c + r_c, z_c)$ to each location. Consider a point (x_n, z_n) located in the first quadrant on the circle. We can determine angle A_n, where

$$A_n = arc_c\ tan\left(\frac{z_n - z_c}{x_n - x_c}\right).$$ (A.35)

As long as (x_n, z_n) is located in the first quadrant, Equation A.35 can be used. However, the equation for a circle is not a function because the inverse of a circle is not unique. The arctangent function will not correctly identify the location of a point in all quadrants. The simplest way to determine the subtended arc is to normalize the distances, effectively translating the point into the first quadrant, then adding or subtracting appropriate values to place the angle in the correct quadrant.

To compute A_i, take the absolute value of the ratio of the distances:

$$A_n' = arctan\left(\frac{z_n - z_c}{x_n - x_c}\right).$$ (A.36)

Next, determine the quadrant of the point by lookup in Table A.1. This table shows a correction factor to be added to A_n', resulting in the true angle.

TABLE A.1.
Quadrants of Various Angles

$x_a - x_c$	$z_a - z_c$	Quadrant	Correction of A_n
Positive	Positive	First	$A_n = A_n'$
Negative	Positive	Second	$A_n = \pi - A_n'$
Negative	Negative	Third	$A_n = \pi + A_n'$
Positive	Negative	Fourth	$A_n = 2\pi - A_n'$

Angles A_i and A_f can be determined from Equation A.36 and Table A.1. There are two arcs connecting A_i and A_f: the clockwise arc and the counterclockwise arc. Given that the SWIMMER travels faster in the forward direction than in reverse, the arc taken depends on the orientation of the SWIMMER at arrival. To determine the direction of travel along the arc, note that the *heading* of the line segment connecting the center and final destinations can be determined by using the Z axis as the horizontal axis:

$$A_h = arctan \left(\frac{x_f - x_c}{z_c - z_f} \right). \qquad (A.37)$$

If the heading of the line segment plus $\pi/2$ is equal to the SWIMMER's heading, the SWIMMER will be traveling clockwise; otherwise the direction of travel will be counterclockwise. Angles A_i and A_f are measured in a clockwise direction. The clockwise arc A_r between the initial and final points is

$$A_r = A_i - A_f \qquad \text{if } A_i - A_f > 0 \qquad (A.38)$$

or

$$A_r = 2\pi - (A_i - A_f) \qquad \text{if } A_i - A_f < 0. \qquad (A.39)$$

The angle of the counterclockwise arc is simply $2\pi - A_r$. The length of each arc is computed by multiplying by r_c, the radius of the circle. Also, travel time can be computed by dividing the appropriate length by S, the SWIMMER's speed.

Finally, the SWIMMER's orientation at the beginning of the path must be determined. To make the correct arc, the SWIMMER must begin on the tangent to the circle at the point of origin, facing in either the clockwise or counterclockwise direction. Fortunately, the change in heading of the SWIMMER is equal to the degree of arc traversed by the SWIMMER. Thus, the initial heading Q_i is $Q - A_r$.

The formulas in this section are universal, but they may not be applied under some conditions. Specifically, division by zero is considered to result in undefined numbers and must be avoided. In some conditions a program might apply the formulas in this section and generate zero-divide errors. This occurs explicitly in Equation A.31, where the z displacement may be zero; in Equation A.30, where $Q + \pi/2$ is zero leading to a zero tangent value; and implicitly in Equation A.30, where $Q + \pi/2$ is $\pi/2$. In the latter situation the tangent of the angle is undefined because it requires a number to be divided by zero.

Whenever $z_f = z_i$, the z_{disp} term is zero. This implies that the perpendicular bisector of the two points is parallel to the z axis with an equation of the form $X = x_m = (x_f + x_i)/2$. Since x_m is known, it may be used directly in Equation A.30 to compute z_i; the pair (x_m, z_t) will be the center of the circle $(x_c, /z_c)$. A related simplification occurs whenever $x_f = x_i$ and the x_{disp} term equals zero. In this case, the equation for the perpendicular bisector line is

$$Z = z_m = \frac{z_f + z_i}{2}.$$ (A.40)

This relation may be substituted in Equation A.30 and the equation solved for x_t. The pair (x_t, z_m) is the center of the circle.

When the angle of orientation at arrival Q is either 0 or π, the orientation radius line will be parallel to the X axis. The equation describing this line is simply $Z = z_f$. This value may be substituted in Equation A.31, obtaining a value for x_p. If Q is either $\pi/2$ or $3\pi/2$, the orientation radius is parallel to the Z axis. The corresponding equation will be $X = x_f$. Again, this may be substituted directly into Equation A.31. The circle is centered at (x_f, z_p).

A.4. ROUTE PLANNING

The navigation problems we have discussed only required the generation of a single heading to maneuver the SWIMMER from the starting point to the destination. In situations where obstacles or other impediments to free motion are present, the simple straight-line course is not sufficient. This section discusses

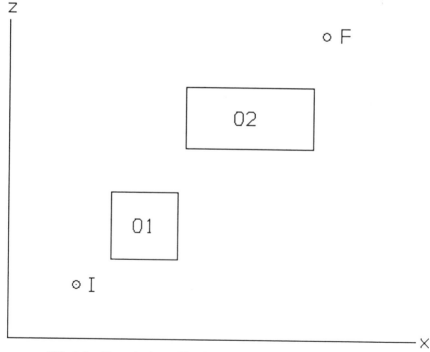

FIG. A.7. The navigation problem further complicated by the addition of obstacles in what otherwise would have been a straight-line navigation situation.

some simple route-planning problems and their automatic solution. Unfortunately, route-planning problems can become quite complex, and the solutions we propose are only sufficient to solve relatively trivial ones. The literature on route planning is extensive, discussing more sophisticated solutions than can be covered here. Chapter XV of the *Handbook of Artificial Intelligence* (Cohen & Feigenbaum, 1983) surveys general planning tasks.

Consider the situation shown in Figure A.7 where a SWIMMER is attempting to maneuver from initial location I to the target location F. Obstacles 0_1 and 0_2 block the straight-line path from one location to another. This situation is usually referred to in the robotics and artificial intelligence (AI) literature as the *find-path problem,* and may be stated more precisely: Given an object with an initial location and a set of obstacles whose spatial location is known, find a continuous path from the initial position to the goal that avoids collision with obstacles along the way.

A simple solution would be to project the line segment connecting the initial and final points, then determine whether any obstacles intersect that line. This solution is not adequate, because if makes no allowance for the width of the SWIMMER, which may then collide with edges of obstacles. A more robust algorithm must factor in required clearances due to all sources of potential

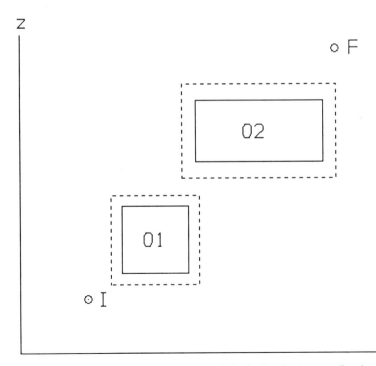

FIG. A.8.   "Bloomed" obstacle boundaries (broken lines) surrounding the original object descriptions (solid lines).

imprecision. One common solution to this problem is to enlarge the boundaries of all obstacles by half of the largest dimension of the SWIMMER plus an extra amount for uncertainty in the SWIMMER's location. This is referred to as *blooming* object descriptions. Given these corrections, the SWIMMER can be mathematically treated as a single point (Figure A.8).

Route planning proceeds in a simple recursive fashion. The straight-line path connecting the SWIMMER location and the goal is computed. If any object obstructs this path, hypothetical lines are drawn from the starting point to each of the observable vertices (edges) of the expanded obstacles. Each vertex is considered to be a potential starting point for a new path: Straight lines are drawn from these points to the target, obstructing obstacles identified, and so on. This expansion results in a series of paths connecting the starting and destination points (Figure A.9). Path lengths can be computed by adding the lengths of path segments. Most AI systems select the shortest path, although many other factors may be considered in choosing the best path.

The recursive find path algorithm we have described is useful when maneuvering room is not at a premium. Under restrictive conditions with lots of objects

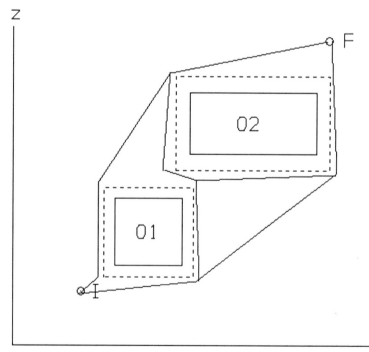

FIG. A.9.   Possible paths taken from the initial point *I* to the destination point *P* in an obstacle-filled environment.

located close to one another, the algorithm may fail to identify useful paths. The problem arises because obstacle boundaries are bloomed according to the largest dimension of the SWIMMER. Assume that the SWIMMER is rectangularly shaped, with a length L that is twice the width W. Two obstacles may be farther than W apart, yet the distance separating the objects could be narrower than L. Because the largest dimension is used to bloom obstacle boundaries, the algorithm will fail to detect a negotiable gap. This is usually termed the *piano mover's problem* (see Schwartz & Sharir, 1983). Treatments generalized to three-dimensional obstacles and paths are presented in Brooks (1983), Donald (1983, 1987), and Lozano-Perez (1983).

The underwater environment often permits a trivial solution to the find path problem: The SWIMMER may simply maneuver over the obstacle unless it is almost at the surface.

Route-planning algorithms are based on prior knowledge of obstacle locations. When a new environment is explored, obstacle locations probably cannot be determined a priori. A few investigators have dealt explicitly with exploration tasks. Iyengar et al. (1986) build up a model of the environment through experience. If a SWIMMER is required to work in one general location, their algorithms can be of assistance in acquiring a model of the environment and using it to guide later navigation. Crowley (1985) describes a similar system. Finally, McDermott and Davis (1984) discuss the situation where the exact positions and orientations of objects are not known. Their SPAM system creates a *fuzzy map* that constrains objects to lie within a range of values. The certainty of object locations increases as new data are encoded. SPAM can create paths to navigate through the terrain and update them as new information is acquired.

REFERENCES

Ade, F. (1983). Characterization of textures by eigenfilters. *Signal Processing 5,* 451–457.

Ait-Kheddache, A., & Rajala, S. (1988). Texture classification based on higher-order fractals. *Proceedings of the IEEE, 9,* 1112–1119.

Aloimonos, J. & Shulman, D. (1989). *Integration of visual modules.* San Diego, CA: Academic Press.

Anderson, N. H. (1981). *Foundations of information integration theory.* New York: Academic Press.

Argyle, E. (1971). Techniques for edge detection. *Proceedings of the IEEE, 59*(2), 285–287.

Bachmann, T. (1980). Genesis of subjective image: acta et commentatione. *Universitat Tancuensis #522 Problems of Cognitive Psychology,* 102–126 (Tartu Estonia, USSR).

Bachmann, T. (1992). *Psychophysiology of Visual Masking.* Commack, N.Y.: Nova Science Press.

Bajesty, R., & Lieberman, L. (1974, August). Computer description of real outdoor scenes. *Proceedings of the Second International Joint Conference on Pattern Recognition, Copenhagen.* Pp. 174–179, Denmark.

Barnard, S. T., & Thompson, W. B. (1980). Disparity analysis of images. *IEEE Transactions on Pattern Analysis and Machine Intelligence, 2*(4), 333–340.

Bennett, B. M., Hoffman, D. D., & Prakash, C. (1989). *Observer mechanics: A formal theory of perception.* San Diego, CA: Academic Press.

Blake, A., & Zisserman, A. (1987). *Visual reconstruction.* Cambridge, MA: MIT Press.

Braunstein, M. L., Hoffman, D. D., Andersen, G. J., Shapiro, L. R., & Bennett, B. M. (1987). Minimum points and views for the recovery of three-dimensional structure. *Journal of Experimental Psychology: Human Perception and Performance, 13*(3), 335–343.

Bremermann, Hans J. (1977). Complexity and transcomputability. In R. Duncan & Miranda Weston-Smith (Eds.), *The encyclopedia of ignorance* (pp. 167–174). New York: Pocket Books.

Brodatz, P. (1966). *Textures—A photographic album for artists and designers.* New York: Dover.

Brooks, R. A. (1983). Solving the find-path problem by good representation of free space. *IEEE Transactions on Systems, Man, and Cybernetics, SMC-13,* 190–197.

Busby, F., & Vadus, J. R. (1990). Autonomous underwater vehicle R&D trends. *Sea Technology, 31,* 65+.

Carlucci, L. (1972). A formal system for texture languages. *Pattern Recognition, 4*, 53–72.

Clark, M., Bovik, A. C., & Geisler, W. (1987). Texture segmentation using gabor modulation/demodulation. *Pattern Recognition, 20*, 261–267.

Clark, J. J., & Yuille, A. L. (1990). *Data fusion for sensory information processing systems.* Boston, MA: Kluwer.

Cohen, P. R., & Feigenbaum, E. A. (1982). *The handbook of artificial intelligence* (Vol. 3). Los Altos, CA: William Kaufmann.

Coleman, G. B., & Andrews, H. C. (1979). Image segmentation by clustering. *Proceedings of the IEEE, 67*(5).

Crowley, J. L. (1985). Navigation for an intelligent mobile robot. *IEEE Journal of Robotics and Automation, RA-1*, 31–41.

Darling, E. M., & Joseph, R. D. (1968). Pattern recognition from satellite altitudes. *IEEE Transactions on Systems, Man, and Cybernetics, SMC-4*, 38–47.

Davis, P. J. (1975). *Interpolation and approximation.* New York: Dover.

Donald, B. R. (1983). *Hypothesizing channels through free space in solving findpath problem* (AI Memo No. 736). Cambridge, MA: MIT.

Donald, B. R. (1987). A search algorithm for motion planning with six degrees of freedom. *Artificial Intelligence, 31*, 295–353.

du Buf, J. M. H., Kardan, M., & Spann, M. (1990). Texture feature performance for image segmentation. *Pattern Recognition, 23*, 291–309.

Enrich, R., & Foith, J. P. (1976). Representation of random waveforms by relational trees. *IEEE Transactions On Computers, C-25*, 725–736.

Galloway, M. (1974). Texture analysis using grey level run lengths. *Computers Graphics and Image Processing, 4*, 172–199.

Geman, S., & Geman, D. (1984). Stochastic relaxation, Gibbs distributions, and the Bayesian restoration of images. *IEEE Transactions on Pattern Analysis and Machine Intelligence, PAMI-6*, 721–741.

Gibson, J. J. (1966). *The senses considered as perceptual systems.* Boston: Houghton Mifflin.

Gibson, J. J. (1979). *The ecological approach to visual perception.* Boston: Houghton Mifflin.

Gleick, S. (1987). New images of chaos that are stirring a science revolution. *Smithsonian, 18*(9), 122–137.

Graham, N. V. S. (1989). *Visual pattern analyzers.* New York: Oxford University Press.

Gramenopoulos, N. (1973). Terrain type recognition using ERTS-1 MSS Images. *Symposium on Significant Results Obtained from the Earth Resources Technology Satellite*, NASA SP327, 1229–1241.

Grimson, W. E. L. (1981). *From images to surfaces: A computation study of the human early visual system.* Cambridge, MA: MIT Press.

Gupta, J. N., & Wintz, P. A. (1975). A boundary finding algorithm and its application. *IEEE Transactions on Circuits and Systems 22*(4), 351–362.

Haralick, R. M. (1971). Statistical and structural approaches to texture. *Proceedings of the IEEE, 67*(5).

Haralick, R. M., Shanmugam, K., & Dinstein, I. (1973). Texture features for image classification. *IEEE Transaction on Systems, Man, and Cybernetics, SMC-3*, 610–621.

Haralick, R. M., Shanmugam, K., & Dinstein, I. (1972, August). On some quickly computable features for texture. *Proceedings of the 1972 Symposium on Computer Image Processing and Recognition, 2*.

Haralick, R. M., & Shanmugam, K. (1973). Computer classification of reservoir sandstones. *IEEE Transactions on Geoscience Electronics, GE-11*, 171–177.

Heeger, D. J., & Pentland, A. D. (1986). Seeing structure through chaos. *Proceedings of the IEEE, 6*, 131–136.

Henderson, M. R., & Anderson, D. C. (1984). Computer recognition and extraction for form features: A CAD/CAM link. *Computers in Industry, 5*, 329–339.

Horn, B. K. P., & Brooks, M. J. (Eds.). (1989). *Shape from Shading.* Cambridge, MA: MIT Press.

Hough, P. V. C. (1962). *Method and means for recognizing complex patterns* (U.S. Patent No. 3069654).

Hsiao, J. Y., & Sawchuk, A. A. (1989). Unsupervised textured image segmentation using feature smoothing and probabilistic relaxation techniques. *Computer Vision, Graphics, and Image Processing, 48*(1), 1–21.

Hubel, D., & Wiesel, T. N. (1962). Receptive fields, binocular interaction and functional architecture in the cat's visual cortex. *Journal of Physiology, 160,* 106–154.

Iyengar, S. S., Jorgensen, C. C., Raop, S. V. N., & Weisbin, C. R. (1986). Robot navigation algorithms using learned spatial graphs. *Robitica, 4,* 93–100.

Jernigan, M. E., & D'Astous, F. (1984). Entropy-based texture analysis in the spatial frequency domain. *IEEE Transactions on Pattern Analysis and Machine Intelligence, PAMI-6,* 237–243.

Julesz, B. (1964). Binocular depth perception without familiarity cues. *Science, 145,* 356–362.

Julesz, B. (1962). Visual pattern discrimination, *IRE Transactions on Information Theory, 8,* 84–92.

Julesz, B. (1981). Textons, the elements of texture perception, and their interactions. *Nature, 290,* 91–97.

Kaizer, H. (1955). A quantification of textures on aerial photographs. *Boston University Research Laboratories.* Boston, MA, Technical Note 221.

Kartikeyan, B., & Sarkar, A. (1989). A unified approach for image segmentation using exact statistics. *Computer Vision Graphics and Image Processing, 48,* 217–229.

Kirsch, R. (1971). Computer determination of the constituent structure of biological images. *Computers and Biomedical Research, 4,*(3), 315–328.

Kirvida, L., & Johnson, G. (1973). Automatic interpretation of ERTS data for forest management. *NASA SP327.*

Kirsh, R. (1974). Constituent structure of biological images. *Biomedical Research, 4,* 315–328.

Klaus, B., & Horn, P. (1986). *Robot vision.* Cambridge, MA: MIT Press.

Koenderink, J. J. (1990). *Solid shape.* Cambridge, MA: MIT Press.

Landy, M. S., & Bergen, J. R. (1991). Texture segregation and orientation gradient. *Vision Research, 31*(4), 679–691.

Lappin, J. S., Doner, J. F., & Kottas, B. (1980). Minimal conditions for the visual detection of structure and motion in three dimensions. *Science, 209,* 717–719.

Laws, K. I. (1980). *Textured image segmentation* (Tech. Rep. No. 940). Los Angeles: University of Southern California, Image Processing Institute.

Lee, D. T., & Schachter, B. J. (1980). Two algorithms for constructing a Delaunay triangulation. *International Journal of Computer and Information Sciences, 9*(3), 219–242.

Livingstone, M. (1988). Art, illusion and the visual system. *Scientific American, 258*(1), 78–85.

Livingstone, M., & Hubel, D. (1988). Segregation of form, color, movement, and depth: Anatomy, physiology, and perception. *Science, 240,* 740–749.

Lozano-Perez, T. (1983). Spatial planning: A configuration space approach. *IEEE Transactions on Systems, Man and Cybernetics, 32,* 108–120.

Lu, S. Y., & Fu, K. S. (1978). A syntactic approach to texture analysis. *Computer Graphics and Image Processing, 7,* 303–330.

Mandelbrot, B. B. (1982). *The fractal geometry of nature.* San Francisco: Freeman.

Marr, D. (1982). *Vision: A computational investigation into human representation and processing of visual information.* San Francisco: Freeman.

Marr, D., & Nishihara, H. K. (1978). Representation and recognition of the spatial organization of three-dimensional shapes. *Proceedings of the Royal Society of London B, 200,* 269–294.

Marr, D., & Hildreth, E. C. (1980). Theory of edge detection. *Proceedings of the Royal Society of London B, 207,* 187–217.

Marr, D., & Poggio, T. (1979). A theory of human stereo vision. *Proceedings of the Royal Society of London B, 204,* 301–328.

Marroquin, J. L. (1985). *Probabilistic solution of inverse problems.* Unpublished master's thesis, Massachusetts Institute of Technology, Cambridge, MA.

Massaro, D. W., & Friedman, D. (1990). Models of integration given multiple sources of information. *Psychological Review, 97*(2), 225–252.

Maurer, H. (1974). Texture analysis with fourier series. *Proceedings of the Ninth International Symposium on Remote Sensing of Environment,* (pp. 1411–1420). Ann Arbor, MI: Environmental Research Institute of Michigan.

McClelland, J. L., Rumelhart, D. E., and the PDP Research Group (1988). *Parallel distributed processing: Explorations in the microstructure of cognition* (7th ed.): *Vol. 2: Psychological and Biological Methods.* Cambridge, MA: MIT Press.

McCormick, B. H., & Jayaramamurthy, S. N. (1975). A decision theory method for the analysis of texture. *International Journal On Computers and Information Sciences, 4,* 1–38.

McDermott, D., & Davis, E. (1984). Planning routes through uncertain territory. *Artificial Intelligence, 22,* 107–156.

Miller, J. (1981). Global precedence in attention and decision. *Journal of Experimental Psychology, 7,* 1161–1174.

Mitchell, O., Myers, C., & Boyne, W. (1977). A max-min measure for image texture analysis. *IEEE Transactions On Computers, C-25,* 408–414.

Moore, E. F. (1956). Gedanken-experiments on sequential machines. In C. E. Shannon & J. McCarthy (Eds.), *Automata studies* (pp. 129–153). Princeton, NJ: Princeton University Press.

Nagy, G. (1969). Feature extraction on binary patterns. *IEEE Transactions on Systems Science and Cybernetics, 5*(4), 273–278.

Navon, D. (1977). Forest before trees: The precedence of global features in visual perception. *Cognitive Psychology, 9,* 353–383.

Nawrot, M., & Blake, R. (1989). Neural integration of information specifying structure from stereopsis and motion. *Science, 244,* 716–718.

Nevatia, R., & Binford, T. O. (1977). Description and recognition of curved objects. *Artificial Intelligence, 8*(1), 77–98.

Nielson, G. M. (1979). The side-vertex method for interpolation in triangles. *Journal of Approximation Theory, 25,* 318–336.

Nielson, G. M. (1983). A method of interpolating scattered data based upon a minimum norm network. *Mathematics of Computation, 40*(161), 253–271.

Nielson, G. M. (1987). A transfinite, visually continuous triangular interpolant. In G. Farin (Ed.), *Geometric modelling: Algorithms and new trends* (221–233). SIAM.

O'Gorman, L. (1988). An analysis of feature detectability form curvature estimation. *IEEE Conference on Computer Vision and Pattern Recognition,* 235–240.

Østerberg, G. (1935). Topography of the layer rods and cones in the human retina. *Acta Ophthalmologica (supplement), 6,* 1–103.

Peleg, S., Naor, J., Hartley, R., & Avnir, D. (1984). Multiple resolution texture analysis and classification. *IEEE Transactions on Pattern Analysis and Machine Intelligence, PAMI-6,* 518–523.

Poggio, T., Gamble, E. B., & Little, J. J. (1988). Parallel integration of vision modules. *Science, 242,* 436–439.

Posner, M. I., Petersen, S. E., Fox, P. T., & Raichle, M. E. (1988). *Science, 240,* 1627–1631.

Pratt, W. K. (1978). *Digital image processing.* New York: Wiley.

Prewitt, J. M. S. (1970). Object enhancement and extraction. In B. S. Lipkin & A. Rosenfeld (Eds.), *Picture processing and psychopictorics.* New York: Academic Press.

Ramachandran, V. S. (1990). Visual perception in people and machines. In A. Blake & T. Troscianko (Eds.), *AI and the Eye.* San Diego, CA: Wiley.

Ratliff, F. (1965). *Mach bands: Quantitative studies on neural networks in the retina.* San Francisco, CA: Holden-Day, Inc.

Ratliff, F. (1976). On the psychophysical basis of universal color terms. *Proceedings of the American Philosophical Society, 120,* 311–330.

Ratoosh, P. (1949). On interposition as a cue for the perception of distance. *Proceedings of the National Academy of Science (Washington), 35,* 257–259.

REA (1978). *Handbook of Mathematical, Scientific, and Engineering Formulas, Tables, Functions, Graphs, Transforms.* New Jersey: Education Association.

Read, J. S., & Jayaramamurthy, S. N. (1972). Automatic generation of texture feature detectors. *IEEE Transactions on Computers, C-21,* 803–812.

Roberts, L. G. (1965). Machine perception of three-dimensional solids. In J. T. Tippett et al. (Eds.), *Optical and electroptical information processing* (pp. 159–197). Cambridge, MA: MIT Press.

Rosenfeld, A. (1980). Iterative methods in image analysis. *Pattern Recognition, 10,* 181–187.

Rosenfeld, A., & Kak, A. C. (1976). *Digital Picture Processing.* New York: Academic Press.

Rosenfeld, A., & Troy, E. (1970). *Visual Texture Analysis (Report No. 70-116).* College Park, MD: University of Maryland.

Rosenfeld, A., & Thurston, M. (1971). Edge and curve detection for visual scene analysis. *IEEE Transactions on Computers, 20*(5), 562–569.

Rosenfeld, A., Thurston, M., & Lee, Y. H. (1972). *Edge curve detection: further experiments. IEEE Transactions on Computers, 21*(7), 677–715.

Rumelhart, D. E., McClelland, J. L., and the PDP Research Group (1986). *Parallel distributed processing: Explorations in the microstructure of cognition* (8th ed.): Vol. 1. Foundations. Cambridge, MA: MIT Press.

Schwartz, J. T., & Sharir, M. (1983). On the "piano movers" problem I. The case of a two-dimensional rigid polygonal body moving admist polygonal barriers. *Communications on Pure and Applied Mathematics, 36,* 345–398.

Shamos, M. I. (1977). *Computational geometry.* New York: Springler-Verlag.

Stevens, K. A. (1981). The information content of texture gradients. *Biological Cybernetics, 42,* 95–105.

Stevens, K. A. (1986). Interring shape from contours across surfaces. In A. P. Pentland (Ed.), *Pixels to Predicates* (pp. 93–110). Norwood, NJ: Ablex.

Stockmeyer, L. J., & Chandra, A. K. (1979). Intrinsically difficult problems. *Scientific American, 240,* 140–159.

Sutton, R., & Hall, E. (1972). Texture measures for automatic classification of pulmonary disease. *IEEE Transactions On Computers, C-21,* 667–676.

Terzopolous, D. (1986). Integrating visual information from multiple sources. In A. P. Pentland (Ed.), *Pixels to predicates: Recent advances in computational and robotic vision* (pp. 111–143). Norwood, NJ: Ablex.

Tomita, F., Yachida, M., & Tsuji, S. (1973). Detection of homogeneous regions by structural analysis. *Proceedings of the Third International Joint Conference on Artificial Intelligence,* 564–571.

Triendl, E. E. (1972). Automatic terrain mapping by texture recognition. *Proceedings of the 8th International Symposium on Remote Sensing of Environment,* Ann Arbor, MI: Environmental Research Institute of Michigan.

Tsotsos, J. K. (1990). Analyzing vision at the complexity level. *Behavioral and Brain Sciences, 13,* 423–469.

Tsuji, S., & Tomita, F. (1973). A structural analyzer for a class of textures. *Computer Graphics, Vision, and Image Processing, 2,* 216–231.

Turing, A. M. (1936). On computable numbers with an application to the *entscheidungs* problem. *Proceedings of the London Mathematical Society (2), 42,* 230–265.

Turner, M. R. (1986). Texture discrimination by Gabor fitters. *Biological Cybernetics, 55,* 71–82.

Uhr, L. (1974). *A model of form perception and scene description* (Tech. Rep. No. 231). Madison: University of Wisconsin.

Ullman, S. (1979). *The interpretation of visual motion.* Cambridge, MA: MIT Press.

Unser, M. (1986). Local linear transforms for texture measurements. *Signal Processing, 11,* 61–79.

Uttal, W. R. (1975). *An autocorrelation theory of form detection.* Hillsdale, NJ: Lawrence Erlbaum Associates.

Uttal, W. R. (1981). *A taxonomy of visual processes.* Hillsdale, NJ: Lawrence Erlbaum Associates.

Uttal, W. R. (1983). *Visual form detection in 3-dimensional space.* Hillsdale, NJ: Lawrence Erlbaum Associates.

Uttal, W. R. (1985). *The detection of nonplanar surfaces in visual space.* Hillsdale, NJ: Lawrence Erlbaum Associates.

Uttal, W. R. (1987). *The perception of dotted forms.* Hillsdale, NJ: Lawrence Erlbaum Associates.

Uttal, W. R. (1988). *On seeing forms.* Hillsdale, NJ: Lawrence Erlbaum Associates.

Uttal, W. R. (1990). Theory and evaluative reviews: On some two-way barriers between models and mechanisms. *Theory and Evaluative Reviews, 48*(2), 188–203.

Uttal, W. R., Davis, N. S., Welke, C., & Kakarala, R. (1988). The reconstruction of static visual forms from sparse dotted samples. *Perception & Psychophysics, 43,* 223–240.

van de Grind, W. A. (1984). Decomposition and neuroreduction of visual perception. In Andrea J. van Doorn, W. A. van de Grind, & J. J. Koenderink (Eds.), *Limits in Perception* (pp. 431–494). New Science Press: Utrecht.

Van Essen, D. C. (1985). Function organization of primate visual cortex. In A. Peters & E. G. Jones, *Cerebral cortex* (Vol. 3, pp. 259–329).

Wang, L., & He, D. C. (1990). A new approach for texture analysis. *Photogrammetric Engineering and Remote Sensing, 56,* 61–66.

Watson, A. B. (1983). *Detection and recognition of simple spatial forms* (Tech. Memo No. 84353). Moffett Field, CA: NASA.

Westheimer, G., & McKee, S. P. (1977). Interactions regions for visual hyperacuity. *Vision Research, 17,* 89–93.

Wojcik, Z. (1987). Approximation of shapes in pattern recognition. *Computer Vision, Graphics and Image Processing, 5*(4), 273–279.

Wu, R., & Stark, H. (1985). Rotation-invariant pattern recognition using optimum feature extraction. *Applied Optics, 24,* 179–184.

Yoerger, D. R., & Slotine, J. J. E. (1985). Robust trajectory control of underwater vehicles. *IEEE Journal of Oceanic Engineering, OE-10,* 462–470.

Zeki, S. M. (1978). The cortical projections of foveal striate cortex in the rhesus monkey. *J. Physiology (London), 277,* 227–244.

Zwillinger, D. (1989). *Handbook of differential equations.* San Diego, CA: Academic Press.

Author Index

Subject Index